Kadi on Trial

The judgments of the European Court of Justice concerning the *Kadi* case have raised substantive and procedural issues that have caught the attention of scholars from many disciplines including EU law, constitutional law, international law, and jurisprudence. This book offers a comprehensive view of the *Kadi* case, and explores specific issues that are anticipated to resonate beyond the immediate case from which they derive.

The first part of the volume sets out an analysis of the new judgment of the Court, favouring a 'contextual' reading of what is the latest link in a judicial chain. The following three parts offer interdisciplinary accounts of the decision of the European Court of Justice, including legal theory, constitutional law, and international law. The book closes with an epilogue by Ernst-Ulrich Petersmann, who studies the role of the *Kadi* case in the methodology of international law and its contribution to the concept of global justice.

The book brings together legal scholars from a range of fields, and discusses pressing topics such as the European Union's objective of 'the strict observance and the development of international law', the EU as a site of global governance, constitutional pluralism, and the protection of fundamental rights.

Matej Avbelj is Assistant Professor of European Law at the Graduate School of Government and European Studies, Slovenia, where he also acts as a Dean.

Filippo Fontanelli (LLM, PhD) is Lecturer in Law at the University of Surrey.

Giuseppe Martinico is a García Pelayo Fellow at the Centro de Estudios Politicos y Constitucionales (CEPC), Madrid and Lecturer in Law at the Scuola Superiore S. Anna.

Routledge Research in EU Law

Local Government in Europe
The 'Fourth Level' in the EU Multi-Layered System of Governance
Carlo Panara and Michael R. Varney

The Legitimacy of the European Union through Legal Rationality
Free Movement of Third Country Nationals
Richard Ball

Forthcoming titles in this series include:

New Governance and the European Strategy for Employment
Samantha Velluti

Human Rights and Minority Rights in the European Union
Kirsten Shoraka

The Legal Order of the European Union
The Institutional Role of the European Court of Justice
Timothy Moorhead

Kadi on Trial
A Multifaceted Analysis of the Kadi Trial
Matej Avbelj, Filippo Fontanelli and Giuseppe Martinico

The Governance of the European Union and the Internal-External Nexus
Paul James Cardwell

Turkey's Accession to the European Union
The Politics of Exclusion?
Edel Hughes

Kadi on Trial

A Multifaceted Analysis of the Kadi Trial

Edited by
Matej Avbelj, Filippo Fontanelli,
and Giuseppe Martinico

Routledge
Taylor & Francis Group

LONDON AND NEW YORK

First published 2014
by Routledge
2 Park Square, Milton Park, Abingdon, Oxon, OX14 4RN

and by Routledge
711 Third Avenue, New York, NY 10017

Routledge is an imprint of the Taylor & Francis Group, an informa business

First issued in paperback 2016

© 2014 Matej Avbelj, Filippo Fontanelli and Giuseppe Martinico

The right of Matej Avbelj, Filippo Fontanelli, and Giuseppe Martinico
to be identified as editors of this work has been asserted by them in
accordance with sections 77 and 78 of the Copyright, Designs and
Patents Act 1988.

British Library Cataloguing in Publication Data
A catalogue record for this book is available from the British Library

Library of Congress Cataloging-in-Publication Data
Kadi on trial : a multifaceted analysis of the Kadi judgment/Matej
Avbelj, Filippo Fontanelli, Giuseppe Martinico.
pages cm. – (Routledge research in European Union law)
Includes bibliographical references and index.
ISBN 978-0-415-64031-2 (hardback) – ISBN 978-0-203-79619-1
(ebk) 1. El Kadi, Yasin, 1956—Trials, litigation, etc.
2. Terrorism–Prevention–Law and legislation–European Union
countries–Cases. 3. Judicial review of administrative acts–Law and
legislation–European Union countries–Cases. 4. International and
municipal law–Law and legislation–European Union countries–
Cases. I. Avbelj, Matej, editor of compilation. II. Fontanelli, Filippo,
editor of compilation. III. Martinico, Giuseppe, editor of compilation.
KJE927.8.E4K33 2014
344.2405'325172–dc23
2013044933

ISBN13: 978-0-415-64031-2 (hbk)
ISBN13: 978-1-138-68509-3 (pbk)

Typeset in Garamond
by Cenveo Publisher Services

Contents

Notes on contributors

Antonella Angelini is a PhD Candidate at the Graduate Institute of International and Development Studies (Geneva) and Research Assistant at the Faculty of Law of the University of Geneva.

Matej Avbelj is Assistant Professor of European Law at the Graduate School of Government and European Studies, Slovenia, where he also acts as a Dean.

Paolo Busco is Assistant Legal Counsel, Permanent Court of Arbitration, and a PhD candidate, Scuola Superiore Sant'Anna, Pisa.

Federico Fabbrini is Assistant Professor of European and Comparative Constitutional Law, Tilburg Law School.

Filippo Fontanelli is Lecturer in Law at the University of Surrey.

Jennifer Hendry is Lecturer in Jurisprudence and Deputy Director, Centre for European Law and Legal Studies, University of Leeds School of Law.

Joris Larik is Senior Researcher at The Hague Institute for Global Justice and Associate Fellow, Leuven Centre for Global Governance Studies, KU Leuven.

Nikos Lavranos is Dr jur., LLM, both from Maastricht University. He is currently a senior adviser and is a former Max Weber fellow at the EUI.

Giuseppe Martinico is García Pelayo Fellow, Centro de Estudios Politicos y Constitucionales; Lecturer, Scuola Superiore Sant'Anna, Pisa; Researcher at the Centre for Studies on Federalism, Turin; and Editor of *Sant'Anna Legal Studies*.

Luke Mason teaches jurisprudence and EU law at the University of Surrey and is a researcher at the University of Oxford.

Petros Constantinos Mavroidis is Edwin B. Parker Professor of Law at Columbia Law School, New York City, currently on leave at the European University Institute, Florence.

Ernst-Ulrich Petersmann is Emeritus Professor and former Head of the Law Department, European University Institute (EUI), Florence (Italy). He is a former secretary, member, or chairman of numerous GATT/WTO dispute settlement panels; former German representative in UN and European institutions; and former legal consultant for GATT, the WTO, UNCTAD, the OECD, the EU Commission, and the European Parliament.

Arman Sarvarian is Lecturer in Law (University of Surrey) and Director of the Surrey International Law Centre.

Antonios Tzanakopoulos is Associate Professor of Public International Law, University of Oxford, and Fellow in Law, St Anne's College, Oxford.

Mihail Vatsov holds an LLB summa cum laude in International and European Law, The Hague University and is an LLM Candidate in European Law, Maastricht University.

Nele Yang is a PhD candidate at the University of Frankfurt/Main, Germany, and a Research Fellow at the Max Planck Institute for Comparative Public Law and Public International Law.

Foreword

The EU officials take pride in underscoring their multilateral credentials whenever they have the opportunity to do so around the world. It is true that they do not often have the chance to do that, as the EU competence in the field of external relations is quite limited and confined to a few areas of economic relations.

The *Kadi* decisions bring the game back inside the EU courts. Roughly, it stands for the proposition that international law will be effectively implemented in the EU legal order, if it does not run afoul the EU fundamental rights. Were *Kadi* to adopt an ex ante control, there would not be much to talk about. It became an issue because international law, generated by the EU as well, risks becoming a *non lieu* inside the EU legal order, unless the EU Courts (in case of challenge) accepts its consistency with the foundations of EU law.

This could be a tall order for various reasons. Questions could be (and indeed, are) legitimately asked regarding the wisdom of this approach. There are legal issues of course, as there are wider policy concerns that have emerged as a result of the first *Kadi* judgment and everything that followed ever since.

In the classic economics literature, human rights are normal goods, and, other things equal, one would expect 'wealthier' nations to have 'beefed up' regimes, and less affluent nations to enjoy more prosaic institutions. International law thus, would be some sort of 'minimal' harmonization. In this context, some (a lot?) of it could be 'unacceptable' by EU standards.

On the other hand, why spend time and effort to contract with the EU if the outcome risks being subverted by the EU Courts? Worse, what if other constitutional courts adopt the same strategy, and condition implementation of international law on their own legal perceptions? What if similar orders are even more basic than international law of today? Why would 'enlightened elites' in that part of the world be willing to commit national policies at the international plane, if their domestic courts were to undo them at one stroke *à la Kadi*?

Critics will ask similar question, and defendants of *Kadi* will respond that, absent this construction, there would be no gains for the EU from participating in the international integration process. The EU is not an international actor in order to eviscerate its current level of protection, but in order to induce others to follow its example, to mimic its manifold achievements.

The editors of this book should be credited with providing a very comprehensive questionnaire of the various legal and policy issues involved and selecting a remarkable group of authors to address it. Avbelj, Fontanelli and Martinico managed to put together a volume which, in my view, will provide the reference for the issues debated here, as well as the standard for this type of collaborative endeavours.

Petros C. Mavroidis
Edwin B. Parker Professor of Law at Columbia Law School, New York City
(currently on leave at the European University Institute, Florence)

1 Introduction

*Matej Avbelj, Filippo Fontanelli
and Giuseppe Martinico*

This book, as the title intimates, revolves around one single object of study: the *Kadi* proceedings before the courts of the European Union (EU). The very idea of several chapters being written on the same topic, and published back to back, conjures up the work of Raymond Queneau, who wrote the same story (a man has a discussion with a stranger on the bus; he then meets a friend by the railways station) 99 times in a row.[1] His purpose was to explore all conceivable writing styles. The underlying story was not the real motive for the writing (*causa*), but an accident (*occasio*).[2] Reading the book cover to cover is mortally boring for the non-linguist.

We are hopeful that this book will not end up being an exercise in style. Also, although we do not necessarily recommend that it is read all at once, we trust that nobody would think that it just juxtaposes variations of the same old *Kadi* story. We also hope that nobody will be bored to death.

The idea behind the collection of essays contained in this book dates back to the workshop on 'How "constitutional" is transnational law?' which took place in September 2011 at the Scuola Superiore S. Anna in Pisa under the auspices of the Sant'Anna Legal Studies (STALS) Programme, the School of Government and European Studies of Kranj, and the European Faculty of Law of Nova Gorica. The workshop revealed the centrality of the *Kadi* case to our understanding of transnational law, but it also disclosed its contested character and the consequences for the theory and practice of transnational law. As such the *Kadi* case, almost by way of necessity, called for further study and scholarly discussion. This book is intended to fulfil these expectations.

The *Kadi* case has raised substantive and procedural issues that have caught the attention of scholars of different backgrounds (EU lawyers, constitutional lawyers, public international lawyers, legal theorists, administrative law scholars, etc.). While the book stays faithful to a broad interdisciplinary approach characteristic of the field, the editors' ambition was to move beyond

---

1 Raymond Queneau, *Exercises de style* (Gallimard, Paris: 1947).
2 The reference is to the Thomistic distinction unearthed by AG Cruz Villalón in his Opinion to case C-617/10 *Åkerberg Fransson* [2013] ECR I-0000 (see para. 61).

the existing scholarship. Rather than merely codifying the state of the art in this area, the book offers a fresh and original multi-perspective analysis of the *Kadi* saga, including the latest link in this protracted judicial chain at the time of writing: the Court of Justice of the European Union (CJEU, or the Court) ruling in the case of 18 July 2013.

The editors invited scholars with different backgrounds who could confront the complex issues raised by the case from different angles. The structure of the book consequently reflects the plurality of interests of the authors engaging in a fascinating and ubiquitous debate. The volume is, accordingly, divided into four parts.

The first part provides, by way of introduction, an analysis of the new judgment of the Court, favouring a 'contextual' reading of the latest link in the *Kadi* judicial chain. It consists of three chapters. The first, by Filippo Fontanelli, compares the most recent judgment with the three previous decisions. It contextualizes the 2013 pronouncement, accounts for the judicial 'developments' traceable in the various decisions and opinions of the Advocates General, and offers a mapping of the different standards of review which were discussed in the proceedings and the scholarship. In the second, Antonella Angelini dwells on the 2010 decision of the General Court (somewhat neglected by the literature), to underscore its crucial role in the judicial mosaic of the *Kadi* affair as a whole. Finally, Paolo Busco's contribution is concerned with the arguments brought before the CJEU by the intervening states, and with their role in the litigation at large.

By contrast, the other three parts of the volume zoom out and offer an interdisciplinary account of the decision of the CJEU. Each of them is dedicated to a different theme. The first thematic cluster belongs to legal theory and consists of three contributions. Matej Avbelj examines how the developments in the *Kadi* case bear on our modern concept of law. Jennifer Hendry analyses the case from a systems theory perspective, whereas Luke Mason emphasizes the Kafkian elements in *Kadi* and reflects on the experience of law in postmodernity that the *Kadi* saga might be an example of.

The third part of the book contains three chapters that observe the importance of the *Kadi* saga with respect to the issue of the international obligations of the EU. Arman Sarvarian provides a discussion of the very possibility of subjecting UN Security Council resolutions to scrutiny and judicial review. He tracks the main elements of the debate in the texts of the *Kadi* decisions relating to *Kadi* and casts *Kadi II* as a cautious model for other jurisdictions engaging with the dilemmas of judicial review. Nikolaos Lavranos and Mihail Vatsov provide an original reading of *Kadi II* as an instance of back-tracking. After the bold judgments of the Court of Justice in *Kadi I* and the General Court in *Kadi II*, they detect a silent return to a more conservative position on the respect of general international law. Antonios Tzanakopoulous tackles squarely one of the most debated aspects of the *Kadi* judgments: the potential margin for a *Solange*-like deference with respect to improved (and yet to come) UN procedures.

The fourth group of contributions deals with the constitutional implications of the decision. Federico Fabbrini and Joris Larik examine the dialogue between the Strasbourg and Luxembourg Courts about due process principles within the broader context of the anti-terrorism strategy of UN Security Council. Giuseppe Martinico offers a joint reading of *Kadi II* and *Van Gend en Loos* (on the occasion of its 50th anniversary), framing these two judgments in the light of the principle of autonomy. Finally, Nele Yang insists on the 'administrative tone' of *Kadi II* and compares it with the 'constitutional rhetoric' adopted in *Kadi I*.

The book closes with an epilogue authored by Ernst-Ulrich Petersmann, who studies the role of the *Kadi* case in the methodology of international law and its contribution to the concept of global justice at large. The epilogue is deliberately distinct from the chapters of the book. Instead of focusing on the details of the *Kadi* saga, it takes a step back and observes it as detail of a general process – an apt way to spare the reader from claustrophobia.

The book thus offers to its readers both a broad oversight of the *Kadi* case as well as a detailed treatment of some specific issues that merit special attention, as they are anticipated to resonate beyond the immediate case from which they derive. The contemporary socio-legal world is, apparently, in flux. The *Kadi* case is a testimony to that and a harbinger of a new socio-legal constellation in the making. Legal theorists, constitutional, EU, and international lawyers are thus facing unprecedented conceptual and practical challenges. This book, as a timely and critical-intellectual engagement with these challenges, might help in resolving some of them, but it will certainly invite its readers to think creatively about the problems of the present that can and will determine our future.

The editors would like to thank the respective institutions (the School of Government and European Studies, Kranj, Surrey University School of Law, the Scuola Superiore S. Anna, Pisa, and the Centro de Estudios Políticos y Constitucionales, Madrid), as well as the contributors and the publisher for allowing them to work this atypical project into a successful story.

Kranj London Madrid, 6 November 2013

Part 1

Kadi II of the European Union Court of Justice

An introduction

2 Kadieu: connecting the dots – from Resolution 1267 to Judgment C-584/10 P

The coming of age of judicial review

Filippo Fontanelli

Officer '[The Condemned Man] has had no opportunity to defend himself... Guilt is always beyond a doubt. Other courts could not follow this principle, for they are made up of many heads and, in addition, have even higher courts above them. But that is not the case here...'

The Traveller looked at the harrow with a wrinkled frown. The information about the judicial procedures had not satisfied him...

Officer 'You are trapped in a European way of seeing things... That's my plan. Do you want to help me carry it out?...'

[The Traveller] hesitated a moment. But finally he said, as he had to, 'No.'[1]

Introduction

On 18 July 2013, the Grand Chamber of the Court of Justice of the European Union (CJEU, or the Court) delivered judgment in the second round of the *Kadi* proceedings.[2] The Court dismissed the appeals brought by the Council, the Commission, and the UK against the General Court's judgment of 30 September 2010. In so doing, it confirmed that the European Union (EU) breached Mr Kadi's fundamental rights by including him in the list of subjects whose resources must be frozen on account of their potential relationship with Al-Qaida. Therefore, the Court upheld the annulment of Commission Regulation 1190/2008, in the part providing for Kadi's renewed enlisting in the blacklist found in Annex 1 to Regulation 881/2002.

The two-level *Kadi II* litigation follows on the heels of the first *Kadi* diptych, comprising the decisions of the then Court of First Instance (CFI) in 2005 and of the then European Court of Justice (ECJ) in 2008. This chapter gives an account of this decade-long saga and provides the necessary background to

---

1 From Franz Kafka, *In the Penal Colony* (1981) (translation by Ian Johnston, The Kafka Project).
2 Joined Cases C-584/10 P, C-593/10 P, and C-595/10 P. For two early commentaries, see Erika de Wet 'From Kadi to Nada: judicial techniques favoring human rights over United Nations Security Council sanctions', (2013) 12 *Chinese Journal of International Law*; Hayley J. Hooper 'An unsteady middle ground' (2014) 20 (3) *European Public Law*, forthcoming.

the following chapters, while offering a retrospective analysis of how the standard of judicial review applied by EU courts has evolved.

The road to the *Kadi I* judgment of the ECJ

In 1999, the United Nations (UN) Security Council passed Resolution 1267 under ch. VII of the UN Charter. This act ordered inter alia the freezing of the assets of individuals and organizations suspected of having links with the Taliban.[3] Resolution 1330 (2000) extended the sanctions regime to Al-Qaida and all subjects linked thereto, regardless of a connection with Afghanistan or the Taliban. States can ask the Al-Qaida Sanctions Committee to include a subject in the Consolidated List, providing the relevant supporting evidence.[4] A number of resolutions have been passed since, refining and correcting the system,[5] up to Resolution 2083 (2012), whose 19 pages provide the most comprehensive overview of the sanctions machinery.

Resolution 1730 (2006) established a focal point entrusted with the channelling of delisting applications to the Sanctions Committee. To assist with these requests, Resolution 1904 (2009) established the Office of the Ombudsperson, replacing the focal point with respect to Al-Qaida sanctions. Under the current system, the Ombudsperson can recommend delisting and the Committee can reject the recommendation within 60 days, but only at unanimity.[6] However, the Committee can always refer the issue to the Security Council, the decision of which is subject to the permanent members' veto.

After 9/11, Saudi national Yassin Abdullah Kadi, supposedly upon the USA's request, was listed by the Sanctions Committee, on the grounds of his suspected association with Usama bin Laden. He was subsequently listed in the European Community (EC) Council Regulation[7] implementing Security Council resolutions. The EU had acted swiftly under the Second Pillar[8] to endorse both Resolution 1267 and 1330 through successive common positions,[9] and subsequently acted under the First Pillar (the Community one) to regulate the obligations of EC member states in keeping with the Security Council's instructions. To this end, arts. 301 and 60 of the Treaty on

---

3 See art. 4 (b).

4 An updated overview of the listing process is in the report of the UN Special Rapporteur on the promotion and protection of human rights and fundamental freedoms while countering terrorism (Ben Emmerson), see UN doc. A/67/396, paras. 25 ff.

5 See resolutions 1333 (2000), 1363 (2001), 1373 (2001), 1390 (2002), 1452 (2002), 1455 (2003), 1526 (2004), 1566 (2004), 1617 (2005), 1624 (2005), 1699 (2006), 1730 (2006), 1735 (2006), 1822 (2008), 1904 (2009), 1988 (2011), and 1989 (2011).

6 See Resolution 1989 (2011), paras. 23, 27.

7 Regulation 467/2001, then repealed and substituted by Regulation 881/2002 (see Annex I).

8 Concerned with the Common Foreign and Security Policy (CFSP).

9 See, respectively, Common Position 1999/727/CFSP (OJ 1999 L 294, p. 1) and Common Position 2001/154/CFSP (OJ 2001 L 57, p. 1).

the European Community (TEC)[10] served as legal basis. These articles endowed the Council with the exceptional power to interrupt economic relations with a third country and limit the freedom of movement of capitals within the Community, in situations of urgency certified by a Common Foreign and Security Policy (CFSP) measure (such as a common position). The regulations aimed to enforce economic sanctions against individuals and organizations identified by the Sanctions Committee.

Kadi brought proceedings in 2001 before the CFI seeking annulment of Regulation 467/2001 and Regulation 2062/2001,[11] in so far as he was directly concerned. He claimed violation of his rights to be heard, property, and effective judicial review, as well as a breach of proportionality. He also purported that the Community had no competence to adopt the regulations: in Kadi's view, only the Union could have adopted similar acts, using a CFSP source.[12] In 2005, the CFI dismissed Kadi's claims.[13] It held, in essence, that the regulations (duly adopted under the First Pillar) enjoyed immunity from judicial review, since they intended to implement international obligations which left no margin of discretion to the EU. The Tribunal declared itself content to note that no breach of *jus cogens* had occurred. Kadi appealed this decision before the ECJ.

Advocate General Maduro, in his Opinion, criticized the CFI's decision and urged the ECJ to review the regulation, to ensure the respect of fundamental rights within the EU. The indefinite maintenance of the sanctions, even if the shortage of available information and the lack of effective judicial review made it impossible to tell whether they were proportionate or misdirected, was for the AG 'anathema in a society that respects the rule of law' (para. 53). Therefore, Maduro vouched for the reversal of the CFI's judgment.

In 2008, the ECJ reversed the CFI's decision.[14] It referred to a core of constitutional principles buttressing the rule of law in the EU, which cannot be prejudiced by unconditional compliance with international obligations (para. 288). Since the legality of EU acts depends on their conformity with the minimum standards of fundamental rights protection, EU courts can review them on that basis. Regarding the nature of the review, the ECJ held that it must ensure 'in principle the full review' of EU legal acts, including those implementing Security Council's resolutions (para. 326). Accordingly, the ECJ found a breach of Kadi's rights to property and judicial protection, mainly caused by the EU's absolute failure to inform him of the reasons for the listing. Hence, he could not effectively submit his views to challenge the

---

10 Now 215 and 75 TFEU, respectively.
11 Which amended Regulation 467/2001 and ordered Kadi's listing therein.
12 The CFI and the ECJ rejected this claim, with slightly different reasoning. On the issue of trans-pillar litigation before the ECJ, see Andrea Gattini's comment (2013) 46 *Common Market Law Review*, 213; Nikolaos Lavranos 'UN sanctions and judicial review' (2007) 76 *Nordic Journal of International Law* 343, 351 ff.
13 Case T-315/01 *Kadi* v. *Council and Commission* [2005] ECR II-3649.
14 Joined Cases C-402/05 P and C-415/05 *Kadi and Al Barakaat* v. *Council* [2008] ECR I-6351.

freezing: he was deprived of the rights to defence and effective judicial review. The ECJ annulled the regulation, allowing for the maintenance of its effects for three months, to afford EU institutions with the time to remedy the procedural wrongdoing. Up to this stage, the ECJ had not actually reviewed the merits of the Security Council's decisions: the blatant failure to safeguard the individual's rights was deemed a sufficient cause for annulment, regardless of whether the listing was warranted or at least justifiable. In essence, this lack of protection did not require a review based on proportionality: whatever the competing interest, the absolute obliteration of Kadi's right to know the grounds for his listing was fatal for the EU measure implementing it.

Shortly after this judgment, the Sanctions Committee authorized the transmission to Kadi of the narrative summary of the reasons for his listing.[15] In a nutshell, Kadi was listed because he had founded and directed the Muwafaq Foundation, which allegedly belonged to the Al-Qaida network and supported mujahidin groups in Bosnia during the Yugoslavian war. Moreover, a foundation's director allegedly had contacts with Usama bin Laden for the provision of military training to Tunisian mujahidin. Kadi was also a shareholder of a Bosnian bank where a terroristic plot might have been planned and of other Albanian firms which allegedly funnelled money from and to extremists. The Commission referred to these reasons to motivate the non-removal of Kadi from the freezing-list and allowed him to submit comments. Through this concession, the Commission attempted to bring the listing procedure in line with the ECJ's requirements and impair the human rights deficiencies. The Commission, in Regulation 1190/08, considered that Kadi's submissions could not warrant delisting.

Again, Kadi sought the annulment of the regulation before the General Court. In its 2010 decision,[16] the General Court referred – with some perplexity – to the dictum of the ECJ, which had called in 2008 for 'in principle full review' of all EU acts. It held that the delisting procedure available before the Sanctions Committee failed to offer the minimum guarantees of judicial protection, nor had the EU system offered any additional protection of Kadi's rights. The General Court also noted that judicial review could not be limited to the merits of the contested measure, but should necessarily extend to the evidence supporting its adoption and could not be dispensed with for secrecy reasons. The review hypothesized by the Commission, limited to the formal correctness of the listing, would be tantamount to 'a simulacrum' of effective judicial review (para. 123). Ultimately, the General Court considered that the Commission's evaluation of Kadi's views was superficial

---

15 Summaries of reasons are available on the Sanctions Committee website of the UN Sanctions Committee (see http://www.un.org/sc/committees/1267/individuals_associated_with_Al-Qaida.shtml). The summary of reasons regarding Kadi was removed after the 2012 delisting. It is reproduced at para. 28 of the 2013 CJEU's judgment.

16 Case T-85/09 *Kadi* v. *Commission* [2010] ECHR II-0000.

and formalistic. Crucially, Kadi had still not been given access to any of the information used against him, other than the summary of reasons. Therefore, the violations highlighted by the ECJ had not been remedied. The General Court annulled the 2008 Regulation.

The CJEU's judgment of 2013

The Council, the Commission, and the UK appealed the General Court's judgment before the CJEU.[17] Thirteen member states intervened in their support. The grounds of appeal can be summarized as follows: 1) the General Court failed to recognize the regulation's immunity from review; 2) the review was in any event too intrusive; and 3) the General Court failed to appreciate – on the merits – the counterbalancing elements that alleviate or justify the violation of Kadi's rights (essentially, the need for confidentiality and the existence of UN and EU procedures allowing Kadi to protest the listing).

In October 2012, the Sanctions Committee delisted Kadi, following an application channelled through the Ombudsperson. The applicants did not relinquish their appeal, seeking to obtain a precedent narrowing down the effects of the General Court's judgment. Likewise, the CJEU did not discontinue the case for being 'devoid of purpose', a choice worthy of further elaboration.[18] In March 2013, AG Bot opined that the General Court's decision should be reversed, in the light of the sanctions' preventative nature and of the improved system of fundamental rights protection at the UN level. In particular, the creation of the Ombudsperson office, which had proved successful, should warrant a presumption of human rights-compliance to the Sanctions Committee's decisions. Accordingly, by virtue of a *Solange*-like mechanism, the CJEU should not interfere with UN acts that do not appear to entail manifest infringements of human rights (para. 90). The thrust of Bot's argument was that the General Court had misinterpreted the ECJ's generic reference to judicial review, endorsing an 'intensive review' (para. 87) which must indeed apply to the external review of the act (its procedural regularity), but not to the

---

17 Joined Cases C-584/10 P, C-593/10 P, and C-595/10 P *Commission and Council* v. *Kadi* [2013] ECR I-0000.

18 Art. 149 of the Rules of Procedure reads: 'If the Court declares that the action has become devoid of purpose and that there is no longer any need to adjudicate on it, the Court may at any time of its own motion, on a proposal from the Judge-Rapporteur and after hearing the parties and the Advocate General, decide to rule by reasoned order.' See Martinico, ch. 12 this volume and Avbelj, ch. 5 this volume. Note that the situation in *Kadi II* was different from a case like C-239/12 P *Abdulrahim* v *Council and Commission* [2013] nyr, in which delisting occurred pending the annulment proceedings before the General Court. The question, there, was whether the General Court could discontinue the case or, instead, the applicant had a right to see the listing annulled retrospectively. In *Adbulrahim*, the CJEU reversed the decision of the General Court, which had disposed of the annulment proceedings with an order after the delisting.

internal review (its opportunity on the merits). The appropriate standard of *internal* review, in the AG's view, hinged upon the ascertainment that the challenged measures be based on reasons that are not 'manifestly inadequate or erroneous' (para. 89), without going as far as second-guessing the decision of the Sanctions Committee.[19]

The CJEU dismissed the immunity claim perfunctorily, recalling its own reasoning in *Kadi I*: the EU is a legal order based on the rule of law, in which the protection of fundamental rights is essential (para. 66). Therefore, all EU acts must be amenable to judicial review for compliance with fundamental rights, without prejudice to the primacy of UN Security Council's resolutions (para. 67). This brief remark represents the consecration of the dualist approach inaugurated in *Kadi I*: the safeguard of EU's constitutional values prevails over the risk of incurring international responsibility for breach of international obligations. When push comes to shove, the Court will strike down abhorrent EU acts, regardless of their UN-stamp. Likewise, the Court dismissed the argument on the review's intensity: review must be full, in principle, and art. 275 (2) of the Treaty on the Functioning of the European Union (TFEU) squarely empowers the Court to carry it out, without there being any suggestion that certain acts deserve more leniency (para. 97).

The crucial determination concerned the merits, i.e. whether Kadi's rights to judicial protection and property had been unjustifiably restricted in the light of the available reasons for the listing (in the AG's taxonomy, an aspect of *internal* review). The EU Charter of Fundamental Rights lists the right to be heard, the right to have access to the file, and the right to ascertain the reasons upon which a decision is taken (see arts. 41 (2) and 47). Article 52 (1), on the other hand, allows for restriction of Charter's rights, subject to the requirements of necessity, proportionality, and contribution to objectives of general interest.

Within this legal framework, the Court turned to the listing procedure and identified the fundamental source of problems: whereas the EU is bound to respect fundamental rights (in all circumstances, and therefore also when it implements Security Council resolutions), the Sanctions Committee is under no obligation to disclose to anyone the information used to adopt its decisions, the only exception now being the publication of the summaries of reasons (para. 107). All issues arise from the gulf between the duties of the EU and the UN bodies' lack of duties. Specifically, the Court noted that the right to effective judicial protection under art. 47 of the Charter requires an ascertainment that decisions affecting individuals be taken on sufficiently solid factual bases (para. 119). Hence, the review cannot stop at the logical cogency of the reasons stated in the decision (as advocated by Bot), but must assess whether they are substantiated on the basis of reliable evidence. In the present case,

19 See Lavranos and Vatsov, ch. 9 this volume.

the Commission could rely on only the summary of reasons. The task of the Court, therefore, was to ascertain whether such a document, in the absence of further supporting information, justified Kadi's listing.

Importantly, the Court did not equate the failure to disclose the evidence supporting the summary of reasons to an automatic violation of the right to defence (para. 137): EU institutions are under no general obligation to submit this information to the Court. If they do not (and in the present case they *could* not, because the Sanctions Committee would refuse to share it), the risk of violation is proportional to the summary's vagueness, but this should not prejudge the review. The Court accepted that the nature of the information might require its non-disclosure for security reasons but reserved for itself the power to ascertain whether non-disclosure is warranted. If it is not the case, the Court will examine the measure's lawfulness solely on the basis of the disclosed information (para. 127). Otherwise, a balance must be struck between the need for confidentiality and the principle of equality of arms – and the Court will again have the exclusive power to determine whether the balance was struck or, to the contrary, the rights of the person concerned are disproportionately restricted (para. 129).

The Court also criticized the General Court for dismissing wholesale the probative value of the summary of reasons for lack of detail (para. 140) and for inferring an automatic breach from the Sanctions Committee's failure to disclose the information to anyone, let alone to Kadi. In fact, in the abstract, a summary of reasons could provide sufficient evidence for the listing, and that more detailed information is not disclosed is not per se decisive. The Court agreed with the General Court that one of the reasons of the summary (about the unspecified Albanian firms) was irredeemably vague, but found that the others were sufficiently detailed, as they specified the identity of the persons involved and the nature of the wrongdoing alleged. The Court then examined these allegations, together with Kadi's comments and the Commission's replies (paras. 151–63). It noted that, invariably, the Commission did not answer Kadi's exculpatory submissions satisfactorily. Therefore, the contested regulation was confirmed as being unlawful, and the errors committed in first instance did not affect the correctness of the annulment (paras. 164–65).

The Court reaffirmed the 2008 judgment, in spite of the mounting pressure by the member states and of the risk to set a precedent for several similar delisting cases. Far from being a decision of principle, it is nevertheless a decision based on principles:[20] its value lies in its systemic impact, as it incarnates the idea that certain fundamental rights cannot be silenced under the cover of generic security concerns, or of knee-jerk deference to the UN Security Council's action.

---

20 Robert Nozick, 'Decisions of principle, principles of decision' in G.B. Peterson (ed.), *Tanner Lectures on Human Values* (University of Utah Press, 1991) 117.

At the time of writing (October 2013), Kadi's legal team is still considering whether to bring an action against the EU institutions for damages under art. 340 TFEU. Since the unlawfulness of EU's action and the existence of damages directly caused thereby are established or easy to argue, success would depend on the proof that EU institutions committed a 'sufficiently flagrant violation of a superior rule of law for the protection of the individual'.[21] The test of seriousness of the breach, recently adjusted to match the standard of responsibility of the EU institutions with that applicable to member states for breach of EU law,[22] calls for a determination based on a matter of degree.

Matters of degree, indeed, are ubiquitous in the narrative chain made up of the *Kadi I* and *Kadi II* links.[23] In the next section, I focus on one of them: the judicial review of EU measures implementing UN Sanctions Committee's decisions.

Judicial review

References to the nature or the degree of judicial review are legion in all judgments and AG opinions mentioned hitherto. They are not *obiter dicta*: they purport to define the EU judiciary's power to take issue with the impugned regulations. In other words, the very outcome of the annulment is presented as a function of the correct standard of judicial review variously suggested. I intend to map these proposals, not before sketching a conventional understanding of judicial review and the range of standards that are customarily referred thereto in domestic regimes. It will be easier to locate where the various proposals fit in the spectrum that, roughly, runs from absolute deference to unfettered intrusiveness.

In the absence of more precise indications, one must expect that the formula 'standard of judicial review' is used in the *Kadi* proceedings in keeping with its common usage in municipal systems. Therefore, it is apposite to note that 'the primary concern of standards of review is to measure the degree of deference owed to the decision-maker on the particular issue under review'.[24] When it comes to a discussion of the various models of review, municipal systems can differ, and a comparative overview is beyond the limits

---

21 Case 5/71, *Zuckerfabrik Schöppenstedt* v *Council* [1971] ECR 975, para. 11.
22 Kathleen Gutman, 'The evolution of the action for damages against the European Union and its place in the system of judicial protection' (2011) 48 (3) *Common Market Law Review* 695. See Case C-352/98 P, *Bergaderm* v. *Commission* [2000] ECR I-5291, para. 41.
23 See Angelini, ch. 3 this volume.
24 Martha S. Davis, 'Basic guide to standards of judicial review' (1988) 33 *South Dakota Law Review* 469, 471.

of the present exercise. Mindful of the fallacies lurking in formulaic exercises,[25] one can tentatively list the following standards:[26]

- *No review*: this standard is self-explanatory.
- *Abuse of discretion review*: the reviewer ascertains that the discretion granted by law to the decision-maker was not exceeded, regardless of the substantive outcome achieved through its exercise. This review is premised on the existence of rules or guidelines that define the legal exercise of discretionary powers.
- *Arbitrary and capricious review*: a decision will be sustained unless the decision-maker is unable to show any rational basis for its decision.
- *Reasonableness review*: the reviewer must simply ascertain that there was sufficient/substantial evidence for the decision under review (for instance, the verdict of a jury). This standard – which starts from a presumption of correctness of the decision at issue – is customarily applied in the review of administrative decisions, especially when they take the form of rulemaking. The meaning of this formula in UK administrative law is somewhat different, and will be referred to below, where appropriate.
- *Clearly erroneous review*: the reviewer can reverse evidently erroneous decisions (not applicable to agency decisions, except those reached through a quasi-judicial procedure).
- *Full review*: the reviewer can second-guess every aspect of law and fact, except those determinations made in the exercise of strict discretion (for instance, on the allocation of economic resources).
- De novo *review*: the reviewer can make anew the determination of the decision-maker.

Note that the CJEU's power of review under art. 263 (and 275) TFEU is not subject to provisos or limitations. In *Kadi II* the CJEU confirms its power of full review of legality of EU measures and rejects all invocations of a lesser standard. Also Maduro, the ECJ, and the General Court had previously vouched for full review, but judicial economy led them to draw conclusions comparable to those applicable under more deferential standards (see below). The parties, the CFI,

---

25 See Chief Judge Posner's remark: 'There are more verbal formulas for the scope of appellate review (plenary or de novo, clearly erroneous, abuse of discretion, substantial evidence, arbitrary and capricious, some evidence, reasonable basis, presumed correct, and maybe others) than there are distinctions actually capable of being drawn in the practice', in *United States* v. *Boyd*, 55 F.3d 239, 242 (7th Cir. 1995).

26 This classification refers to the US system and is taken from Davis, 'Basic guide'. Classification from other jurisdictions might be proposed. For the UK system, see Andrew Le Sueur, 'The rise and ruin of unreasonableness?' (2005) 10 *Judicial Review* 32; Paul Craig, *Administrative Law* (7th ed., Sweet & Maxwell, 2013) 624–25; 645. In general, see Paul Daly, *A Theory of Deference in Administrative Law: Basis, Application and Scope* (Cambridge, 2012), ch. IV, 137 ff.

and Advocate Generals advanced alternative standards reading inherent limits into the Treaty provisions. The reason for this apparent stretch is clearly reflected in the CFI's words: 'Any review of the internal lawfulness of the contested regulation... would... imply that the Court is to consider, indirectly, the lawfulness of [UN Security Council] resolutions' (para. 215). This is not an unintended consequence of the review of EU acts, but a necessary element of its effectiveness: 'the review carried out by the Community judicature of Community measures to freeze funds can be regarded as effective only if it concerns, indirectly, the substantive assessments of the Sanctions Committee itself and the evidence underlying them' (General Court, para. 129).

The quest for the right standard, therefore, was prompted by the awareness that the annulment of the regulation would frustrate an act (the UN resolution) that, in principle, allows *no review*. The difficulty lay in the moderation between the *full review* and the *no review* standards, which would alternatively apply, in the *Kadi* cases, depending on whether one looked at the measures directly challenged or at the indirect effect of their review. Unsurprisingly, as deference makes way to full (*de novo?*) review, the very outcome of the case may vary, since the reviewer is increasingly empowered to second-guess the merits of the decision. In *Kadi*, this process is visible in the gradual substitution of the UN Sanctions Committee's understanding of the relationship between Kadi's rights and security concerns with the balancing performed by the CJEU. In the following paragraphs, I set out to illustrate how this proportionality assessment gradually crept over and took the fore in 2013.

No review

The CFI's pronouncement was one of full deference. It did not even consider testing whether the balance attained by the Sanctions Committee was viable. The *jus cogens* argument was merely *per absurdum*, as it is evident from a reading of the judgment: the CFI disregarded or ignored what *jus cogens* means under international law.[27] It set arbitrarily (but conveniently) the gravity threshold high enough ('in the stratosphere'[28]) to show how the case presented no such seriousness.

Abuse of discretion

This standard lends itself to various interpretations, ranging from the review of legal errors, to the correction of unreasonable outcomes,[29] to the strict

---

27 Elizabeth F. Defeis, 'Targeted sanctions, human rights, and the Court of First Instance of the European Community' (2006) 30 *Fordham International Law Journal* 1449, 1454.

28 See *A, K & others* v. *HM Treasury* [2008] EWCA Civ 1187, para. 18.

29 In the UK, the unreasonableness review is indeed defined by reference to the boundary of the discretion of the decision-makers. In the present classification, this standard is discussed as a *species* of reasonableness review.

policing of extravagant decisions.[30] In this chapter, it is useful to pick a feasible definition of abuse of discretion, using the customary notion of abuse of power. *Ultra vires* review is customary in settings where deference is the baseline. It limits the possibility of reversal to cases where the decision-maker has exceeded its conferred powers.[31] The terms of reference for the review are the rules delimiting the powers of the decision-maker. Special Rapporteur Scheinin suggested that the Security Council acted *ultra vires*, by taking on 'a judicial or quasi-judicial role'[32] that overlooked due process guarantees (see art. 1 (3) and the obligation of art. 24 (2) of the UN Charter[33]). National courts and various commentators made a similar point,[34] sometimes lamenting the EU judiciary's tendency to use instead internal terms of reference for the review, exacerbating the rupture between the UN and EU systems. This kind of review is external and does not engage in a proportionality assessment. It is also reminiscent of the idea of unreasonableness for inappropriate purposes (one strand of the *Wednesbury* test[35]): since the Security Council acted in view of improper purposes, its decision must be vacated.

Arbitrary and capricious review

The review could be limited to absurd errors of judgment, decisions deprived of any rational basis and formal errors. This is commonly referred to as *Chevron* standard, in the USA,[36] or the *Wednesbury* irrational (substantive) standard, in the UK. The EU institutions advocated for this standard in the General Court proceedings: the Commission suggested limiting the review to 'wholly manifest errors of fact or assessment, such as an error as to the identity of the person designated' (para. 96).[37] Again, this standard does not trigger a proportionality test, as the merits of the decision are left beyond scrutiny.

---

30 Martha Davis, 'Standards of review: judicial review of discretionary decisionmaking' (2000) 2 *Journal of Appellate Practice and Process* 47, 57.

31 *Ultra vires* of EU measures by member states is threatened by the Bundesverfassungsgericht in the judgments *Lisbon* (2 BvR 2661/06) and *Antiterror Database* (1 BvR 1215/07). Courts are routinely empowered to set aside *ultra vires* arbitral awards (see for instance ICSID Convention, art. 52 (1) (b)).

32 See UN Doc. A/65/258, Report of the Special Rapporteur on the promotion and protection of human rights and fundamental freedoms while countering terrorism, Martin Scheinin, para. 57.

33 According to which 'the Security Council shall act in accordance with the Purposes and Principles of the United Nations'.

34 See also the Commission's pleading before the CFI (see paras. 269–70). See Gattini, *Common Market Law Review*; Yang, ch. 13 this volume; Francesco Francioni, 'Kadi and the vicissitudes of access to justice' (2009) EUI Working Paper AEL 2009/10 19, 29.

35 *Associate Provincial Picture Houses Ltd* v *Wednesbury Corp* [1948] 1 KB 223.

36 *Chevron*, 467 U.S. at 843.

37 See also the position of the council in paras. 102 ff.

Reasonableness review

This is the standard *enforced* by the ECJ in 2008. Granted, the ECJ claimed to be entitled to exercise full review, after AG Maduro's panegyric,[38] irrespective of the fact that the measures originated from the UN Security Council.[39] However, it was not necessary to go the whole nine yards. The drastic lack of information available to Kadi made it 'a relatively simple task'[40] to conclude that his rights 'were patently not respected' (para. 334). In other words, the absence of UN countervailing measures compensating the breach of Kadi's rights rendered the proportionality balancing redundant. Interestingly, this was also the standard of review advocated in 2013 by Bot, who tried to demonstrate that the Ombudsperson procedure had tilted the balance in favour of a presumption of reasonableness of the Committee's action,[41] and therefore the EU judiciary could confidently decline to exercise the *internal* review of the measures implementing UN decisions. Whereas the common view is that this standard requires no scrutiny of proportionality, Craig rightly observed that a finding of unreasonableness based on the insufficiency or insubstantiality of the relevant evidence is, in and of itself, the result of balancing between relevant factors. This perceptive idea suggests that even deferential standards normally trigger proportionality analysis.[42] Finally, consider a passage from *Korematsu*, a US Supreme Court case mentioned by Maduro to discard the idea that judicial review could not apply to 'political questions':

> like other claims conflicting with the asserted constitutional rights of the individual, the military claim must subject itself to *the judicial process of having its reasonableness determined* and its conflicts with other interests reconciled... It is difficult to believe that reason, logic, or experience could be marshalled in support of [the assumption underlying the impugned decision].[43]

---

38 On Maduro's endorsement of a full power of indirect review, see Gráinne de Búrca, 'The European Court of Justice and the international legal order after Kadi' (201) 51 *Harvard International Law Journal* 1, 30.

39 Takis Tridimas, 'Terrorism and the ECJ: empowerment and democracy in the EC legal order' (2009) *EUI Working Paper* 99, 110.

40 Juliane Kokott, Christoph Sobotta, 'The Kadi case – constitutional core values and international law – finding the balance?' (2013) 23 (4) *European Journal of International Law* 1015, 1016.

41 See how Bot refers to the idea of 'sufficient evidence,' which is a classic proxy for reasonableness review, at paras. 82 and 84: 'listing and delisting procedures must now be implemented on the basis of a sufficient level of information... decisions are taken on the stronger foundations'.

42 Paul Craig, 'The nature of reasonableness review' (2013) 66 *Current Legal Problems* 131.

43 *Korematsu* v. *United States*, 323 U.S. 214, 233-234 (1944) (Murphy, J., dissenting) (emphasis added).

Clearly erroneous review

The General Court carried out the review in line with this standard (again, it needed not to unfold the 'in principle full review' which it had duly reassessed). It took notice of the progress at UN and EU level, most importantly the establishment of the Ombudsperson mechanism and the process of submission of views to the Commission. In conclusion, however, these improvements were virtually insignificant and clearly insufficient to balance the breach of fundamental rights entailed by the freezing.[44] In this case, the General Court engaged for the first time in a summary assessment of proportionality, which was however only *prima facie*. Indeed, Kadi's rights of defence had 'been "observed" only in the most formal and superficial sense' (para. 171), and '*no balance* had been struck between [Kadi's] interests and the need to protect the confidential nature of the information'.[45] The merits of the decision taken by the Sanctions Committee were closely examined for the first time, but the General Court did not appraise the underlying balance, because none was found. When attempting to go beyond the merits and look at the supporting evidence for the listing, the General Court considered the information available (in the summary of reasons) to be insufficient. Granted, the General Court did not set out to reconsider the merits of the evidence available with a view to reformulate the evaluation of the Sanctions Committee. It would have possibly endorsed the allocation of weight carried out by the decision-maker, had it been possible to detect some kind of balancing – which was not. Compare this approach with the standard advocated in the *Miss Behavin'* case before the UK House of Lords:

> Had the Belfast City Council expressly set itself the task of balancing the rights of individuals… against the interests of the wider community, a court would find it hard to upset the balance which the local authority had struck. *But where there is no indication that this has been done, the court has no alternative but to strike the balance for itself,* giving due weight to the judgments made by those who are in much closer touch with the people and the places involved than the court could ever be.[46]

Full review

After the admonishments of 2008 and 2010, the EU judiciary actually engaged in full review in 2013. The CJEU showed indeed little deference, as

---

44 See para. 127: 'the re-examination procedure operated by the Sanctions Committee *clearly fails* to offer guarantees of effective judicial protection' (emphasis added).

45 Lisa Ginsborg, Martin Scheinin, 'You can't always get what you want: the *Kadi II* conundrum and the Security Council 1267 terrorist sanctions regime' (2011) 8 *Essex Human Rights Review* 7, 16.

46 *Belfast City Council* v. *Miss Behavin' Ltd (Northern Ireland)* [2007] UKHL 19, see Baroness Hale [37] (emphasis added).

evidenced by the alignment between the review exercised on regulations implementing Resolution 1267 sanctions and on regulations implementing Resolution 1373 (2002) sanctions.[47] Whatever deference could be warranted in the application of inter-systemic comity, the CJEU has disregarded it by equating UN-ordered and in-house listings.[48] Once the possibility of full review is admitted, the outcome depends on a legal/factual determination based on the proportionality test. In the UK experience, this standard is commonly ventilated in cases impinging on fundamental rights.[49]

Therefore, it is fair to say that the final determination is a value judgment (a question of degree): the CJEU acknowledges the evidentiary value (albeit minimal) of the summary of reasons, the improvements of the UN system, the cogency of security reasons, and the secrecy concerns, as well as the lower degree of certainty that can justify precautionary measures such as freezing sanctions. The scale, however, still tips in favour of fundamental rights. Differently from the previous decisions, the EU judiciary is not simply chastising the apparent lack of balance of the UN decisions. In 2013, the CJEU concluded that the balance offered by the UN system was unsatisfactory under the EU standard. It confirmed that what matters is not *some* balance, but the *EU-preferred* balance (which incidentally is very much influenced by the rulings of the European Court of Human Rights (ECtHR)).[50] A recent enunciation of the EU balance is found in the *ZZ* judgment of the Grand Chamber.[51] It confirmed that lawful limitations to the right under art. 47 of the Charter cannot entail its annihilation: 'the person concerned must be informed, in any event, of the essence of the grounds on which a decision [that affects them] is based' (para. 65).

47 For a discussion of this alignment already in the General Court's judgment, see Hayley Hooper, 'Liberty before security' casenote on Case T-85/09 *Kadi* v. *Commission* (2012) 18 (3) *European Public Law* 457, 463. The parallel is already visible in the General Court's decision, para. 138 ff. See de Wet, 'From Kadi to Nada', 14. For an analysis of this review, see Takis Tridimas, Jose A. Gutierrez-Fons, 'EU law, international law, and economic sanctions against terrorism: the judiciary in distress?' (2008) 32 *Fordham International Law Journal* 660.

48 But see Asier Garrido Muñoz, in 'On AG Bot's opinion in Kadi (IV)' (2013) *EJIL:Talk!*, who points to a realignment of the review of Resolution 1373 listings with the standard of manifest error.

49 *R* v. *Secretary of State for the Home Department; Ex parte Daly* [2001] 2 UKHL 26.

50 Since *Kadi I* (see para. 344), the CJEU has referred to *Chahal* v. *U.K.*, 23 Eur. H.R. Rep. 413 (1996). On the relevance of the ECtHR's case-law on the relationship between the need for confidentiality and the right to defense, see Fabbrini and Larik, ch. 11 this volume. A pending case before the ECtHR regarding extraordinary renditions, *Husayn (Abu Zubaydah)* v. *Poland*, Application no. 7511/13, is likely to further specify the legitimate balance that must be struck when secrecy is used to preclude accountability of public authorities. Thanks to Kasja Granat for the indication.

51 Case C-300/11 ZZ v. *Secretary of State for the Home Department* [2013] ECR I-0000. See Hooper [2014], supra n. 2.

De novo review?

Through a comparison with the standard of review applied on Resolution 1373 listings, it can be argued that the margin of discretion left to the EU Council (the institution responsible for EU listings) might even be *wider* than afforded to the Sanctions Committee in *Kadi II*. In *OMPI II* the CFI acknowledged that, when reviewing EU sanctions, 'it must not substitute its own assessment of what is appropriate for that of the Council'.[52] This warning is not explicitly made in the CJEU's *Kadi II*, and it was rehearsed verbatim by the General Court (para. 142) but only limitedly to the discretion of the *Union* institutions (not of the UN ones). The impression is that the EU Courts are not equally benign to the discretion of the other Council, sitting in New York.[53] Whether full review, through proportionality, would also entail covert *de novo* review (that is, the second-guessing of the Sanctions Committee's determination regarding the opportunity to list), is now unclear. EU courts declare that their target is the balance between values, but their scrutiny of the evidence supporting the listing calls into question the very appropriateness of the listing, not just its negative externalities.

My name is review, in principle full review

To avoid that the standard mutate further, and entail *de novo* review on the merits, the only option seems for the Security Council to change its procedures and bring them in compliance with the European Convention of Human Rights, in order for resolutions to survive indirect review in Luxemburg.[54] Whether there is some space for comity or *Solange* presumptions is too early to say,[55] the only fascinating evidence in that respect being the CJEU's pertinacious clinging to the odd mantra of 'review, in principle full review' inherited from *Kadi I*, which betrays a reluctance to let go of some margin of deferential *manoeuvre*.

---

52 Case T-256/07 *OMPI II* [2008] ECR II-03019 para. 138.

53 See Bot's Opinion para. 71.

54 On this issue, see Iain Cameron, 'The European Convention on Human Rights, due process and United Nations Security Council counter-terrorism sanctions', report for the Council of Europe, 2 June 2006, available at http://www.coe.int/t/dlapil/cahdi/Texts_&_Documents/ Docs 2006/I. Cameron Report 06.pdf. The European Parliament has recently confirmed that secrecy concerns cannot shield breaches of fundamental rights from judicial review. See European Parliament resolution of 11 September 2012 on alleged transportation and illegal detention of prisoners in European countries by the CIA: follow-up of the European Parliament TDIP Committee report (2012/2033(INI)), art. 3.

55 See Kokott and Sobotta n 40. See Tzanakopolous ch. 10 this volume. AG Maduro hinted at this possibility, see para. 54 of his Opinion.

3 Playing Chinese whispers

The *Kadi II* decision of the General Court of the European Union

Antonella Angelini

Introduction: on chains of readers in the *Kadi* story

If only for the ink spilled on it, the '*Kadi* saga' is well worth the name. Few judicial instances have numbered as many tellers as *Kadi* has. The plot set by both European Union (EU) Courts has circulated and been retold among international, human rights, and constitutional lawyers. Although multi-authorial, the saga of Mr Kadi has mainly been construed as one single story, whose unfolding recalls the 'chain novel' metaphor coined by Dworkin to describe legal practice.[1] In his account, each novelist in the chain is to contribute a chapter to a collective work – a task they can do at their best only by first interpreting what has already been written.[2] Yet, the past is not the only source of constraints. The success of their contribution depends also on future contributors: what these latter will identify as the themes they have treated, whether such themes will be dropped, or how they will be continued.[3] The chain novel metaphor thus captures both a process and the (thoroughly constrained) position of each participant in it.

Reading the 2010 *Kadi* decision of the General Court of the European Union (GC)[4] places us at the heart of such a collective enterprise. The decision itself clearly qualifies as one chapter of our chain novel – or saga. The GC's main business is indeed about making the best case for its own understanding of the *Kadi I* decisions,[5] while expounding, unusually at length, on the doctrinal and judicial aftermath of these pronouncements. It is less straightforward, though, that our position as commentators is also internal to the enterprise,

---

1 Ronald Dworkin, 'Law as interpretation' (1982) 60 *Texas Law Review* 527 and *Law's Empire* (Harvard University Press, 1986), 228–32.

2 As stressed by Stanley Fish, the position of the first contributor is as constrained as that of future contributors by the accepted canons of the activity (see Stanley Fish, 'Working on the chain gang: interpretation in the law and in literary criticism' (1982) 9 *Critical Enquiry*, 201, 203).

3 The point is made specifically by Gerald Postema, '"Protestant" interpretation and social practices' (1987) 6 *Law and Philosophy*, 283, 311–12.

4 Case T-85/09 *Kadi* v. *Commission* [2010] ECR II-05177 (*Kadi II GC*).

5 Case T-315/01 *Kadi* v. *Council and Commission* [2005] ECR II-03649 (*Kadi I GC*) and Joined Cases C-402/05 P and C-415/05 P, *Kadi and Al Barakaat* [2008] ECR I-06351 (*Kadi I ECJ*).

involving the same structure of constraints, albeit not the same constraints in substance, as those of the GC. Hence, one's interpretation of *Kadi II GC* comes with an audience, synchronically and diachronically addressed and sensitive to what other readers, and not lastly the Court of Justice (ECJ) in its *Kadi II* pronouncement,[6] have been making of that part of the story.

The main theme of *Kadi II GC* is consensually identified in the intensity of the judicial review of the EU measures implementing Security Council (SC) binding sanctions-related resolutions. From the blunt question of whether to exercise control, the spotlight thereby moves to the more nuanced one of how to do so.[7] In truth, rather than marking a shift of focus, the GC presented the two aspects as falling in the purview of the ECJ *Kadi I* decision, which it excluded to be in the position to revise. And, while discussing at length the intensity of review, it hinted that judicial control remained the core of contention in the scholarly debate it evoked with vibrant strokes.[8] The intensity of review endorsed in *Kadi II* thus seems to involve no higher stake than the application of a fairly established aspect of a precedent. Yet, if only from the arguments of the respondents, one is adverted of the 'continuum of options and interpretive modes' to which judicial review lends itself.[9] How did the Court underpin its construction of the appropriate one? It is claimed that digging into this aspect is crucial in order to assess in substance the position of the GC and, in turn, the import of its *Kadi II* decision.

Our interpretation traces two paths of the Court's approach as both a reader of Kadi's previous chapters and an author addressing its audience. The first concerns the relationship with the *Kadi I* decisions. A few commentators have stressed how 'grudgingly' the GC followed the ECJ.[10] It is, however, less noted to what extent the GC sought to tap into the authority of the Court of Justice to articulate its discourse on the intensity of the standard of review, while developing part of its reasoning from premises akin to those of its 2005 pronouncement. Our goal will be to bring to light this thick backward-looking interaction. The second path traces a more synchronic aspect of the GC reasoning. As further support to the standard of review chosen, the GC took up an

---

6 *Commission, Council and United Kingdom* v. *Kadi*, judgment of 18 July 2013, nyr. See also *Kadi II*, Opinion of AG Bot of 19 March, nyr.

7 In the *Kadi II* ECJ decision, the claimants requested to reconsider the principles set out in regard to immunity from jurisdiction of the contested regulation, but the ECJ refrained from doing so (see *Kadi II* ECJ paras. 60–9; see also Fontanelli, ch. 2 this volume).

8 *Kadi II GC*, paras. 112–22.

9 The expression is borrowed from Jose Alvarez, 'Judging the security council' (1996) 90 *American Journal of International Law* 1, 39.

10 Antonios Tzanakopoulos, 'Kadi II: the 1267 sanctions regime (back) before the General Court of the EU' blog post of November 16, 2010, *EJIL Talk!*, available at http://www.ejiltalk.org/kadi-ii-the-1267-sanctions-regime-back-before-the-general-court-of-the-eu/, last visited on February 25, 2014. See also Tim Stahlberg, 'Case T-85/09, *Kadi II*', blog post of October 28, 2010 (CourtofJustice.eu), available at http://courtofjustice.blogspot.ch/2010/10/case-t-8509-kadi-ii.html, last visited on February 25, 2014.

individual-centred register, in tune with a trend of judicial decisions then blossoming with particular effervescence. In so doing, it is claimed, the GC attempted not only to strengthen its discourse, but also to mitigate the image of 'unfair players' attached to the European judicature in one strand of critiques to the previous ECJ decision.

The diachronic interaction: on reviewing the intensity of review

As the ECJ handed down its 2008 *Kadi* decision, one could have anticipated the likelihood of new proceedings. To be sure, the EU institutions took action to comply with their obligations. The Commission, upon obtaining the summary of reasons from the Sanctions Committee, informed Mr Kadi that his listing would remain in place, and gave him the possibility to submit comments before taking a final decision. Ultimately, Regulation no. 1190/2008, while acknowledging Mr Kadi's submissions, confirmed the restrictive measures against him.[11] Shortly afterwards, Mr Kadi brought a new request for annulment before the GC, advocating for an 'intensive and anxious' standard of judicial review. The defendant institutions and intervening states, on the contrary, held the ECJ had not set the extent or intensity of the standard of review. Mindful of the nature of the measures at stake, the GC should adopt the agreed standard for complex and broadly defined objectives, deferring the assessment of the evidence for listing to the Sanctions Committee.[12]

Both parties agreed that the intensity of review should be established upon an interpretation of the *Kadi ECJ* decision. The GC set out to do so with self-restraint: because the ECJ 'clearly intended to deliver a judgment establishing certain principles',[13] it was for the latter to address what questions may arise therefrom. That extends to the intensity of review, which the Court resolutely denied had been left undecided.[14] The ECJ had indeed endorsed 'in principle [a] full review' of EU measures. Yet, to apply such standard to the procedure set by the Commission implied establishing which substantial elements of the measure fell in the purview of EU institutions. As in 2005, the GC thus found itself at the edge of action, although this time potentially in a more advantageous position. The *Kadi I ECJ* decision provided a shield to put forward major developments of principle, while still claiming to act in someone else's name. In this light, the GC reluctance at endorsing the ECJ

---

11 For the details of the procedure, comprising the text of the summary of reasons provided to Mr Kadi, see *Kadi II GC*, paras. 49–62.

12 The defendants further maintained their claim invoking the 'primacy of the role of the Security Council in that [of international security] area' recognized by the ECJ in *Kadi I* (see *Kadi II GC*, paras. 103–7).

13 *Kadi II GC*, para. 121.

14 *Kadi II GC*, para. 131.

approach plays a twofold role: on the one hand, it shows the awareness of an audience, and disposes of the critiques that may come from the latter by invoking the authority of precedent; on the other hand, it conceals behind a curtain of strict abidingness the GC indulging in its own approach to review.

The pillars of the reasoning – implicitly, the distinction between EU and UN measures, and, explicitly, the full review to be exercised upon the former – are borrowed from the ECJ. Two passages bridge between such principles and the rest of the Court's findings. In the first, it is claimed that the ECJ clearly endorsed a standard of review extending 'not only to the apparent merits of the contested measure, but also to the evidence and information on which the findings made in the measure are based'.[15] In the second, the parallel is drawn between *Kadi ECJ* and *OMPI GC*,[16] inferring that the same standard of review applies in both cases.[17] This leads to the further conclusion that the lack of full disclosure to the Court of the information motivating the restrictive measures amounts to a breach in the right to effective judicial protection.[18] In the view of the GC, none of the improvements in the sanctions regime called for a mitigated intensity of review. As long as a fully-fledged judicial mechanism is not in place at UN level, EU courts should control all the aspects of a measure.[19] Upon these premises, the GC concluded that the procedure adopted by the Commission still failed to meet the human rights guarantees of the EU legal order; Mr Kadi's listing remained illegal and Regulation no. 1190/2008 had to be annulled.

The conclusion reached is no novelty, but the GC pushes some themes of *Kadi ECJ* far in their implications. There is a certain tension in the passages inferring the characteristics of the applicable standard of review from the allegedly clear approach of the ECJ in *Kadi*. One is left dubious that the full

15 *Kadi II GC*, para. 135. To support the conclusion that the ECJ intended that its review should extend to the evidence and information on which the findings made in the measure are based, the GC relies on the reference to *Chahal* v. *United Kingdom*, Application no. 22414/93, Eur. Ct. H. R. [GC], judgment of 15 November 1996, made by the ECJ in para. 344.

16 The *OMPI* case concerned the sanctions regime established under United Nations Security Council Res. 1373 (28 September 2001). Unlike the regime provided under United Nations Security Council Res. 1267 (15 October 1999), the listings under the 1373 regime are left to the discretion of the implementing states. Case T-228/02 *Organisation des Modjahedines du peuple d'Iran* v. *Council* [2006] ECR II-4665 (*OMPI*).

17 The GC considers that certain passages of *Kadi ECJ* 'at the very least reproduce the substance' of certain paragraphs in *OMPI* and therefore 'the Court approved and endorsed the standard and intensity of review as carried out by the General Court in *OMPI*' (*Kadi II GC*, para. 138). In truth, the GC implicitly assimilated the 1267 and the 1373 regime in para. 137, referring to the ECJ pronouncement in case C-5550/09 *E and F* [2010] ECR-1-0000. The GC maintains that the pronouncement confirms the ECJ endorsement of a standard of review comprising the evidence and information in support of the measure.

18 The GC had established so in *PMOI II* (see *Kadi II* GC, para. 145).

19 The GC stresses that a full judicial review must remain in place 'at the very least, so long as the re-examination procedure operated by the Sanctions Committee clearly fails to offer guarantees of effective judicial protection'. For the *Solange* aspect of the Kadi story, see Tzanakopoulos.

disclosure of the evidence and information for listing may accord with what the GC presented as the gist of the ECJ message – namely, to accommodate 'legitimate security concerns about the sources of information' with a 'sufficient measure of procedural justice'.[20] It is also baffling, if not contradictory, that the Court first extended the *OMPI* precedent to cases under Resolution 1267, and then quashed as insufficient the very same procedural guarantees put in place by the Commission which had been deemed to pass the muster in *OMPI*-like cases.[21] From being a judge-made criterion for broaching the different contexts of EU action, the distinction between 1373 and 1267 types of cases becomes a vector of conceptual incoherence inasmuch as the degree of decentralization respectively allowed under the two regimes is cancelled out for certain aspects of review and resuscitated for others. The one-fits-all approach to review, justified by juxtaposing some extracts from *Kadi ECJ* and *OMPI*, thus proves shaky in the lapse of a few paragraphs. But, more than in these aspects, the tensions that the GC interpretation of *Kadi* exposes are those potentially cloaked in the folds of the ECJ reasoning.

Indeed, to insist on the full review of EU measures either proves practically impossible or thwarts the backbone distinction between EU and UN measures. The reason resides in the architecture of the 1267 regime. Behind the formal distinction between the EU and the UN measures of listing lies the fundamental question of who holds the power to decide on the substantive aspects of the respective freezing measures. When it comes to the EU measure, the requirement of full disclosure of evidence cannot simply be met when the EU institutions – and, as the case may be, the Sanctions Committee itself – lack access to the confidential information motivating a listing.[22] Piercing the veil of the procedural guarantees set by the Commission brings the Court into the Sanctions Committee's room, and the distinction between the two measures comes to naught. Yet, the GC at no point enters into the merits of either the summary of reasons or the assessment made by the Commission upon Mr Kadi's submissions. In spite of its self-declared retreat from the hemisphere of principles, the GC is indeed by large involved in establishing the criteria which should characterize judicial review. Its analysis rests at a high level of abstraction, which entails a degree of automaticity in the exercise of review. In acknowledging the lack of full disclosure, and the generality of the reasons for listing, a violation of the claimant's rights is

20 *Kadi II GC,* para. 134.
21 The Commission argued that the procedural guarantees established to comply with the ECJ decision corresponded to those put in place by the Council after the GC *OMPI* decision, which were endorsed by the GC in *PMOI I*. To quash such an argument, the GC holds that 'it disregards the marked procedural differences between the two Community regimes [i.e. the 1267 and the 1373] for the freezing of funds' (*Kadi II GC,* para. 185).
22 See Lisa Ginsborg, Martin Scheinin, 'You can't always get what you want: the *Kadi II* conundrum and the Security Council 1267 terrorist sanctions regime' (2011) 8 *Essex Human Rights Review* 7, 17–19.

forthwith established. Judicial review becomes tantamount to rubber-stamping decisions for annulment.

Counterintuitive as it may seem, the foregoing echoes in some respects the posture of the GC in its 2005 pronouncement. Among the critiques recalled early in the judgment, it is observed that the distinction between the EU and the UN acts proves altogether artificial when a resolution affords no latitude in implementation,[23] and that the ECJ in fact reviewed the conformity of the UN sanctions regime with the system of protection guaranteed at EU level. In this respect, while the focus of the GC's analysis refers only to the impugned regulation, the latter is envisaged as a complex act,[24] akin to what the Court did in *Kadi I*. Interestingly enough, in the second GC decision, the thrust of the EU measure only implicitly comprises SC Resolution 1267. As witnessed in discussing the full disclosure of evidence, the continuity runs from the EU measure to the listing decision by the Sanctions Committee. Whereas the gateway between the two is inevitably the Council act, the Court glossed over this aspect, avoiding all reference to Resolution 1267. The thorny question of reviewing a formal act of the Council is thereby altogether eclipsed by the shift in focus to the assessment of the specific decisions consensually reached by the Committee in tackling the less transparent chain of the mechanism for the imposition of sanctions.

Another *fil rouge* between the two pronouncements is the very conception of judicial review. Admittedly, certain passages of the decision suggest the contrary. The Court assimilated the standard proposed by the defendants into its own in *Kadi I*, holding they both amounted to a 'simulacrum' of judicial review.[25] The ECJ had clearly set the bar of protection higher than that, as much as the full review accorded in *Kadi II* would do. No resemblance would therefore seem to exist between the two GC decisions. This conclusion, though, is worth qualifying for several reasons. To begin with, in both cases the GC engaged with the content of the impugned measures at an abstract level. In the first pronouncement this is due partly to the complete eclipse of the domestic measure and to the absolute primacy accorded to binding SC resolutions, no matter what their specific content may be and, therefore, to what extent they may prevail over EU law *in casu*.[26] Partly, it is the consequence of a review based on the broad terms of *jus cogens*. While resting on altogether different premises, the second pronouncement is no more sensitive to the factual context of the case: as soon as lack of full disclosure is taken as entailing a breach of

23 *Kadi II GC*, paras. 116–17. See Riccardo Pavoni, 'Freedom to choose the legal means for implementing UN Security Council resolutions and the ECJ *Kadi* judgment: a misplaced argument hindering the enforcement of international law in the EC', in *Challenging the EU-Counter-Terrorism Measures through Courts*, (2009/2010) EUI Working Papers, 31, 32–7.

24 Stressing the continuity between the two measures (see Tzanakopolous).

25 *Kadi II GC*, para. 123.

26 *Kadi I GC*, paras. 183–5.

individual rights, all further consideration becomes moot. The upholding of the impugned measure in one case is as predictable as its annulment in the other. Measured against the ECJ approach, the continuity between the GC decisions is even more evident. A thorough analysis of facts is probably one of the traits characterizing the ECJ *Kadi II* decision,[27] but a hint at the context of adoption, and especially at the UN mechanisms for the management of restrictive measures, is to be found also in *Kadi I*.[28] It is, thus, telling that the GC did little but recite the findings of the ECJ in this respect, while not expounding on this direction of analysis.

Aside from the foregoing, a further reason to nuance the sharp distinction between the 2005 and 2010 approaches to review is that the comparison between the *Kadi I* GC's and the defendants' approach is misleading. As to their conceptual premises, the two lack continuity. The GC endorsement of *jus cogens* as a parameter of review had been dropped by the ECJ, which avoided all references to any normative corpus other than EU law. In line with the latter, the defendants advocated for a standard of review based on the EU guarantees of individual rights protection, implicitly conceding the distinction between the Council act and the EU implementing measure. The comparison drawn by the GC is also shaky with respect to the issue of intensity of review. The gist of the 'simulacrum' argument is that the defendants' approach has to be rejected because it only allows a façade review, as the one of the GC itself in *Kadi I*. Yet, far from dodging the scrutiny of the impugned measure, the GC went at length (if not always soundly) to show that the SC and EU institutions had not breached *jus cogens* with their respective acts. Its exercise of review was a genuine one. In addition, to hold that *Kadi I GC* does not provide for an effective judicial review conflates two distinct aspects. That an SC provision is unlikely to be found in breach of *jus cogens* is one thing; that such a review is doomed to ineffectiveness is yet another. It is so not only because obviously, in case of violation, the measure at stake would become null and void, but also because to invoke *jus cogens* as a parameter of review entails making this notion operational in instances of international practice.[29] In other words, inasmuch as the possibility of annulling a measure is a parameter of effectiveness of what is commonly understood as judicial review, a scrutiny based on *jus cogens* scores relatively low. But the very use of such a normative body has marked a crucial stage in the articulation of a notion of judicial review in which international law norms are invoked more with a 'signalling' function towards the Council, than in view of annulment. This appears only between the lines of *Kadi I GC*, which is still much annulment-centred, but has later ripened into the discourse

---

27 *Kadi II ECJ*, paras. 143–65; see also Fontanelli, ch. 2 this volume.
28 *Kadi I ECJ*, paras. 318–25.
29 See Andrea Bianchi, 'Human rights and the magic of jus cogens' (2008) 19 *European Journal of International Law*, 491, 499.

of other courts which have relied on human rights obligations to broach the acts of the SC.[30]

The synchronic interaction: the GC contribution to a trend in the control of sanctions-related measures

Beyond the interaction with the European judicature, the *Kadi* decision is evidence of the GC's interest in addressing a broader audience. Several sources external to the EU institutional context are generously cited, ranging from the judgments of other Courts to the Report of the UN High Commissioner on Human rights.[31] Such references are primarily aimed at backing up the standard of review endorsed by the GC. It is notably so with respect to the full disclosure of the evidence and information justifying restrictive measures,[32] and to the negative assessment of the improvements made in the UN system of sanction management up to the creation of the Ombudsperson.[33] In a less conventional fashion, the enterprise of external actors also provides the background for a somewhat self-reflective analysis. Before broaching the intensity of review, the Court recounted some then recently handed down decisions exhibiting different approaches towards the judicial review of SC acts.[34] This posture profiles, if not of dialogue, at least of interaction with other international and domestic courts, and brings to light a crucial dimension of the *Kadi II* decision: namely, the GC's attempt at making European courts active participants in a 'trend', mainly, but not only, judicial, on the control of measures related to the SC activity.

After the *Kadi I* decision, many commentators have criticized the ECJ for blotching the reputation of European courts as supporters of international law or,[35] even more starkly, for expressing 'constitutional hegemony'.[36] To blunt the edges of this image, the GC borrowed a much individual-centred tone

---

30 See particularly the Al-Jedda (*Al-Jedda* v. *The United Kingdom*, Application No. 27021/08, Eur. Ct. H. R. [GC]) judgment of 7 July 2011 and the Nada (*Nada* v. *Switzerland*, Application No. 10593/08, Eur. Ct. H. R. [GC]) judgment of 12 September 2012. On the latter, see also Fabbrini and Larik, ch. 11 this volume.

31 *Kadi II GC*, paras. 135, 149–50.

32 *Kadi II GC*, paras. 135, 146, referring to *Chahal* v. *United Kingdom*, Application no. 22414/93, Eur. Ct. H. R. [GC], judgment of 15 November 1996, para. 131.

33 *Kadi II GC*, para. 149, referring to the Ahmed case (*Her Majesty's Treasury (Respondent)* v. *Mohammed Jabar Ahmed and Others (Appellants), Her Majesty's Treasury (Respondent)* v. *Mohammed al-Ghabra (Appellant),* and *R (on the application of Hani El Sayed Sabaei Youssef) (Respondent)* v. *Her Majesty's Treasury (Appellant)* [2010] UKSC 2 *(Ahmed and Others),* paras. 60, 192).

34 *Kadi II GC*, para. 122.

35 Particularly, Gráinne de Búrca, 'The road not taken: the European Union as a global human rights actor' (2011) 105 *American Journal of International Law* 649.

36 P. Takis Tridimas, Jose A. Gutierrez-Fons, 'EU law, international law and economic sanctions against terrorism: the judiciary in distress?' (2009), Queen Mary University of London, School of Law Legal Studies Research Paper no. 11/2009, 1, 23.

from some of the domestic pronouncements mentioned in the decision. Particularly telling are the passages on the nature of the restrictive measures imposed in conjunction with blacklisting. For instance, the GC cited the UK Supreme Court position that designated persons are 'prisoners of the state', or it drew on the Report of the UN High Commissioner to corroborate its observations on the serious impact of restrictive measures in the scale of a human life.[37] The GC still used its own palette to depict the image of the sanctions regime in *Kadi*. The merits of the claims are decided on the basis of the substantive provisions enshrined in the EU legal order.[38] Yet, the Court's tapping into several external authorities is aloof from the strongly autonomous tone of the ECJ.

It is, then, no surprise if the GC *Kadi II* decision has contributed to rethinking the mark of defiance attached to regional (and domestic) courts controlling SC resolutions implementing measures. Much of the initially popular monist/dualist dichotomy to frame the matter has waned in favour of arguments on coordination among different levels of governance.[39] But of course the question of the violation of international law remains. Coming to grips with it, some have ventured that, when a SC resolution leaves no margin of discretion to the state, the annulment of the domestic implementing measures could qualify as a countermeasure against the SC's wrongful imposition of sanctions.[40] Such challenges could count as elements of practice for certain rights to crystallize into *jus cogens* or into some other sort of normative hierarchy.[41] It seems somewhat hard to square the latter interpretation of judicial practice with the fact that courts have fundamentally relied on domestic law to annul implementing measures. Be that as it may, the sliding away from a characterization in terms of defiance represents a major shift in the understanding of the *Kadi*

---

37 The Court cites an extract of the report of the Special Rapporteur on human rights while countering terrorism (UN Doc. A/63/223, para. 16 (footnote 26)).

38 As stressed by Erika de Wet, the principles of judicial protection applied to blacklisted people 'were distilled primarily from EU or domestic law, despite the fact that international human rights instruments such as the European Convention of Human Rights (ECHR) were also applicable to the respective cases' (Erika de Wet, 'Human rights considerations in the enforcement of Security Council sanctions in the EU legal order', in Bardo Fassebender (ed.), *The United Nations Security Council and Human Rights* (Oxford University Press, 2011), 141, 142).

39 See, for instance, Juliane Kokott, Christoph Sobotta, 'The Kadi case – constitutional core values and international law – finding the balance?' (2012) 23 *European Journal of International Law*, 1015. The piece has spurred further comment (see discussion of Kokott and Sobotta at http://www.ejiltalk.org/category/ejil-analysis/). See Tzanakopoulos, ch. 10 this volume.

40 Antonios Tzanakopoulos, *Disobeying the Security Council. Countermeasures against Wrongful Sanctions* (Oxford University Press, 2011).

41 Antonios Tzanakopoulos, 'Collective security and human rights', in Erika de Wet and Jure Vidimar (eds.), *Hierarchy in International Law: The Place of Human Rights* (Oxford University Press, 2012), 42.

story; and the interactive allure of the GC decision has played a crucial role for such a recalibration in the doctrinal debate.

Part of the implications of relying on external authorities still lies elsewhere. The individual-centred register of the Court, in fact, underpins the conclusion that sanctions-related restrictive measures should not be considered as temporary and precautionary when they are not. In calling for the ECJ to revise its finding in this respect, the GC is fundamentally pursuing a battle for qualification. Its strategy is twofold: while the ECJ is the only explicit addressee, the citation of the UN High Commissioner Report and of the UK Supreme Court suggests the GC is trying to collect enough authority for its position to mark a turn in the debate over control, beyond the European judicature. The move is ambitious. Not differently from the ECJ, the GC casted a broad assessment of the system of sanctions maintained by the Council. The conclusion as to the insufficiencies of the sanction system, notwithstanding the creation of the Ombudsperson mechanism, hints at an expressive mode of review, [42] whose focus shifts from the individual acts of the Council to its procedures at large. Yet, the stakes of the battle for qualification are higher. In commenting about the open-ended duration of individual listings, the GC endorsed the claim of the Special Rapporteur that such a course of action 'threatens to go well beyond the purpose of the United Nations to combat the terrorist threat posed by an individual case'.[43] To say so targets the Council in the very exercise of its functions, suggesting the measures taken with respect to sanctions are *ultra vires*. That the Court probably took a step too wide is proved by the cold reaction of both doctrine and the ECJ in its *Kadi II* decision.[44] The move of the GC nonetheless marks an important moment: the culmination of an approach towards the characterization of sanctions-related restrictive measures which had until then remained scattered among different sources of judicial and UN authority.

Conclusion: the essential is in the folds

Since the GC decision, new chapters have been added to the *Kadi* story, and the ECJ has entered again the chain of contributors with its recent appeal decision. If one had to apprehend the contribution of *Kadi GC* from such an angle, it would most probably conclude that the GC approach towards judicial review has stirred a rather cold reaction in the doctrinal debate, and met with little success in the ECJ. Indeed, the parallel between the 1267 and the

---

42 See Jose Alvarez, commenting on the function of the dissenting opinions of a number of judges in the *Lockerbie* case of the International Court of Justice ('Judging the Security Council' (1996) 90 *American Journal of International Law* 1, 39).

43 *Kadi II GC,* para. 150.

44 The ECJ confirmed the preventive nature of the restrictive measures; see *Kadi II ECJ*, paras. 130, 132.

1373 regime, a crucial point of the GC reasoning on the intensity of review, has been dropped altogether by the ECJ, after having been quashed by the Advocate General in his Opinion.[45] In doctrinal circles, the GC insistence on the full disclosure of evidence has led to warnings against the adoption of too blunt a posture towards the SC.[46] That, in turn, has contributed in pointing towards the political character of the issues at the heart of the counterterrorism sanctions regime. But limiting oneself to these considerations would do no justice to the complexity of the GC enterprise in *Kadi*. The developments probably most fruitful of the GC decision lie in the folds of its reasoning. As to judicial review, the attention towards the Sanctions Committee is evidence of the (still cautious) attempt to grasp the layering of decision-making authority within the UN. If the first phase of *Kadi* marked the centrality of SC resolutions as authoritative texts, with *Kadi II GC* the informal decisions taken by the Council subsidiary bodies come to forefront. This finds confirmation in *Kadi II ECJ*, with the in-depth analysis of the summary of reasons provided to the Commission. Another aspect between the lines of the GC decision concerns the shaping of the discursive resources of the current debate on the nature of restrictive measures. The qualification proposed by the GC has encouraged a flurry of responses, ranging from the UN Special Rapporteur on Human Rights while countering terrorism, to the ECJ. In the light of the *Kadi II ECJ* decision, a similar process may in the future concern the qualification of the adequacy of the reasons motivating a restrictive measure, as well as the very character of the procedural guarantees established at UN level. In expressly addressing the issue of qualification, the GC decision brings to light the importance of the spill-over effects of judicial review.

---

45 *Kadi II*, Opinion of AG Bot of 19 March, nyr, para. 63.
46 E.g. Lisa Ginsborg, Martin Scheinin, 'You can't always get what you want: the Kadi II conundrum and the Security Council 1267 terrorist sanctions regime' (2011) 8 *Essex Human Rights Review* 7, 19.

4 Thou shalt only partly judge! Jurisdictional review in the opinion of the intervening states in *Kadi II*

Paolo Busco[1]

> I am not interested in picking up crumbs of compassion thrown from the table of someone who considers himself my master. I want the full menu of rights.[2]

Introduction

This contribution canvasses the positions of the intervening states in the *Kadi II* trial, before the Court of Justice[3]. As will emerge from the discussion, member states[4] are split into two groups. Apart from certain common argumentative grounds shared by all the appellants, some states insisted on the necessity to recognize full immunity from jurisdictional review to European Union (EU) measures that blindly replicate the content of Security Council resolutions. Others, on the contrary, did not challenge the right of the Court to perform its scrutiny, but constrained it within very limited margins. It may seem surprising that some of the intervening parties advocated an interpretation that the Court had previously disproved. As a matter of fact, the judges had already clarified that excluding *tout court* judicial review of EU acts is not a viable option in the context of the constitutional order of the Union.[5]

However, the General Court in its *Kadi II* judgment seemed to adhere to this dictum more out of respect for the hierarchical relationship between the two judicatures than out of genuine conviction. The judges hinted more than

---

1 The views expressed in this chapter are strictly personal.
2 Archbishop Desmond Tutu, *Today* (9 January 1985), NBC TV.
3 It does not feature, on the other hand, the various positions of the intervening states before the General Court. The richness of the arguments of the appellants before the Court of Justice suggests that the analysis be focused solely on that phase.
4 Issues of confidentiality require that in some cases the positions of the states cannot not be disclosed in full. In this article, when a certain argument is attributed specifically to a named state, it means that such a position has already been made public elsewhere. In all other cases, the position of the state will be explained, but it will be generally attributed to 'a country' or 'an EU government' or anyway outlined by means of similarly generic references.
5 Joined Cases C-402/05 P and C-415/05 *Kadi and Al Barakaat* v. *Council* [2008] ECR I-6351, para. 300.

once at the fact that if the soundness of the principle stated by the Court of Justice needed further assessing, it would be for the Court itself to do so, and not for a lower tribunal.[6] Some states must have read into this behaviour a classic case of *excusatio non petita, accusation manifesta*. Why did the General Court feel the need to bring again on to the table the issue of the full immunity from review? Was it perhaps suggesting that someone should raise it afresh before the Court of Justice? It seems that Ireland, Italy, and Spain thought so.[7]

Ireland, Italy, and Spain: the case for full immunity from review

The opinion that the contested regulation should enjoy *full and absolute* immunity from judicial review is the contention of the most categorical nature among those brought forward by the intervening states. Surprisingly enough, the position of greatest deference towards the decisions of the Security Council has not been voiced by the states that hold a permanent seat therein, but rather by those that retain a comparatively stronger position at the EU level.[8] To outline such a 'political' point is not irrelevant, if one only considers that the sets of arguments articulated by many states rest at a crossing point between legal and international-relations-oriented considerations and develop specifically along the lines of well-defined United Nations (UN) Charter and EU law perspectives.

The Republic of Ireland, building upon the Council's stands, paved the way for reopening the question of the very legitimacy of the review. It affirmed that, despite the fact that the issue had previously been addressed by the Court in *Kadi I*, the decision did not amount to *res judicata* and could therefore be the subject of renewed analysis.[9] The consequential point raised by the Kingdom of Spain and the Italian Republic was that the contested regulation blindly replicated the content of a Security Council resolution, leaving no margins of appreciation to EU organizations as to the scope of its implementation.[10] As a matter of fact, whereas in some cases the Security Council limits

---

6 Case T-85/09 *Kadi v. Commission* [2010] ECHR II-0000, para. 121.

7 This emerges quite straightforwardly from the pleading of the Italian Republic. The text of the intervention is reported in full in Maurizio Fiorilli, 'Il caso Kadi. La legittimazione dei giudici comunitari a sindacare le risoluzioni del Consiglio di Sicurezza' (2011) 3 *Rassegna Avvocatura dello Stato* 1, 17.

8 A possible explanation could be that the permanent members feel that the right to veto resolutions gives them full control of the 'normative' powers of the Security Council. It is not clear, on the contrary, why non-permanent members would support the idea of totally excluding the review of an act that they cannot as effectively oppose at the moment of its adoption.

9 On file with author. For a summary of this position, see generally *Report for the Hearing*, Joined Cases C-584/10 P, C-593/10 P, and C-595/10 P, para. 54.

10 See Fiorilli (n7) 11. On file with author. For a summary of these positions, see *Report for the Hearing*, para. 53.

itself to setting out the criteria according to which states should identify suspected terrorists, Resolution 1267 (1999), under which the case of *Kadi* falls, already featured the exact list of people to be targeted by the asset freezing.

In a case like this, judicial review of the regulation in the light of the principles of a 'municipal legal order of transnational dimension'[11] would only formally concern an EU act. Substantially, it would reverberate its effects on the merits of the Security Council resolution. From a political perspective, this result is unacceptable. The Council is the organ with the primary responsibility for assessing and responding to threats to international peace and security. Allowing a regional judicature to challenge its evaluations would deprive it of its statutory functions and also jeopardize the effectiveness of the whole system put in place by ch. VII of the UN Charter. Massive annulments would undermine the uniformity and immediateness of actions undertaken. They could lead to the very dismantling of the anti-terrorism strategy.[12]

These policy considerations provide the contextual background to more legally oriented arguments. Encroaching upon the Security Council's prerogatives in this way, and, for instance, considering one of its resolutions to be illegal, implies the breach of the primacy in international law of the obligations placed upon states by art. 25 of the Charter and guaranteed by the provision of its art. 103.[13] In the constant interpretation of the International Court of Justice, obligations that stem from a decision of the Security Council 'prevail over any other international agreement' and, in the case of conflict between 'regional, bilateral and even multilateral arrangements' and a Security Council decision, the former 'must always be made subject to the provisions of art. 103 of the Charter'.[14]

In the case of *Kadi*, the contrast is very evident. As explained by two national governments[15], on the one hand, member states would be bound by the decision of the EU judicature to annul and deprive of any effect the contested regulation. On the other hand, however, they should recognize it full force as a binding act of the UN. The Italian Republic described this irreconcilable contradiction in detail. It clarified that art. 103 of the Charter would normally provide a possible way out of the impasse, by enabling states to override their obligations under EU law and give precedence to those under the Charter. However, allowing states to act in areas that have long been devoted to the exclusive competence of the Union would be much more than simply bypassing a discrete standoff that derives from the incompatibility of two sets of obligations. It would imply the large-scale dismantling of the

---

11 Samantha Besson, 'European legal pluralism after Kadi' (2009) 5 *European Constitutional Law Review* 237, 264.
12 See generally *Report for the Hearing,* para. 55. To the same effect, see Fiorilli (n7) 12 ff.
13 On file with author.
14 *Nicaragua* v. *United States of America,* Judgment of 26 November 1984, *ICJ Reports* 392.
15 On file with author.

principles of functioning of the EU and, in particular, of the intangible rule of the prevalence of community law over national law.[16]

The only solution would seem to be that of preventing a situation like this from occurring in the first place. For some of the interveners, this can only be achieved by limiting or, better still, excluding the supervising powers of the Union tribunals. Italy explained that the EU should treat the question of the review of the decisions of the Security Council in the same way as a domestic jurisdiction would.[17] This is the case because the Union does not have the 'competence of its competence' and, in observance of both the principle of attribution and of the rule *nemo plus iuris transferre potest quam ipse habet*, it is not in a position to do what would individually be prohibited to each single state. Competence and limits to competence stay and fall together, and the process of devolution is not also one of degradation, whereby a non-discretionary duty to act in a certain way is transformed into a mere option.

To this end, the Italian Republic expounded that case law is quite consistent in ruling out the possibility that domestic judges may replace their own assessment with the decisions of the political body of the UN.[18] In *Dubsky* v. *Ireland* the High Court refused to exert any form of control over Resolution 1368 (2001), holding that 'it is neither permissible nor appropriate for this court to seek to even interpret a Security Council Resolution'.[19] Similarly, and specifically with regard to Resolution 1267, the Turkish Council of State in *Al-Qadi* declared itself incompetent to pronounce over the legitimacy of domestic acts of mere implementation of the resolution, owing to arts. 24 (1), 25 (e), and 48 (2) of the UN Charter.[20] For the same reason, in *Sayadi and Vinck* the Brussels court held, albeit incidentally, that it had no jurisdiction to interfere with Security Council resolutions.[21]

Exclusive competence of the EU and member states' responsibility

There is, however, more. The considerations made above must be contextualized within a normative background that requires states to devolve some competencies to the EU in an exclusive way, but still places responsibility for the violation of the duties associated with those competencies upon their original holders. Some countries may feel trapped by this mechanism: as one national government explained, once competences are transferred to the EU,

16 See Fiorilli (n7) 23.
17 *Ibid.*, 18.
18 *Ibid.*
19 *Dubsky* v. *Government of Ireland* [2005] IEHC 442, para. 91.
20 Quoted in Antonios Tzanakopoulos, 'Domestic court reactions to UN Security Council sanctions', in August Reinisch (ed.), *Challenging Acts of International Organizations before National Courts* (OUP, 2010), 64.
21 *Ibid.*, 20, 64.

member states can no longer exercise them, nor retrieve them.[22] The consequence of this situation is that if communal action fails when it is necessary, the EU itself pushes states in a position of illegality. It is clear for two of the interveners that financial-freezing measures have the potential of affecting the functioning of the common market, an area reserved to the exclusive regulation of the EU. In this case member states would have no alternative but to stand back and watch as the very EU engages its international liability for not implementing a binding measure of the Security Council that it could not implement autonomously.[23]

In conclusion, the argument voiced by the first group of the intervening states can be articulated as follows: 1) arts. 25 and 103 oblige member states to abide by Security Council resolutions; 2) the practice of states that declare that they want to abide by their international duties rules out any review of acts of mere implementation of such resolutions; 3) when exercising one of its attributed competencies, the EU has to do so with the same width and limits as members states; 4) member states, in any case, could not enact the asset-freezing measures individually, since implementing financial sanctions autonomously would deal a serious wound to the common market and ultimately invade the exclusive prerogatives of the EU; and 5) the EU could not act (or, as in this case, fail to act) in such a way as to engage its members' liability for breach of those international obligations, for which they retain responsibility.

A full and rigorous standard of review?

The position that the contested regulation should enjoy full and absolute immunity was brought forward by a limited number of states. However all the interveners agreed, some as a subordinate argument and others as their main contention, that the General Court erred in law in interpreting the Court of Justice's decision as requiring a thorough, full, and rigorous review of the asset-freezing measure.

According to the Republic of Bulgaria, the Czech Republic, the Kingdom of Denmark, the French Republic, the Republic of Ireland, the Italian Republic, the Grand Duchy of Luxembourg, the Republic of Hungary, the Kingdom of the Netherlands, the Slovak Republic, and the Republic of Finland, the Court of Justice in *Kadi I* did not take a position on the depth of the review that the Union judicature should entertain with respect to an act that implements a decision of the Security Council.[24] Quite the contrary, all the Court did was to exclude that in a constitutional legal order where fundamental human rights have a central role, there may exist pockets of

---

22 On file with author.
23 On file with author.
24 See generally *Report for the Hearing*, para. 58. The pleadings of all the intervening states support this position. Proof on file with author.

complete immunity from jurisdictional control of provisions of a potentially ablative nature as regards those rights. The real scope of the assertion of this rule would emerge quite clearly, according to the interveners, from the specificity of the language used by the Court of Justice. The judges held that judicial review simply 'cannot be *excluded*'[25] and '*generalized* immunity from jurisdiction' [26] within the internal legal order of the community cannot be granted and, again, acts implementing Security Council's decisions cannot escape 'all review by community judicature'.[27]

In other words, only *the absolute lack of any form* of jurisdictional control is incompatible with the principles of EU law.[28] Identifying the actual level of the pervasiveness of the scrutiny, however, is quite another matter, which the Court did not venture to explore in *Kadi I*. On the contrary, it spoke very generically of 'review, *in principle* full review' of the measures at issue.[29] According to the Republic of Bulgaria, the Kingdom of Denmark, the Republic of Ireland, and the Kingdom of the Netherlands, the nuanced language and, in particular, the usage of the expression 'in principle', leave significant margins of appreciation as to the actual standard of assessment required. This will fall somewhere between the two extremes of absolute immunity and complete, rigorous scrutiny.[30]

How intense in practice the review should be depends on the sorts of conflicting interests that are at stake in each single case. The Republic of Bulgaria[31] believed, for example, that the flexible language of the Court is an indication that the scrutiny should be such as to reconcile the need to guarantee international peace and security with the respect of fundamental human rights. A standard of review 'full and rigorous', on the other hand, would unduly make a disproportionate and far too abstract choice about which values to give preference to, excluding the possibility of performing the essential 'delicate act of balancing'.[32] Other interpretations are offered, too. The Republic of Finland, for instance, claimed that the Court of Justice only made use of the cited expression in order to disprove the General Court's position in *Kadi I* that non-conformity to *jus cogens* is the only parameter under which the assessment of an implementing measure can be performed.[33] Another European country held that the adjective 'full', as a specification of the term review, should not be referred to the intensity of the review but rather to the 'ambit of the fundamental rights that will be considered' under such an analysis.[34]

---

25 *Kadi and Al Barakaat* v. *Council*, n. 5, para. 374.
26 *Ibid.*, para. 321.
27 *Ibid.*, para. 343.
28 See generally *Report for the Hearing*, para. 59
29 *Kadi and Al Barakaat* v. *Council*, n. 5, para. 326.
30 See generally *Report for the Hearing*, para. 58; see also Fontanelli, ch. 2 this volume.
31 *Report for the Hearing*, para. 59.
32 On file with author.
33 See generally *Report for the Hearing*, para. 59.
34 On file with author.

The (bad) consequences of a full review

The interveners felt that with the line of thought explained above they could rule out that the Court of Justice *imposed* a full and rigorous standard in the examination of the regulation. They also believed it was useful to reinforce their arguments with a *'quasi ad absurdum'* reasoning, which would unveil the dramatic consequences of the application of the contested standard of scrutiny. It is very telling, as is discussed in the concluding remarks of this chapter, that the arguments voiced by the states that convened on the necessity of a limited review overlap with those that pushed for full immunity. So again, according to all the appellants, a full enquiry into the regulation would be equal to denying that the EU must comply with international obligations, in particular those enshrined in the UN Charter. This is untenable, especially in the light of the recent inclusion of the said obligations in the preamble of the Treaty on the Functioning of the EU.[35] In the opinion of the United Kingdom, furthermore, the provision of the first part of art. 351 of the treaty does not allow any activity that, even indirectly, sterilizes the prescriptive content of the norm and the prevalence of certain international agreements over EU law, as authorized therein.[36]

According to a European government, a full and rigorous standard of analysis neglects the differences between the autonomous and non-autonomous sanction regime, as seen above, nullifying *de facto* a difference which is most evident in international law, and treating as homogeneous dissimilar situations which should not be disciplined by mechanical analogical extensions of methodological approaches.[37] In the opinion of the United Kingdom, faced with the inaction of the EU, states may have to implement autonomously measures which constitute a hindrance to the free circulation of capital (such as the asset-freezing orders), trespassing into the EU's exclusive prerogatives.[38] Also politically, the consequences would be grave: one country warned that the Security Council could be discredited and paradoxically portrayed as an enemy to 'human rights', the very same rights that it actively seeks to protect by means of smart sanctions.[39]

The correct standard of review

What is, then, the correct standard of review to which asset-freezing measures should be subject? The guiding principle should be that of reconciling the two conflicting goals of guaranteeing the right to defence with the maintenance of international peace and security.[40] And also, as another government said, that

---

35 This contention is shared by all the intervening states. Proof on file with author.
36 See generally *Report for the Hearing*, para. 63.
37 On file with author.
38 See generally *Report for the Hearing*, para. 63.
39 On file with author.
40 On file with author.

Security Council's resolutions have to be complied with in any case.[41] This means that although in general terms member states are free to choose how to enact a Security Council's decision, the more detailed and precise resolutions are, the more limited the margins of appreciation in their implementation and, by the same token, the more restricted the scope of the judicial review.

According to one government, in order to identify the specific obligations placed upon states, a preliminary interpretation of Security Council resolutions is required.[42] This should conform to the standards set out by the European Court of Human Rights in *Al Jeddah*: it must be presumed that resolutions are, and therefore should be interpreted, in compliance with the prescriptions of human rights law.[43] It is not possible to exclude a priori however, that, given the role of the UN main political body in keeping international peace and security, a different interpretative outcome may still be feasible. This is especially the case when the wording of a resolution so requires, because what is certain is that an interpretation *contra legem* of the resolution would not in any case be sustainable.[44] Therefore, a judicial review so pervasive as to allow for the *de facto* disapplication of the Security Council resolution would not be permissible, because it would put the state in flagrant breach of its obligation under the Charter.

In essence, as explained by one government:

> the review should not go beyond the bounds of that applicable, under the case law of the Court of Justice, in cases where the EU institutions are required to adopt complicated {*sic*} of a political nature, in a sphere in which they enjoy a broad discretion.[45]

Practically speaking, this would happen in very few cases. According to the Republic of Bulgaria, the Czech Republic, and the United Kingdom, one case would be a review of the manifest error of assessment (which would for instance occur in the case of the erroneous application of the asset-freezing measure to people other than the addresses identified by the Security Council). In the Kingdom of Spain's position, the limited review is tantamount to proposing a correct interpretation in cases where the terms of the resolution may be ambiguous.[46] France spoke of 'errors of such significance that the EU should have informed the Sanctions Committee of them', whereas the Republic of Hungary wanted to limit the review to 'clear infringements of fundamental rights'.[47] The various declinations of this approach, according to the interveners,

---

41 On file with author.
42 On file with author.
43 ECtHR, *Al-Jedda* v. *The United Kingdom*, App. no. 27021/08, 7 July 2011. 50 ILM 950 (2011).
44 On file with author.
45 On file with author.
46 *Report for the Hearing*, para. 63.
47 *Ibid.*

are also the only ones that strike a balance between the primacy of UN Charter obligations and the importance to protect fundamental human rights.[48]

The nature of the sanctions

The Czech Republic, the French Republic, the Republic of Ireland, the Italian Republic, the Republic of Hungary, the Republic of Austria, and the UK also challenged the qualification of the asset-freezing orders provided by the General Court. Contrary to the Tribunal's view, which recognized in the measures the typical traits of a criminal, *ex-post-facto* sanction, the intervening states stressed the non-punitive, markedly preventative nature of the provisions.[49] These would be aimed at pre-empting possible future threats to international peace and security and not punish an already perfected violation of the international order. France stressed that measures of the kind affecting Mr Kadi were administrative in nature since they left untouched the right to property of the owner, and simply implied a constraint on the possibility of exercising such right.[50] Another member state pointed to the limited efficacy, time-wise, of the measures at issue, which, unlike punitive sanctions, are revoked when the threat they aim to prevent is no longer present.[51]

The exact classification of the asset-freezing measures is not a sterile exercise of taxonomy, but determines the exact width of the remedies that must be ensured to bring the imposition process within the dominion of procedural legality. As stressed by the Italian Republic[52] and the Slovak Republic[53], the intensity of the review against a regulation that infringes upon a certain right must be calibrated proportionally to the level of aggression that it determines against such a right. The deeper the compression of the individual position is, the more intense the judicial review has to be. When an individual is faced with a criminal charge and, subsequently, a criminal sanction, the full set of guarantees of art. 6 (1) of the European Convention on Human Rights (ECHR) apply, which entail the necessity to subject the imposition mechanism to the control of an independent judicial tribunal. In the case of a mere administrative measure, on the contrary, the affected party may be entitled to a fair hearing or to just a review by an administrative authority.[54] Again, whereas the principle of *ne bis in idem* is operative in the field of criminal sanctioning, it does not activate in the case of administrative measures.[55] Along these lines of thought, therefore, the review process of the asset-freezing orders

---

48 On file with author.
49 *Report for the Hearing*, para. 66.
50 *Ibid.*
51 *Ibid.*
52 See Fiorilli (n7) 31.
53 *Report for the Hearing*, par. 66.
54 On file with author.
55 See Fiorilli (n7) 32.

could stop at a sub-jurisdictional stage and hence be performed through the mechanism set up at UN level.

Improvements in the mechanism at UN level

As for this mechanism, all member states essentially pointed out that after the procedural improvements which characterized its development over the last few years, this would have afforded Mr Kadi a degree of protection of his interests on a par with that guaranteed by a fully-fledged judicial procedure.[56] In 2005, in particular, the General Assembly demanded that fair and clear procedures exist for placing individuals and entities on sanctions lists and for removing them, as well as for granting humanitarian exceptions.[57] Since then, what used to be an essentially diplomatic and intergovernmental procedure to seek delisting gradually turned into a solution able to offer the guarantees of impartiality, transparency, independence, and fairness to applicants seeking to be removed from freezing-asset lists.

For example, the Republic of Finland and the UK explained that in the past sanctions against an individual could only be lifted with the unanimous deliberation of all the members of the Sanction Committee.[58] Nowadays, on the other hand, the delisting is an automatic outcome if after 60 days of the Ombudsperson recommendation to delist, the Sanction Committee has not unanimously decided to the contrary. Similarly, the Ombudsperson does not comprise states' representatives, but independent and impartial members.

In the light of these developments, intervening members found it remarkable that Mr Kadi never availed himself of the UN delisting procedure. For some, institutionally wise, this would amount to a breach of the principle of cooperation between the UN and the EU.[59] For others, like the Kingdom of Denmark, Mr Kadi was under an obligation to exhaust the prior remedies offered by the administrative procedure.[60] This is the case because according to the principles of administrative due process, the review is not just in the interest of the claimant, but also in that of the Sanctions Committee. As a matter of fact, in the interest of peace and security, the organization should be put in the situation to remedy its own potential misjudgments. This phase of the procedure, therefore, could not simply be skipped.[61]

For the Italian Republic, the institution of a review procedure at the UN level, just as the setting up of an international tribunal, are measures adopted under ch. VII with a view to protecting peace and security and could not simply

---

56 See generally *Report for the Hearing*, para. 79 ff.
57 A/RES/60/1 (2005), para. 109. See also Fiorilli (n7) 34.
58 See generally *Report for the Hearing*, para. 79.
59 On file with author.
60 See generally *Report for the Hearing*, para. 79.
61 See Fiorilli (n7) 42.

be circumvented on the consideration that other remedies may be more convenient for the private interests of one party.[62] This is why two countries also warned against the risk of a 'judicial forum shopping' if each applicant was to be allowed to choose the review mechanism that best suits their interest.[63] Only for the Czech Republic, in the case of a manifest deficiency of the available mechanisms at UN level, would the claimant be allowed to bring its case before a court straightaway[64] – a condition, however, quite difficult to fulfil when one considers the improvements of the UN review mechanism explained earlier.

Of crumbles and full menus

By now it should be clear why the interveners took a firm stand against the General Court's conclusion that failure by the Commission to provide Mr Kadi access to the evidence produced against him amounted to a violation of his right of defence. It is an issue that is interwoven with the one of the intensity of the review, so much so that it could be considered as the other side of the same coin. A full and rigorous review would require the Court to assess a considerable amount of evidentiary elements related to the merits of the asset freezing-measure, just as much as a totally uncompressed right of defence would demand access to all the elements brought against the suspect. Given that only a *prima facie* review of the regulation would seem allowed in the case at issue, the Italian Republic concluded that Mr Kadi should be satisfied with the communication of the mere reasons of his listing.[65] On the other hand, a request to get the full evidentiary justification behind the decision would not be justifiable. According to the Republics of Bulgaria, Austria, and Finland, the case *Jasper* v. *United Kingdom*[66] confirms the caution of the intervening states.[67] In all cases where disclosure of sensitive information to an accused individual risks dispersing those data to third parties as well, limits may be imposed to the right of the accused to be made knowledgeable of all the evidentiary grounds on which charges against them are brought.

Only the Republic of Austria took a somewhat more flexible approach and clarified that if evidences are in fact to be provided to Mr Kadi, these have to be interpreted in a mere factual way, and not as judiciary evidences, considering that as seen earlier asset-freezing orders are not criminal, but preventative in nature.[68] The Kingdom of Spain, the French Republic, and the Italian Republic also stressed with particular intensity that it would be impossible even from an

---

62 *Ibid.*
63 On file with author.
64 See generally *Report for the Hearing*, para. 79.
65 See Fiorilli (n7) 40.
66 *Jasper* v. *United Kingdom* (2000) 30 EHRR 441.
67 *Report for the Hearing*, para. 71.
68 *Ibid.*, 74.

operational point of view to provide a suspect of international terrorism with all the evidentiary elements brought against him.[69] Such information is in the exclusive possession of the Security Council, and an order of disclosure issued by a court against the supreme organ of the UN would be impossible to envisage, both from a subjective point of view and because of the objective sensitivity of the data, which are legitimately covered by a procedural secret.

The same considerations hold true from the perspective of the implementing phase of the Security Council's regulations. The Commission, simply asked to give effect to an 'external order', is not in possession of any of the elements used by the Sanctions Committee to reach its conclusion on the opportunity to list a person. Therefore, even if it were requested by the Court to preliminary review the merits of the asset-freezing measure, it would not have the elements do so. This would determine a perennial breach of EU law in as much as even when an asset-freezing regulation is annulled for lack of sufficient evidence disclosed to its addressee, the EU institutions could only reissue it on the basis of the same amount of information that they originally had.

Conclusions

The contorted vicissitudes of the *Kadi* trial are a story of petitions of principles and of paying lip service to them. Most of all, they are a story of not calling things by their names. It seems that both parties to this dispute could not resist the temptation to dwell in the comfortable realms of half-truths, euphemisms, and understatements. On the one hand, Mr Kadi contended that review on the merits of an EU measure which blindly replicates a Security Council resolution does not amount to a review of the legitimacy of the resolution itself. This position seems difficult to reconcile with factual reality, and perhaps even more so with common sense. On the other hand, the position of most of the intervening member states tends to draw up artificial distinctions that are hard to grasp in real legal life. This is particularly clear if one sticks to the juxtaposition between the group of states that kept insisting on full immunity from review and those states that restricted the margins of the permitted scrutiny to such limited degrees as to effectively neutralize any chance to assess the compatibility of UN sanctions with the Community legal order.

As a matter of fact, a review confined to procedural blunders such as may be the case of an *aliud pro alio*, or one dealing with issues of interpretation of ambiguous terms, amounts to no review at all – as for the first issue, because in that case the court should only limit itself to assessing a factual element which bears no relevance on the compatibility between asset-freezing measures and human rights. As for the second issue, it genuinely seems too much of a stretch to include in the notion of review of the legality of a norm the mere act

---

69 See Fiorilli (n7) 30.

of interpreting its meaning when this is not clear enough to bestow upon the provision self-executing capabilities. As for the positions of the French Republic and the Republic of Hungary, one could even contend that the sorts of infringements they mention end up proposing again the court-disproved thesis that *jus cogens* is the only legitimate ground of reviewing the legality of a regulation. And, even if this was not the case, they are far too generic expressions void of any operational meaning.

Member states should not have hidden behind any sophistic curtains and should have tackled the dilemma head on. Either UN measures must be subject to the overriding principles of a community legal order that values human rights above all things, or they have to be accepted for what they are, considering that sometimes protecting public order and security comes at a price. The choice to be made was probably more political than juridical, but, unlike politics, in cases like these, it is not possible to envisage third ways.

Part 2

The legal theory perspective

5 The case of Mr. Kadi and the modern concept of law

Matej Avbelj

Introduction

What is a legal theoretical lesson taught by the *Kadi* saga? The *Kadi* case has been discussed widely, in particular regarding its implications for the status and role of, as well as for the relationship between, international and European Union (EU) law. My focus in this chapter is different. I push the investigation to a higher level of abstraction and in so doing try to delve deeper. The chapter therefore asks how the judicial development in the *Kadi* case bears on our modern concept of law. Naturally, this is a big question whose answer will necessarily remain circumspect. It is methodologically unwarranted to draw sweeping theoretical conclusions from a discussion of a single case. Consequently the points developed in this chapter have to be taken as nothing more than hypotheses on the evolving character of the modern concept of law that will either be corroborated by practices in a more or less distant future, or not.

The argument proceeds as follows. The modern concept of law is outlined first. It is argued that this concept of law has been caught in a positivist/non-positivist dichotomy that should, however, be overcome. Instead the modern law should be conceived of in an integrated way. In the second step, the impact of the *Kadi* case on the thus defined modern concept of law is examined. In particular, I study to what extent the core theoretical assumptions underlying the modern concept of law are still warranted in the light of the *Kadi* case. Finally, the chapter juxtaposes competing theoretical approaches aimed at responding to the challenges posed by the *Kadi* case so as to preserve the essence of the modern concept of law. Between the theoretical models of universalism, particularism, and pluralism I argue in favor of the latter.

The modern concept of law

What is understood here by the notion of a modern concept of law is the law as it has been practiced and theoretically grounded since the beginning of the twentieth century, but especially after the WWII, in the geographical and political space conventionally known as the West. In practical terms the modern law so defined has been closely connected to the state. The state has long been considered if not an exclusive, then at least a main source and operating theater of law. There have, admittedly, existed other non-statist sources and therefore bodies of law, most notably international law, but the latter's 'real', rather than derived (of course from the state) legal nature, has always been disputed in theory and in practice.[1] The centrality of the state to the modern concept of law has been so evident, that it has for a long time remained not only unstated but also fairly uncontested.[2] Conceiving the modern concept of law thus meant, almost unexceptionally, thinking of the law in the state: a state law. As is well known, some theorists, in particular Kelsen, even went as far as equating the state with the law.[3]

The self-contained state was thus taken as a natural (re)source of the modern concept of law. The legal theoretical disputes consequently raged elsewhere. Rather than the law's environment, the concept itself was contested. The dividing line has run between the so-called legal positivists and the non-positivists, sometimes known also as natural lawyers.[4] The bone of contention has been formed around two questions: substantive and methodological. The substantive question concerns the meaning of law, whereas the methodological question relates to the way the law can be known. Merging them into one, they essentially pose the following challenge: can the meaning of law be determined in a non-evaluative, descriptive manner?[5] If the answer is yes, as most legal positivists are bound to argue, then the law is an autonomous concept whose legality, within the meaning of its conceptual existence and practical legal validity, is independent from other normative systems, including morality.[6] Otherwise, if the concept of law cannot even be defined (better: interpreted) in normatively neutral terms, as non-positivists argue[7] and even some soft positivist are willing

1   H.L.A Hart, *The Concept of Law* (OUP, 1994) 229, arguing that international law is not a legal system, but merely a set of rules. For an overview of international law's difficulties with its legal character, see Robert Jennings and Arthur Watts (eds), *Oppenheim's International Law* (OUP, 2008) vol. 1, 3.

2   The movement of legal pluralism has been a notable exception: John Griffiths, 'What is legal pluralism' (1986) 24 *Journal of Legal Pluralism and Unofficial Law* 1.

3   Hans Kelsen, *Pure Theory of Law* (Gloucester, 1989). This approach, however, did not go by entirely unquestioned. For an early critique of the statist monopoly over the law, see the institutionalist legal thought of Santi Romano nicely explained in Filippo Fontanelli, 'Santi Romano and *L'ordinamento giuridico*: the relevance of a forgotten masterpiece for contemporary international, transnational and global relations' (2012) 2 *Transnational Legal Theory* 67, 79.

4   Brian Leiter, 'Beyond the Hart/Dworkin debate: the methodology problem in jurisprudence' (2003) 48 *American Journal of Jurisprudence* 17.

5   *The Concept of Law*; Ronald Dworkin, 'Hart's postscript and the character of political philosophy' (2004) 24 *Oxford Journal of Legal Studies* 1.

6   Joseph Raz, *The Authority of Law: Essays on Law and Morality* (OUP, 1979).

7   Dworkin, 'Hart's postscript'; John Finnis, 'On the incoherence of legal positivism' (1999–2000) 75 *Notre Dame Law Review* 1597.

to concede,[8] then both the law's validity and conceptual existence hinge on its fit with other normative systems, most notably morality.

This division has prompted the two theoretical camps into emphasizing their own particular dimensions of the concept of law. The legal positivists are chiefly concerned with the form:[9] with the formal idea of a legal order as a self-referential and hierarchical system of legal norms, whereby the higher norms determine the mode of creation and validity of the lower norms.[10] The formal dimension of the legal order is cherished for its contribution to the values related to the order *lato sensu* (e.g. also to the order beyond a legal order, such as coherence, predictability, transparency, intelligibility, certainty, authority, compliance, and, hence, efficiency etc.).[11]

On the other hand, the non-legal positivists tend to prioritize the substance of a legal order over its form.[12] A legal order must meet certain substantive qualitative standards to qualify as a legal order properly so-called.[13] Hierarchy and self-referentiality are necessary but, insufficient conditions, for a legal order – indeed for its very character of law. A legal order properly so-called must contain substantive standards reflecting a scheme of justice embodied by a legal order. The validity of the legal order's norms depends on their compliance with the said substantive standards. In modern legal orders these substantive standards are known as human rights and fundamental freedoms. According to non-positivists the substance eventually prevails over the form, for even a legal rule which comes into being in a formally correct way can be invalidated, even stripped of its character of law, if it conflicts with or disregards the substantive standards of a legal order.[14]

While the two theoretical camps, by and large, remain entrenched in their respective positions, which are increasingly marked by marginal differences, they should be viewed as two sides of the same coin. The formal and the substantive dimensions of law are indivisible and only together constitutive of the modern concept of law. The modern concept of law is thus an integrated concept with a dual character: the formal and the substantive.[15] The positivist/non-positivist

---

8 Wilfrid J. Waluchov, 'The many faces of legal positivism' (1998) 48 *The University of Toronto Law Journal* 387, 394.

9 However, this is not to say that legal positivism can simply be equated with formalism, though the two are, in my opinion, not entirely unrelated. For a broader discussion, see Anthony Sebok, *Legal Positivism in American Jurisprudence* (CUP, 1998), and a review by Brian Leiter, 'Positivism, formalism, realism' (1999) 99 *Columbia Law Review* 1138.

10 Kelsen.

11 Raz.

12 Even though they must and in fact always do assume the latter's existence.

13 Ronald Dworkin, *Law's Empire* (Harvard University Press, 1986).

14 Perhaps the most representative author of this view is Gustav Radbruch. For the famous Radbruch formula, see Gustav Radbruch, 'Gesetzliches Unrecht und übergesetzliches Recht' (1946) *Süddeutsche Juristenzeitung* 105.

15 Matej Avbelj, 'The EU and the many faces of legal pluralism: toward a coherent or uniform EU legal order?' (2006) 2 *Croatian Yearbook of European Law and Policy* 377.

dichotomy is therefore false. To further their substantive account of law, the non-positivists need to assume, and they indeed do, the existence of a legal order as a form. What counts as a legal norm, as opposed to a norm of another normative system, is, as Dworkin has been willing to concede, part of a pre-interpretative agreement.[16] Only once the latter is in place, and hence the idea of a formal legal frame, can the interpretative disputes about the optimization of the legal order's substantive standards begin. In the absence of a formal legal frame, of the very criteria of the legal, the non-positivists cannot be said to be doing law, to be arguing about the substance of a legal rather than some other normative system. The idea of a legal frame thus demarcates the border between the law as an institutional normative order and other non-institutional normative systems.[17] The substance of a legal order thus must presuppose the legal form. But, the reverse is also true.

The formal frame of a legal order is not an end in itself. It is, as explained above, in the service of values associated with the order *lato sensu*. These values are themselves substantive standards since they guarantee and require not whatsoever a legal order, but such which is just and whose authority (or rather the authority of its legal norms) stems not merely from the form of a legal order but from its overall legitimacy. The latter comes in many forms: as input, procedural and output legitimacy, but irrespective of its exact type, the legitimacy is always at least partly dependent on its fit with and furtherance of the substantive standards of a legal order: the human rights and fundamental freedoms.

The modern concept of law in view of the *Kadi* case

The *Kadi* case questions most of what has just been said about the modern concept of law. It has challenged both the concept of law as well as its environment. To start with the latter first, the *Kadi* case confirms the state's loss of monopoly over the concept of law. The underlying theoretical assumption (but also practice) of the modern concept of law that the state is an exclusive source of law and its ultimate guardian has been defeated. There are other autonomous types of law and legal orders, which are not exclusively of a public let alone statist character. They come into being also independently of individual states and affect them and their residents directly, sometimes even against their will. In other words, the concept of law is now also bred and practiced beyond the state. We are faced with a legal plurality, whose exact character and precise consequences are yet to be fully uncovered and accounted for. But the big question has already been posed: is this factual situation one of a mere plurality of sources of law within a single concept of

---

16 Dworkin, *Law's Empire*, 91.
17 Neil MacCormick, 'Beyond the sovereign state' (1993) 56 *Modern Law Review* 1, 11.

law, or has the shift been more substantial, so that it can already be spoken of a plurality of concepts and not just sources of law?[18]

While the *Kadi* case offers no support to the hypothesis of a plurality of concepts of law, it brings out the plurality of sources of law with full force. We deal with a sanctioning regime grounded into an international legal order of the United Nations (UN), which claims primacy over any other legal order. We are faced with the implementation of the said sanctions by the EU supranational legal order that has also been institutionally and academically defended as its own, autonomous, even constitutional order, equally claiming primacy over the matters falling within its material legal scope.[19] Finally, there are autonomous, constitutional legal orders of the EU member states which have had to apply the adopted smart sanctions against the targeted individual, in our case Mr. Kadi. The state has thus lost the monopoly over the creation of legal rules. The smart sanctions derive from the UN resolutions, which can also be passed against the individual state's will. They are implemented on the basis of the EU regulation, which does not require the consent of all states either. The regulation is, moreover, directly applicable and enjoys by virtue of art. 288 of the Treaty on the Functioning of the European Union (TFEU) explicit treaty-based primacy over the potentially conflicting laws of the member states.

This legally pluralist context, featuring an interaction between a statist and two non-statist legal orders, did not only exhibit the loss of the statist monopoly over the law, but it has also unsettled the modern concept of law in its formal and substantive dimensions. Concerning the formal dimension, it is the notion and practice of the legal hierarchy that have been undermined most. As explained above, hierarchy has been seen as a prerequisite and a guarantee of a single legal order which is ordered thanks to a clear rule of conflict resolution: the higher norm invalidates the lower norm. An ordered hierarchical legal order engenders coherence, consistency, predictability, transparency, it eschews conflicts and ensures its own authority and efficiency. All these values are threatened if and once hierarchy is lost.

Precisely this has occurred with the reversal of the initial ruling of the then Court of First Instance (CFI). That court endorsed a wholesale hierarchal reading of the relationship between EU law and international law, based on the supremacy clause contained in art. 103 of the UN Charter. In so doing, it declared itself *in principle* incompetent to review the EU legal acts which implement the UN resolutions, other than subjecting them to a review for compliance with a yet higher body of rules contained in the so-called *jus cogens* norms.[20]

18 Craig Scott, '"Transnational law" as proto-concept: three conceptions' (2009) 10 *German Law Journal* 859.
19 Matej Avbelj, 'Supremacy or primacy of EU law – (why) does it matter?' (2011) 17 *European Law Journal* 744, 750–4.
20 Case T-315/01 *Kadi v. Council and Commission* [2005] ECR II-03649.

Upon appeal the Court of Justice rejected this hierarchical all-the-way-through approach.[21]

This came as no surprise. The pursuit of formal hierarchy by the CFI basically deprived the EU legal order in the *Kadi*-like scenario of the entire judicially protected substantive standards. To ensure judicial review of EU legal acts, which implement UN resolutions, only against the *jus cogens* norms is like abandoning judicial review completely. Not only are the *jus cogens* norms very much indeterminate in international law,[22] even to the extent their content is well-defined, it is clear that they can offer substantive protection only against the worst transgressions of the most fundamental rights, such as slavery, apartheid, aggression, torture etc.[23] None of these is normally going to happen in the EU and, more concretely, none of these violations was at stake in the *Kadi* case. In short, judicial review against so empty substantive standards amounts to theoretical window-dressing and is practically meaningless.

Unlike some other authors,[24] I am therefore convinced that the TFEU was left with no alternative other than reversing the decision of its lower instance. However, before going into that, let us focus more closely on the CJEU ruling's exact repercussions for legal hierarchy. The CJEU judgment is slightly obscure on this point, but in principle there are two plausible readings of it. Either the CJEU has dispensed with the legal hierarchy between EU law and international law and instituted a heterarchical relationship between the two, or the legal hierarchy was preserved in favor of international law, but made conditional on the latter's compliance with certain EU substantive standards. The former understanding is more plausible than the latter.

The notion of hierarchy, even if conditional, assumes the existence of a single legal order. In this case the international legal order of the UN, whose constitutive, albeit semi-autonomous, part is also EU law.[25] Yet, this conceptualization

---

21 Joined Cases C-402/05 P and C-415/05 P, *Kadi and Al Barakaat* [2008] ECR I-06351.

22 Vienna Convention on the Law of the Treaties, art. 53: *jus cogens* stands for peremptory norms of general international law which are accepted and recognized by the international community of states as a whole as norms from which no derogation is permitted.

23 For an overview, see Rafael Nieto-Navia, 'International peremptory norms (*jus cogens*) and international humanitarian law', in Antonio Cassese, Lal Chand Vohrar (eds.), *Man's Inhumanity to Man: Essays on International Law in Honour of Antonio Cassese* (International Humanitarian Law Series, vol. 5, Martinus Nijhoff, 2003), 619.

24 Tridimas P. Takis, Gutierrez-Fons A. Jose, 'EU law, international law and economic sanctions against terrorism: the judiciary in distress' (2009) 11 *Queen Mary University of London, School of Law, Queen Mary School of Law Legal Studies Research Paper* 1, 23.

25 This understanding would be close to the conception of EU law as a partial legal order (*ordre juridique partiele*), which is familiar to French legal theory. See Allain Pellet, 'Les fondement juridique internationaux du droit communautaire', in Academy of European Law (ed.), *Collected Courses of the Academy of European Law*, vol. V, Book 2 (Kluwer Law International, 1997). According to this Kelsenian teaching, the EU legal order is partial, incomplete, and has a relative autonomy, since it is a creation of international law and since it is, in comparison with the national legal orders, limited only to those competences which are necessary for the achievement of its objectives. See Kelsen Hans, *Das Problem der Souveranität* (Scientia Aalen, 1960) 286.

finds relatively little support in EU legal theory and practice. The CJEU has long held, as it was nicely restated by AG Maduro in his Opinion to the first *Kadi* case,[26] that EU law is a new legal order distinct from the existing legal order of public international law, with its own basic constitutional charter.[27] The two legal orders, however, do not exist in mutual isolation. In practice they are closely related, and yet independent so that effects of international law, without prejudice to its autonomy, are determined in the EU by the EU legal order and its courts.[28]

Unlike AG Maduro, who favored the heterarchical relationship between legal orders, the CJEU ruling in the *Kadi* case was far less clear. While it openly rejected an unconditional supremacy of international law over the EU's primary law, including fundamental rights, it appeared content to recognize the international law's primacy over the EU's secondary law.[29] By turning the *Solange* rationale against international law, the CJEU mimicked the practice of national constitutional courts in avoiding a clear-cut hierarchy between EU law and national law.[30] Yet, the result achieved, the conditional hierarchy is in conceptual terms much less convincing and logically defensible than the heterarchical conception. Hierarchy is either unconditional or it is lost; and a legal order is either autonomous, or it does not exist as a legal order in its own right. The conditionally hierarchical conception of a legal relationship between legal orders is thus entrapped in conceptual and logical problems that are avoided by its heterarchical alternative.

However, irrespective of the CJEU's exact approach to international law, it is patent that the conventional understanding of legal hierarchy as unconditional supremacy of international law over other legal orders lost ground. Legal hierarchy as one of the fundamental pillars of the modern concept of law was thereby undermined by the *Kadi* case. But was that done for good reasons? As intimated above, I am convinced that the court had no alternative. Had it confirmed the CFI approach, it would have caused grave consequences for the affected individuals, such as Mr. Kadi, for the EU's own system of fundamental rights protection, and ultimately for the EU's very character of (the rule of) law.

The reason for this lies in an apparent gap in substantive legal standards between EU law and international law. Since the 1970s, the EU has been developing its own system of fundamental rights protection which is now comparable to the national system of its member states.[31] No other non-statist legal order has reached this level of sophistication of substantive standards and so is true of

26 Joined cases C-402/05 P and C-415/05 P, *Kadi and Al Barakaat*, Opinion of AG Poiares Maduro [2008] ECR I-06351.
27 Case 294/83 *Les Verts* [1986] ECR 1339, para. 23.
28 Joined Cases C-402/05 P and C-415/05 P, *Kadi and Al Barakaat*, Opinion of AG Poiares Maduro (2008).
29 Joined Cases C-402/05 P and C-415/05 P, *Kadi and Al Barakaat*, para. 308.
30 Matej Avbelj, 'Supremacy or primacy?', 744.
31 Gráinne de Búrca, 'The road not taken: the European Union as a global human rights actor' (2011) 105 *American Journal of International Law* 649.

the UN sanctioning regime. As confirmed by the CFI ruling in the first *Kadi* case, none of the rights relied upon by Mr. Kadi – the right to a fair hearing, the right to respect for property, and the right to effective judicial review – was guaranteed by the Security Council's Sanctioning Committee.[32] In contrast, they are protected in the EU, but the CFI refused to effectuate them out of fear of defeating the EU's international obligations that, in its view, reign supreme over EU law. In other words, had the Court followed the CFI path, the rights of individuals formally recognized in the EU could not have been protected against those segments of EU legislation which implement UN resolutions due to the latter's supposedly formally supreme, but clearly inferior substantive character. The EU system of protection of fundamental rights would hence need to devaluate, perhaps even drop, its substantive standards of protection. With the proliferation of such cases, the EU law would find it increasingly difficult to continue meeting its presently well-established substantive standards of the rule of law, eventually putting its very character of law into question.

The CJEU had apparently foreseen this threat and reversed the CFI ruling, stressing that:

> the review by the Court of the validity of any Community measure in the light of fundamental rights must be considered to be the expression, in a community based on the rule of law, of a constitutional guarantee stemming from the EC Treaty as an autonomous legal system which is not to be prejudiced by an international agreement.[33]

Contrary to CFI, the CJEU held that EU legislation, including that which implements UN resolutions, must be 'in principle subject to full review' in light of the fundamental rights as protected in the EU.[34] The Court hence saved the EU substantive legal standards, the rule of law in the Union, and its own character of the modern law. However, these 'achievements' turned out to be nothing but abstract and nominal. In practice the CJEU too left Mr. Kadi's rights *de facto* unprotected, making its adherence to substantive standards of law merely theoretical rather than practical.

In finding Mr. Kadi's rights violated, the Court did invalidate the contested EU implementing regulation, but it simultaneously limited the scope of its ruling, leaving the regulation's effects against Mr. Kadi in place for three more months.[35] This allowed the Commission to adopt a new implementing measure, putting Mr. Kadi back on the list.[36] A new case was soon brought to

---

32 Case T-315/01 *Kadi v. Council and Commission* [2005] ECR II-03649.

33 Joined cases C-402/05 P and C-415/05 P, *Kadi and Al Barakaat*, para. 316.

34 *Ibid.*, para. 326.

35 *Ibid.*, para. 380.

36 Commission Regulation (EC) no. 1190/2008 of 28 November 2008 amending for the 101st time Council Regulation (EC) no. 881/2002 imposing certain specific restrictive measures directed against certain persons and entities associated with Usama bin Laden, the Al-Qaida network, and the Taliban Official Journal (L 322, 02/12/2008 P. 0025–0026).

what was now the General Court, which ruled, albeit reluctantly, in Mr. Kadi's favor.[37] But since the Commission and the intervening parties appealed, Mr. Kadi's name remained on the list. The sanctions thus stayed in effect until he was finally delisted by the Sanctions Committee in October 2012.[38] This meant that Mr. Kadi's EU rights were left violated for more than a decade. That was a strong blow for the substantive dimension of the modern concept of law.

After all, we have witnessed a case of an individual in twenty-first-century Europe whose property has been administratively frozen for a decade without being given the reasons for this and absent of an effective judicial remedy. The substantive standards that exist solely on books and have no practical bite are only paying lip-service to the modern concept of law. This diagnosis grows only worse if one recalls the widespread human rights euphoria in the EU. The EU as well as Europe *lato sensu* is literally replete with *documents* guaranteeing human and fundamental rights. These encompass the member states' constitutions or comparable acts, the EU Charter of Fundamental Rights and Freedoms, the European Convention on Human Rights, and non-written, but legally recognized, general principles of law which embody the rights stemming from these as well as other sources. And yet, in the context of this apparent inflation of rights in books, in practice an individual was deprived of them for many years. This puts the often praised multilevel system of human rights protection in a completely different light.

The existence of a plurality of legal orders, the multiple levels of law making, and the systems of protection of rights might, due to its complexity, enfeeble the individuals against the various authorities. The latter can pursue their objectives in different fora and sites by choosing those that come with less demanding legal constraints. In so doing, they can strategically play different sites against each other and achieve the objectives that could normally not be pursued in the primary locus of law-making, in the state. In this way, the multi-levelness offers much more room for maneuvering *praeter legem* in optimizing strategic political, economic, and above all (and increasingly relevant) security interests, of which the *Kadi* case is a prime example.[39] Yet, even in the absence of such 'strategic' motives, the various sites in a multilevel environment conceptually find themselves, as exemplified by the *Kadi* case, in a vicious dialectics between the legal form and the legal substance.

Staying faithful to the form, apparently, requires compromising the substance whereas, alternatively, emphasizing the substance detracts from the

---

37 Case T-85/09 *Kadi* v. *Commission* [2010] ECR II-05177, para. 197.

38 See http://www.un.org/News/Press/docs//2012/sc10785.doc.htm, last visited 1 March 2013; and http://eur-lex.europa.eu/LexUriServ/LexUriServ.do?uri=OJ:L:2012:278:0011:0 1:EN:HTML, last visited 1 March 2013.

39 Matej Avbelj, 'Security and the transformation of the EU public order' (2013) 14 *German Law Journal* 2857.

form as a bridge between different levels of law-making and as a precondition of the order *lato sensu*. In the pluralist environment the modern concept of law thus appears to be ridden with an internal tension between the form and the substance which (potentially) triggers disintegration rather than integration as a prerequisite for the viability of the modern concept of law. The multi-levelness thus launches a zero-sum game, undermining the modern concept of law and leaving even the bona fide actors at different sites and the individuals affected by their decisions with less than optimal solutions.

The already negative scenario for the modern concept of law existing before the CJEU final ruling, especially its substantive dimension as (un)applied to Mr. Kadi, was bound to deteriorate further following the Opinion by AG Bot. He proposed to reverse the General Court's ruling that conducted a full review of the EU legislation implementing the UN resolution and consequently ruled in Mr. Kadi's favor. While the AG did not plead to abandon completely the judicial review of such EU legislation, he insisted that the standards of review should be toned down.[40] In the cases relating to the global fight against terrorism which require global coordination and consist of preventative measures, exceptions to the full judicial review should be permitted.[41] In short, the AG suggested Mr. Kadi's ordeal to be continued. He was not alone in this. The Commission and the Council, joined by a number of intervening member states, followed suit. The prospects for Mr. Kadi and for the modern concept of law prior to the CJEU final ruling therefore appeared gloomy.

However, the court eventually defeated these negative expectations. It rejected the *opinio juris* formed among the appellants against the General Court's decision[42] and ruled in favor of Mr. Kadi by refining, but ultimately confirming, its ruling. The Court stressed that exercising judicial review of EU legislation implementing UN resolutions is:

> indispensable to ensure a fair balance between the maintenance of international peace and security and the protection of the fundamental rights and freedoms of the person concerned, those being shared values of the UN and the European Union.[43]

---

40 Joined Cases C-584/10 P, C-593/10 P, and C-595/10 P, *Commission, Council and United Kingdom v. Kadi*, judgment of 18 July 2013, Opinion of AG Bot, [2013] ECR I-00000, para. 52.

41 Joined Cases C-584/10 P, C-593/10 P, and C-595/10 P, *Commission, Council and United Kingdom v. Kadi*, Opinion of AG Bot (2013), para 61.

42 It is worth noting that the General Court's ruling was appealed by the Commission, the Council, and the UK, and that these appellants were supported by a considerable number of intervening member states.

43 Joined Cases C-584/10 P, C-593/10 P, and C-595/10 P, *Commission, Council and United Kingdom v. Kadi*, nyr, para. 131.

Finding support in the recent jurisprudence of its national and regional counterparts,[44] it added, by clearly contradicting the Opinion of AG Bot, that effective judicial review is even more essential precisely in the cases such as Mr. Kadi's.

This surprising decision might have been taken because at the time of the court's ruling Mr. Kadi's case was already essentially moot. He had been delisted a few months before in October 2012.[45] The expectations thus grew that the CJEU might even drop the case as this could have become devoid of purpose in virtue of Mr. Kadi's delisting.[46] But it refused to do so. Ruling on the merits of the case, rather than dismissing it on procedural grounds, demonstrates the CJEU apparent belief about the importance of the case. The case has set a precedent governing the implementation of the UN sanctioning regime in the Union and beyond, sending out another impulse for the qualitative reform of this regime. Last but not least, by handing down the final ruling in a described way, the court essentially saved its own face, the EU system of fundamental rights protection, and through that contributed to the preservation of the modern concept of law.

A refined theoretical basis for the modern concept of law

As we have seen, the *Kadi* case has left a deep scar on the modern concept of law, but the eventual intervention by the CJEU left it standing. At the same time it is clear that a new legally pluralist environment, in which the state has lost its long held monopoly over law, contributes to an internal tension inside the concept of law between its formal and substantive dimensions. This tension arises out of disparate substantive standards between different legal orders when they interact. The *Kadi* saga would lose much of its glamour and notoriety if public international law within the UN system adhered and practiced substantive standards that were the same or at least comparable to those of the EU. Provided that institutional actors would in fact implement them, the question of the presence or absence of hierarchy between the two legal orders would not even emerge. The case would be an easy one, as both legal orders would be committed to the same substantive standards that

---

44 *Ibid.*, para. 133; the Court has drawn on the ECHR decision *Nada* v. *Switzerland*, Application No. 10593/08, Eur. Ct. H. R. [GC], judgment of 12 September 2012, endorsing the assessment of the Federal Supreme Court of Switzerland ATF 1A.45/2007/daa, *Nada* v. *SECO*, judgment of 14 November 2007. See Fabbrini and Larik, ch. 11 this volume.

45 http://www.un.org/News/Press/docs/2012/sc10785.doc.htm.

46 Juliane Kokott, Christoph Sobotta, 'The *Kadi* case: response by Juliane Kokott and Christoph Sobotta,' *EJIL Talk*, http://www.ejiltalk.org/the-kadi-case-response-by-juliane-kokott-and-christoph-sobotta/, last visited 2 October 2013. See CJEU Rules of Procedure art. 190 in liaison with art. 149.

would be worked out through the division of labor between the authorities on different levels of global governance.

However, the gist of the problem lies in the fact that substantive standards across different legal jurisdictions are simply not the same. Therefore, provided that we are committed to the preservation of the modern concept of law as an integrated concept whose both dimensions – the formal and the substantive – are equally important, we need a theory that would dispense with the described internal tension arising out of differing substantive standards between the interacting legal orders. This can be done in three ways: following the universalist,[47] the particularist, or the pluralist model.

Pursuant to the universalist model, the substantive standards should be universalized across the globe, so that all legal orders will be committed to the same standards. This is a normative proposal which seeks to overcome the present disparity in substantive standards between legal orders. As such it is subject to the sociological objections about the actual plausibility of the chosen normative agenda, as well as to the normative critique of its desirability. The latter, however, fuels the former. Normative reservations act as a disincentive for the actual harmonization and they are not few. Universalizing substantive standards across the globe requires a choice of a common standard and the giving up of the particular ones. Neither is easy, because the process of universalization will raise concerns of potential hegemony, new imperialism, identity loss etc. All this will protract the actual harmonization or even render it impossible. This makes the universalist alternative not my preferred model. It is normatively unattractive and will most likely never work. The arguments following which the universalist model is already part of reality do not change this conclusion. They are a premature truth.[48]

The universalist model is often contrasted with the particularist model.[49] However, the latter offers no solution to the problem discussed here. In fact, the particularist model lies at the source of the problem by insisting that each legal order should preserve its own substantive standards as part of its identity. This means that in case of interaction between legal orders with different substantive standards each of them will proceed from within the perspective of its own standards and ultimately fall back upon them. In the particularist model, the legal orders are epistemically blind and self-sufficient. They will always prioritize their substance and resort to their form to exclude the incompatible claims

---

47 Universalism should be distinguished from cosmopolitanism which is, as Appiah has observed, marked by two strands: universal concern (that is shared with universalism) and respect for legitimate differences (which is absent in universalism). Cosmopolitanism so understood is thus very close to the concept of pluralism defended in this chapter. See, in particular, Kwame Anthony Appiah, *Cosmopolitanism: Ethics in a World of Strangers* (WW Norton & Company, 2006), xv. and Ulrich Beck, Edgar Grande, *Cosmopolitan Europe* (Polity Press, 2007), 13.

48 Karl Mannheim, *Ideology and Utopia: An Introduction to the Sociology of Knowledge* (Routledge, 1966) 183.

49 The particularist model is sometimes also labelled as communitarian.

of another legal order. This generates a conflicting situation between legal orders, putting at a disadvantage individuals caught between different legal authorities, and also hampers the desired international cooperation.

What is therefore apparently needed is a model that would bridge the universalist and the particularist approach. This can be done by pluralism. Pluralism starts off from the premise of the particularist model by stressing the plurality of legal orders, their distinctiveness, and diversity. However, it then moves beyond the pure particularism, adding a universalist side to it by insisting that these distinctive legal orders always have to open up to their counterparts and put their own substantive standards in the service of a reflexive equilibrium of which the substantive standards of an interacting legal order form one part too. Plurality, as a reflection of the particularist model, combined with the dialectically open-self of a legal order, as an expression of universalism, make up pluralism.

The internal disharmony between the form and the substance in the modern concept of law, caused by plurality of legal orders, as exemplified by the *Kadi* case, can be thus solved through the theoretical model of pluralism. Pluralism preserves, indeed requires, both dimensions of the concept of law. The formal dimension is necessary as a guarantee of the autonomy of a legal order. The substantive dimension is a sign of the distinctiveness of a legal order for the protection of which it requires the autonomy in the first place. However, unlike in the particularist model the form cannot be used as an excuse for the legal order's solipsistic, blind reliance on its own substantive standards. Pluralism requires reflexivity about the legal order's own substantive standards in view of the substantive standards of another legal order. This reflexivity, if genuine, leads to the approximation of substantive standards between legal orders. Since this approximation occurs gradually, through the reflexive engagement, bottom up in the actual practices, normative concerns associated with the universalism drop off.

In that way the pluralist solution posits the modern concept of law on sounder theoretical grounds, that dissolve the tension between the form and the substance conceptually, but in so doing also create the conditions for the improvement of the actual practices. The *Kadi* case, now leaving aside the political geo-strategic considerations that might have considerably influenced its development, would have unrolled differently – and much sooner – had the EU judiciary already at the outset adopted a clearly pluralist perspective.[50] That is to say, the UN sanctioning regime is lacking any kind of substantive standards, therefore to the best of our reflexive capacities we cannot recognize its effects in the EU legal order. This has eventually been said and done after 10 years, during which the UN has started catching up in ensuring the protection

50 Daniel Halberstam, Eric Stein, 'The United Nations, the European Union, and the King of Sweden: economic sanctions and individual rights in a plural world order' (2009) 46 *Common Market Law Review* 13.

of substantive standards first through the so-called focal point and later with the Ombudsperson Office. Yet, this has been long overdue – especially for the affected individual – and, moreover, unsatisfactory in the eyes of the concerned judiciary.[51]

To improve the situation and prevent similar cases from arising in the future, however, the burden of reform rests not only on the judiciary, but on the political actors in all the three involved governing sites: national, supranational, and international. Pluralism offers a theoretical helping hand and breeds hope that the modern concept of law can continue living both in theory and practice.

---

51 The UN Security Council first established the so-called focal point, and then in Resolution 1904 (2009) also the Office of the Ombudsperson. However, none of this has so far been found satisfactory. For the reaction of the British Supreme Court, see its decision in *HM Treasury* v. *Mohammed Jabar Ahmed and ors (FC)*; *HM Treasury* v. *Mohammed al-Ghabra (FC)*; *R (on the application of Hani El Sayed Sabaei Youssef)* v. *HM Treasury* [2010] UKSC 2.

6   *Kadi* in sight of autopoiesis

Jennifer Hendry[1]

Introduction

Over the past decade the name *Kadi* has become well known to legal scholars, especially those with interests in European Union law, –external relations, –constitutionalism, –fundamental rights, global administrative law, international security, international law, and the fight against global terrorism. Indeed, the surname of Mr Yassin Abdullah Kadi has since 2001 come to represent a variety of arguments, approaches and standpoints, and to encompass all of this reasoning and all of these articles and judgments under a single word that is simultaneously representative of and detached from the individual most profoundly affected by the case. The attenuation of the legal hullabaloo from the human individual at its heart is mirrored by this chapter, which will proceed in a similar vein of engagement and detachment in terms of the circumstances and contours of Mr Kadi's particular case,[2] its effects and repercussions, and the scholarly discussion arising from it.

This chapter takes as its core approach and frame the theory of autopoietic social systems (systems theory) established and made famous by Niklas Luhmann,[3] and most notably further developed in relation to law and normativity by Gunther Teubner.[4] While a radically antihumanist, radically antiregional,

1 I am grateful to Clive Walker for his time in discussion of this case, and to Michael Thomson and Tom Webb for their comments on an earlier draft. The usual disclaimer applies.

2 Joined Cases C-584/10 P, C-593/10 P, and C-595/10 P. Also, Cases C-402/05P and C-415/05P, Kadi and Al Barakaat, judgment of the Court (Grand Chamber) of 3 September 2008. In 2008 the Court was still the European Court of Justice (ECJ) but by 2013 it had been renamed the Court of Justice of the European Union (CJEU).

3 See, for example, Niklas Luhmann, *The Differentiation of Society* (Columbia University Press, 1982); *Social Systems* (Stanford, 1995); and *Law as a Social System* (OUP, 2004).

4 See, for example, Gunther Teubner, *Law as an Autopoietic System* (Blackwell, 1998); 'The anonymous matrix: human rights violations by "private" transnational actors' in (2006) 69 *Modern Law Review* 327–46. See also Gunther Teubner, 'Societal constitutionalism: alternatives to state-centred constitutional theory?' (Storrs Lectures 2003/04 Yale Law School) in Christian Joerges, Inger-Johanne Sand, and Gunther Teubner (eds.) *Constitutionalism and Transnational Governance* (Hart, 2004), and *Constitutional Fragments: Societal Constitutionalism and Globalization* (OUP, 2012).

and radically constructivistic theory might appear to be a strange one to utilize when the focus rests, as it does here, upon the respective authority claims of international and EU law, and human rights protection under the EU and United Nations (UN) regimes, systems theory offers a useful different angle on world society (*Weltgesellschaft*), the legal system's (*Rechtssystem*) regulation of the social, and the possibilities and potentialities in functional differentiation, pluralism, and fragmentation. The modest aim of this chapter is to scrutinize and critique from the perspective of systems theory the main strands of the *Kadi* legal saga. The facts have already been covered comprehensively elsewhere in this volume[5] so I will not repeat them beyond what is required for clarity and will instead proceed directly to outline the component parts of this chapter's analysis.

Foremost among these strands is the issue of human rights protection and its corollary of good governance. The Court of Justice of the European Union's (CJEU) decision in *Kadi* can be taken to represent its overt declaration to be a human rights actor *in its own right*. The position taken by the Grand Chamber in July 2013 was to uphold the Court's 2008 casting of the EU as a 'virtuous international actor'[6] and to privilege the rule of law and its protection of individual fundamental rights over compliance with an international regime providing a lesser standard and offering lesser guarantees. While the political motivations of the European Court's judiciary in taking such a hard line on EU legal autonomy could of course be queried, the CJEU's firm stance concerning its 2008 decision in *Kadi* had the effect of reifying the position that, within the EU at least, fundamental rights cannot be eroded 'under the cover of generic security concerns'.[7] Such overt commitment to rights protection and rights compliant action would be viewed in a positive light by both of the main protagonists of systems theory; nevertheless it is important to note that there is no clear consensus between the two as to the scope of rights within the theory. The reason for this is that it is within the field of rights that the differences between the determinedly non-normative sociological approach of Luhmann[8] and the more normatively open standpoint adopted by Teubner[9] are cast in sharpest relief. The 'rights' section of this chapter will tease out the

---

5 See Fontanelli, ch. 2 this volume.

6 Gráinne de Búrca, 'The European Court of Justice and the international legal order after *Kadi*' (2009) 51 *Harvard International Law Journal* 1, 3

7 Filippo Fontanelli, 'Kadi II, or the happy ending of K's trial – Court of Justice of the European Union', http://www.diritticomparati.it/2013/07/kadi-ii-or-the-happy-ending-of-ks-trial-court-of-justice-of-the-european-union-18-july-2013.html, accessed September 2013, 5.

8 Niklas Luhmann, *Grundrechte als Institution* (Duncker & Humblot, 1965). See also Gert Verschraegen, 'Human rights and modern society: a sociological analysis from the perspective of systems theory' (2002) 29 *Journal of Law and Society* 258, 261.

9 Gunther Teubner, 'The anonymous matrix'; also 'Justice under global capitalism', Michael Blecher, Jennifer Hendry (eds) 'Governance, *Civil Society and Social Movements: Special* Issue' (2008) 19 *Law and Critique* 329–34.

differences between the two approaches and relate them both to the issue of fundamental rights in the case of *Kadi* and then to 'good governance' within the EU, which is to say, in terms of the EU's self-description as a virtuous actor.

The next strand to come under scrutiny will be that of the conflict over the locus of ultimate legal authority, which could be phrased as the question of *Kompetenz-Kompetenz*. It can be said that *Kadi* represents a marked departure for the CJEU from its 'traditional embrace of international law' and a reorientation towards a more pluralist approach to the issue of the 'multiplication, overlap and conflict of normative orders in the global realm'.[10] This change of direction is at odds with the more obliging approaches taken by both the European Court of Human Rights (ECtHR) and the Court of First Instance (CFI), which adopted positions that could be described as 'strongly constitutionalist'.[11] However, it cannot simply be downplayed as a misstep on the part of the CJEU. On the contrary, the *Kadi* case appears to have been selected intentionally as the platform for the Court's 'you shall not pass'[12] moment, whereby it asserted the EU's distinctiveness and separation from the international order.[13] It appears that the opportunity presented itself in *Kadi* for a clear statement of EU autonomy in the international realm and this chance was seized upon by the CJEU. From a systems-theoretical perspective, the points of interest here are this robust assertion of autonomy on the part of the CJEU and its result in generating a situation of overt plurality within international (multi-level) governance. A systems approach here not only elides, after a fashion, the hard regime boundaries that lawyers are used to working with and within, but also facilitates the accommodation of such complexity by means of its founding premise of functional differentiation.[14]

Finally, a little attention ought to be paid to the individual-*nominate* of the case in question, Mr Kadi, or rather, to his status and position within systems theory. This will form the focus of the next section, subsequent to which the sections will follow on the topics of human rights and 'good' governance, and will conclude with a discussion of multi-level governance, plurality, and authority.

---

10 de Búrca, 36.

11 *Ibid.*, 19 ff. and 38–42.

12 While this is hardly an obscure reference, I should point out that it comes from JRR Tolkien's Gandalf in *The Fellowship of the Ring* and denotes extreme wizarding stubbornness.

13 de Búrca, 4. Compare, also, the discussion by Martinico, ch. 12 this volume.

14 The founding premise may be more accurately cited as the fundamental distinction between system and environment, from which functional differentiation – that is to say, the differentiation of social subsystems on the basis of their function – can be said to stem. This functional differentiation establishes the boundary between a system and its environment: for example, the legal system (system) and society (environment). Other function systems include: politics, the economy, science, education, religion, the mass media, art, and sport.

Mr Kadi in sight of autopoiesis

As stated above, systems theory is at variance to the majority of sociological theories that, more conventionally, hold the human actor, the human *agent*, to be the protagonist of activity within the social. In spite of being renowned (or notorious) for its ambivalent treatment of human individuals,[15] systems theory is not, as often alleged, an entirely anti-individualistic theory. On the contrary, individual human beings have an important dual role within systems theory: they exist as psychic autopoietic systems in their own right as well as being point of attributions for the elements of the system, communications. This deliberate *decentring* of the individual within systems theory can be explained by reference to what Luhmann was aiming to accomplish, namely to construct a complete theory of society.[16] Taking as his starting premise the idea that 'society... was never human', that 'the notion of a "human being" has always been theoretically problematic and a sociology based upon human terms has always been misguided',[17] Luhmann's approach was an anti-humanist one that attempted to move beyond thinking of society in merely human terms. This decentring required a number of elegant moves on Luhmann's part but the main one was the recognition of *communications* over actions as the systemic elements, which in turn facilitated the all-important distinction to be drawn between system/environment, removing the requirement for further reliance upon the classic dichotomy of subject/object. Luhmann combined these insights to produce an 'overarching epistemological framework' that 'organised and structured communicative processes by providing for the autopoietic linkage of communicative acts to other communicative acts in the form of "codes", "programmes", "media", "expectations".'[18]

Under a systems-theoretical construction, therefore, world society can be described as a 'multitude of self-constituted and functionally differentiated social subsystems',[19] such as politics, the economy, education, law, health, art, and so on, in relation to which individuals participate on a daily basis but within which they are never included nor into which are they ever subsumed. It can be stated

---

15 Zenon Bankowski, '"How does it feel to be on your own?" The person in sight of autopoiesis' (1994) 7 *Ratio Juris* 254–66. For a reply to Bankowski's argument, see John Paterson, 'Who is Zenon Bankowski talking to? The person in sight of autopoiesis' (1995) 8 *Ratio Juris* 212–29.

16 There is an old rumor in circulation about Luhmann, who, it is alleged, on his appointment to the Sociology Department at the University of Bielefeld in 1969, was asked for details about his project. His answer was: project: to develop a theory of society; duration: thirty years; cost: none.

17 Hans-Georg Moeller, *The Radical Luhmann* (Columbia University Press, 2012) 21.

18 Moritz Renner, 'Death by complexity – the financial crisis and the crisis of law in world society' in Paul Kjaer, Gunther Teubner, and Alberto Febbrajo (eds.) *The Financial Crisis in Constitutional Perspective: The Dark Side of Functional Differentiation* (Hart, 2011).

19 Jiří Přibáň, 'Multiple sovereignty: on Europe's self-constitutionalization and legal self-reference' (2010) 23 *Ratio Juris* 41, 42.

that Mr Kadi is neither, nor was he ever, a part of the legal system, and this in spite of his engagement with legal orders of both the UN and the EU. He, along with his lawyers and representatives, the judges and advocates-general, even the academics, has no more physical place within the legal system than he does in any other function system, which is to say, none whatsoever. The interaction of individuals with a system is always-already determined *by* the system; in this fashion a human being can be a point of communicative attribution or a source of systemic perturbation, or can even be *constituted* by a system – indeed, by any number of systems – as actors within it.[20] We can say that Mr Kadi is constituted by the relevant social systems as, among other things, an economic actor, a EU citizen, and a bearer of human rights.[21]

It is concerning the issue of human rights, however, that the role of the individual in systems theory is perhaps the most counterintuitive, as a result of the disconnect between their psychic and social selves. Teubner conveys this as follows:

> The paradoxical circular relationship between society and individual (society constitutes the individual person, who in turn constitutes society) is, as it were, the *a priori* that underlies all historically variable human rights concepts. Flesh-and-blood people, communicatively constituted as persons, make themselves disruptively noticeable, despite all their socialization, as non-communicatively constituted individuals/bodies, and hammer for their 'rights'.[22]

It is important to note here that human rights attach, nay, *belong* to a human being *as a human being*, to the individual instead of the 'person' within a function system. The next section analyses the 'role' of rights within systems theory in more detail and with specific reference to the *Kadi* case.

Human rights

In systems theory, rights are conceptualized as a social institution by means of which society is able to 'protect its own structure against self-destructive tendencies'.[23] For Luhmann, rights operate as political communications that serve to introduce self-limitations to the political system; in essence, they provide a restraint on the potential excesses of the political system (power),

---

20 Richard Nobles, David Schiff, *Observing Law through Systems Theory* (Hart, 2013) 253.

21 Space unfortunately does not permit me to engage with the temporal issue raised by the discrepancy of ruling as far as rights protection is concerned between the CFI, the ECtHR, and the CJEU. For a general discussion of *time* in terms of systems theory, see Niklas Luhmann, *Social Systems* (Stanford UP, 1995) 41–52.

22 Gunther Teubner, 'Societal constitutionalism', 6.

23 Gert Verschragen, 262.

which otherwise would tend to exert too great an influence upon individuals within society, and which in turn would have detrimental effects upon and within the social. This can be best observed in terms of participation or inclusion: property rights facilitate participation within the economy, for example, while freedom of expression provides communications for the systems of the media and art, to name but two, while at the same time ensuring variety within politics.

It is important to note here that Luhmann's conceptualization of rights is neither liberal nor ideological but rather completely sociological, which is to say that he omits any rose-tintedness in favour of a robustly functionalist understanding. To him rights are a social institution with a precise function, namely, to protect the society from the dangers of functional differentiation. Rights represent a curb upon systemic operations in that they comprise coalesced and concretized expectations, which, in their very *concreteness*, take on the nature of fixed points, of *facts*. Fundamental rights therefore have innate facticity – they are universal and individual human entitlements[24] – and operate to 'protect the autonomy of spheres of action from political instrumentalization'.[25] Without such limitations upon its operations, the political system runs the risk of over-extending its influence and imposing thresholds of regulation that undermine 'the ability of other systems to operate in ways that are productive for society'.[26]

The functional importance of rights is easier to recognize when cast against the backdrop of the highly specialized global systems of world society, which is where those excesses relevant to the *Kadi* case can be identified. The iden-tification of the political and economic systems as having been guilty of overstepping their bounds will come as little surprise, although the issue of most interest here is actually the interplay or rather 'structural coupling' of these two systems with each other, and with the resultant effects both upon the general operation of the legal system and more widespread juridification dynamics.

In terms of the political system, fingers can be pointed at the rights-violat-ing (counterfactual) excesses immediately post-9/11, some of which, such as the Guantanamo Bay detention camp, still persist to this day. The ground for these political excesses was cleared by the shock of the 2001 international terrorist attack upon the twin towers of the World Trade Center, which not only sent many of the function systems of global society into spasm or crisis[27]

---

24 This acknowledgment of universal fundamental rights arguably runs somewhat counter to the positivism at the core of Luhmanian systems theory, which has been referred to as the 'daughter of positivism'.

25 Teubner, 332.

26 Richard Nobles, David Schiff, 199–200.

27 See, in particular, Rudolf Stichweh, 'Towards a general theory of function system crises' in the excellent collection by Kjaer *et al.* (eds), which has drawn attention to the issue of crisis and its articulation from a systems-theoretical perspective.

by disrupting their operations,[28] albeit momentarily, but then also contributed to a state of exception whereby the system of international politics was able to expand its sphere of influence. The means by which these particular circumstances gave rise to such developments are straightforward enough to pinpoint: they undermined the conditions under which the systemic safeguards of constitutional and human rights and social movements could operate, thus disrupting the legal system's operation of rights stabilization[29] and removing the demands for systemic self-restriction. In this regard, Teubner's observation that the 'real dangers are posed less by the dynamics of international politics and more by economic, scientific and technological rationality spheres',[30] while being both astute and prescient vis-à-vis the global financial crisis, as will be discussed, nonetheless arguably downplays the destructive potential of international political power, especially when it is asymmetric to law.

This quote from Teubner brings to the fore the difference between his standpoint and that of Luhmann on the issue of the scope of constitutional and human rights. Whereas Luhmann considers the political system to be the only one requiring self-restraint, Teubner insists that *other* social systems need to be subject to the same controls provided for the political system by constitutional and human rights. The dangers of functional differentiation are as apparent and pernicious in other systems, such as the economy, which is 'as capable of distorting the conditional programmes of other systems as is politics'.[31] While recent excesses and crises within the economic system corroborate this claim, it does not immediately follow that the need to curb such expansionist tendencies makes constitutional and human rights the mechanism to do so. This is the 'normative turn' on the part of Teubner, the designation of human rights as the 'line of defence against the structural violence of the logics of systems running amok'.[32] Therefore while Luhmann would restrict the curbing effect of rights to the political system, based upon his descriptive premise and the evolution of human rights through periods of social segmentation, stratification, and, finally, functional differentiation, Teubner detaches rights from the political with the aim of reorienting them

---

28 This notion of systemic 'spasm' toys with the idea that there is some environmental 'noise' or 'irritation' that is simply so great that it has the effect of momentarily disrupting the order created by operational closure. A spasm could arguably be generated through intense and cumulative perturbations to a system's primary function; in terms of the legal system, this primary function is the stabilization of normative expectations, based upon its coding of legal/illegal.

29 As Verschraegen, 263, notes, the legal system operations pertaining to rights are positivization, interpretation, and stabilization.

30 Teubner, 'Societal constitutionalism', 330.

31 Nobles and Schiff, 200.

32 Lyana Francot-Timmermans, Emilios Christodoulidis, 'The normative turn in Teubner's systems theory of law' (2011) 3 *Netherlands Journal of Legal Philosophy* 187, 188.

towards 'the independent logic and independent rationality of diverse social contexts'.[33]

So how do these observations relate to the specifics of the *Kadi* case? Interestingly, what can be observed is actually a situation of congruence of three function systems: politics, economics, and law. To start at the beginning, we can say that UN Resolution 1267 (and indeed any other) is a structural coupling between the political and legal systems, representing the connection between the 'institutionalized politics' of the UN[34] and the normative (regulatory) character of the Resolution. Moreover, as the decision to blacklist on the strength of this Resolution affects the participation of Mr Kadi within the economic system – genuinely limiting his inclusion and participation with that system – then the coupling can also be considered as one connecting the political and economic systems. Insofar as the issue concerns the enforcement of anti-terrorist-financing norms, however, these waters are muddied, for it is less immediately apparent as to whether the Resolution also represents a structural coupling between the legal and economic systems. To put this in another way, while the blacklisting of Mr Kadi under Resolution 1267 and the 'freezing' of his financial assets certainly had *normative* effect by virtue of constituting an economic sanction, the normal operations of the legal system appear to have been disrupted by the excesses of the political system. The decision-making (power) occurs within the political, which in this case – as we can now assert with the benefit of hindsight – bypassed legal due process and overstepped its bounds.

Accordingly, from systems perspective, it is the dominance of the global political system, represented here by the UN, that is problematic in terms of systemic excesses. First, the initial UN inclusion of Mr Kadi on the UN's consolidated anti-terrorism lists under Security Council Resolution 1267 was not rights-compliant either in terms of procedure or in terms of ensuring adequate levels of judicial protection. Second, although the economic 'sanctions' suffered by Mr Kadi appear at first glance to pertain to both the economy and the legal system, these are actually political decisions based upon protectionist ideologies and 'soft power' dynamics that are networked beyond the ambit of the UN and thus also beyond its steering and/or control. In this regard these dynamics resemble more Teubner's 'anonymous matrix'[35] than the exercise of political power by nation states and their international representatives. The danger to individuals' integrity, as he would put it, can be said to arise from 'a multiplicity of anonymous and globalized communicative processes', whereby the anonymous matrix of an autonomized communicative

33 *Ibid.*, 188; also Nobles and Schiff, 200–2.
34 Gunther Teubner, *Constitutional Fragments: Societal Constitutionalism and Globalization* (OUP, 2012) 50.
35 Teubner, 'The anonymous matrix'.

action is the 'fundamental-rights violator'.[36] Finally, it can be asserted that there are inherent flaws within the UN's operation, a situation that was obviously recognized and reacted to by the creation of the UN Office of the Ombudsperson.

Good governance

Whereby the issue of rights within systems theory can be discussed at the level of world society, that of 'good governance' relates specifically to the EU as a 'virtuous actor'. Although systems theory is often understood as an anti-regional theory, like its anti-individualistic reputation this is somewhat overstated. While systems of world society are differentiated from each other on the basis of their function, it is also the case that there is a subsequent *system-internal* differentiation (*Binnendifferenzierung*) that facilitates systemic understanding of environmental complexity in the form of jurisdiction or territorial difference.[37] To be clear, the EU can be considered as being both a legal and political actor. Indeed, its own boundaries and the borders of its constituent member states are communications from the political system,[38] which have an 'irritant' effect[39] upon the secondary operations and programmes of the legal system. It is also important to note here that the virtue or otherwise of a position adopted by any actor, be it the CJEU or the EU more generally, goes effectively 'unseen' by the legal system, which understands its environment in terms of its binary coding of legal/illegal,[40] and it alone.

As discussed above, the standpoint taken by the CJEU in its landmark judgment of September 2008 had the effect of establishing its clear stance on EU-internal human rights protections. While the procedural delay of three months prior to EU Commission implementation[41] reduced the 2008 decision's impact to being more rhetorical than actual, especially insofar as it affected the specifics of Mr Kadi's situation vis-à-vis the 'frozen' assets, I submit that

---

36 Teubner, 'Societal constitutionalism'.
37 Jennifer Hendry, 'The double fragmentation of law: legal system-internal differentiation and the process of Europeanization' in Daniel Augenstein (ed.), *Integration through Law Revisited: The Making of the European Polity* (Ashgate, 2012).
38 Anton Schütz, 'The twilight of the global polis. On losing paradigms, environing systems and observing world society' in Gunther Teubner (ed.) *Global Law without a State* (Ashgate, 1997) 279–94.
39 Gunther Teubner, 'Legal irritants: good faith in British law or how unifying law ends up in new differences' (1998) 61 *Modern Law Review* 11.
40 Niklas Luhmann, 'The coding of the legal system' in Alberto Febbrajo, Gunther Teubner (eds.) *State, Law, Economy as Autopoietic Systems* (Giuffre, 1992).
41 The ECJ followed the reasoning in AG Maduro's Opinion and decided in favour of protecting fundamental rights but stopped short of the immediate invalidation of the challenged EU measures, instead allowing their continuation for another three months and thus providing time for the Commission to become rights-compliant.

this judgment and, more importantly, its subsequent confirmation by the CJEU Grand Chamber in 2013 had the effect of generating and constituting an *unchangeable standard*[42] within the legal system. Having stated its case with such fanfare, the EU has effectively now established a normative standard *for itself* that it now *must* maintain. This self-restraint does not only pertain to the legal system, however, as it also has effects within the political system. The Court's decision had overt political consequences, partly in terms of the EU's relationship with the UN, which will be discussed in the next section, and partly in terms of its own identity as a rights-respecting, rights-compliant polity. When viewed from a system's theoretical perspective, the 2008 legal ruling in *Kadi* has the irritant effect of *constituting* this (restricted) political position for the EU, and thus generating a '"rule of law" relationship between [politics] and law'.[43] In essence, the limitations placed upon the political are simultaneously self-limitations – in a similar sense to those represented by constitutional and human rights, as discussed above – *and* limitations derived from the operations of the legal system.

Even more interesting is the subsequent challenge to this stance in the form of the appeal by the Commission, the Council, and the United Kingdom and its 2013 rejection, as this allows us to chart its development from a 'rule of law' relationship to a constitutional one. Nobles and Schiff outline this trajectory as follows:

> The next step, if one is to move into a 'constitutional' level, is for the legal rules which support a social system to develop a distinction between *changeable and unchangeable law*.[44] This distinction provides a basis for the legal system to limit what support it provides to the social system. For this distinction to operate as a mutual self-limitation, it must be repeated (re-entered) within that social system's own communications, generating structures of communication which identify the system's own version of what is fundamental, and not open to change.[45]

As stated, the requirement for mutual systemic self-limitation is that the distinction between law that is changeable and law that is not is *re-entered* into the system, in this case the political system. This process of re-entry (*Wiedereintritt*) presents us with one of the paradoxes at the heart of systems theory, namely that what is being reintroduced into the system is the very distinction between system and environment upon which the system

---

42 Niklas Luhmann, *Law as a Social System* (OUP, 2004) 17.
43 Richard Nobles, David Schiff, 'Pulling back from the edge? Review of Teubner's constitutional fragments' (2013) 76 *Modern Law Review* 620, 623.
44 My emphasis. Please note that Nobles and Schiff here rely on insights from Luhmann, *The coding* (n40) 17.
45 Nobles, Schiff, 'Pulling back', 623.

depends.[46] The distinction re-entered into the political system, therefore, can be recognized as its (political) systemic understanding of the (legal) judgment, which has the effect of operating as a mutual self-limitation on both of the function systems. The effect of the CJEU setting out their stall in *Kadi* 2008 to characterize the EU as both virtuous and rights-compliant – a stance generally accepted as being political in nature[47] – is that the political system at the EU level is now subject to self-imposed restraints *pertaining to that virtuous declaration of intent*.

Not that this is a new position in terms of EU politics, of course, especially in the field of human rights. These have been employed collectively as jurisdictional and identity determinants for the EU ever since their genesis, developing internally within the EU 'in conjunction with a narrative that sought to construct an identity *with* the Community[, while] externally, the narrative was concerned with the identity *of* the Community'.[48] The EU's self-description in this respect becomes altogether more important when the focus is extended from 'good governance' at the level of the EU to that of global governance, most notably in terms of the apparent disconnect, at least in practical terms, between the respective stances of the EU and the UN. The vagaries of multi-level governance and the attendant issues of authority and plurality are the focus of the next section.

Multi-level governance, plurality and authority

Takis Tridimas recently observed that, when it comes to *Kadi*, we are 'faced... with the problem of *Kompetenz-Kompetenz*, to which there is no conclusive answer'.[49] The clash of legitimate authority claims illuminated by this case has been a subject of much debate since even before the decision was handed down; indeed, it would be disingenuous even now to suggest that the recent appeal judgment has put an end to this debate. In that regard, a systems theorist might be forgiven for the temptation to assert the theory's radically anti-regional character and potential for abstraction: to point to the decentralization and fragmentation of world politics[50] and beat a retreat from the problems of complex structure! But systems theory offers much in terms of fresh perspectives on entrenched debates, so this final section will endeavour to suggest some alternatives to debating the same established tension with reference to the asymmetry between the legal and political systems at the global

---

46 Miguel Torres Morales, *Systemtheorie, Diskurstheorie und das Recht der Transzendentalphilosophie* (Königshausen & Neumann, 2002) 118.

47 de Búrca.

48 Andrew Williams, *EU Human Rights Policies: A Study in Irony* (OUP, 2004) 179.

49 Tridimas P. Takis, 'International law and economic sanctions against terrorism: post-Kadi developments' (2010–11) *Cambridge Yearbook of European Legal Studies* 455, 489.

50 Marcelo Neves, *Transconstitutionalism* (Hart, 2013) 58.

level. It should be noted at this stage that the 'plurality' generated by the decision in *Kadi* is not that of worldwide legal pluralism and the normative diversity that is claimed by and attaches to ethnic and cultural communities[51] but rather one of multiple (dual) authority and competence claims from regulatory regimes at various levels of world society.

First, having mentioned the innate anti-regionality of systems theory, a note on spatial issues. The particular accommodation of territorial considerations within systems theory has already been discussed in the preceding section but this bears some more scrutiny here, especially in terms of how the interaction of different 'levels'[52] of different function systems is understood from systems theoretical perspective. The hard regime boundaries that create such 'levels' are subject to elision by a theoretical approach that differentiates primarily upon the basis of function, but this is not to say that they are vanquished entirely. On the contrary, instead of an absolute 'dismissal of geography',[53] subsequent system-internal processes of differentiation occur to reconstruct jurisdictional and territorial specificity within the relevant function systems on the terms of those function systems. To give an example here: the internally differentiated 'German' part of the legal system will 'see' and operationalize a judgment of the *Bundesverfassungsgericht* differently to equivalent parts corresponding to other EU member states. Any multi-level conflict arising is, therefore, also a system-internal one, thus avoiding any discussion of structural coupling[54] or cross-systemic irritation.

Systems theory consequently offers the opportunity of considering the issue in relation to the legal system and the legal system alone. Following the reasoning above, it can be asserted that the EU legal order is, by means of legal system-internal differentiation, an internal construct that operates according to the system's secondary programmes, which is to say, according to its own rules of operation. This situation is one created by the treaties, binding undertakings on the part of the signatory member states that constitute structural couplings between the legal and the political. Moreover, the particular nature of EU law in relation to that of its member states – which is to say, its penetrative quality resulting from the doctrine

---

51 Gunther Teubner, 'Global Bukowina: legal pluralism in the world-society' in Gunther Teubner (ed.) *Global Law without a State* (Dartmouth, 1997) 3–28. See also Teubner, 'Legal regimes of global non-state actors' in the same volume.

52 This is not to introduce a hierarchical element, which would of course be antithetical to systems theory, but rather to help convey the idea of separate areas within the overarching function system.

53 Schütz.

54 'Function systems can enter into "structural coupling" with each other so that their autopoiesis – though still operationally closed – is in contact with that of another systems… Structural coupling does not violate the operational closure of systems, rather it establishes specific relations between different autopoietic processes.' See Hans-Georg Moellers, *Luhmann Explained: From Souls to Systems* (Open Court, 2006) 37.

of direct effect – means that this internal construct also includes many member state legal operations, and broadly symmetrical ones at that. Legal-systemic unity is untroubled by this arrangement, which is conflict-averse in nature. Things are complicated, however, by the inclusion of UN norms within the system – and I use the term norms specifically here – not least by the issues of procedure, legitimacy, efficacy, enforceability and practicality engendered by the struggle to determine competence. The solution, such as there is one, may be located in the recognition that while UN Security Council resolutions are certainly normative, they lack the requisite robust *legality* in order validly to countermand EU-related systemic operations.

This widespread weakness of law at the international level is in sharp contrast to that of law at EU level; nevertheless, law is not the only function system of relevance in this regard. Instead of viewing the UN from the perspective of the legal system, therefore, it follows that the political system is rather kinder to the UN, which is, after all, a regime of 'institutionalized politics'.[55] In contrast to the legal system, where the EU legal order occupies a position of strength and the UN 'legal' order is comparatively weak, a shift in focus to the political system and, indeed, its interaction with and irritation of the legal system, and the UN's political power comes to the fore. What can be observed here is a general *asymmetry* in terms of the legal and the political on the global scale, to the extent that law finds itself directly subordinated to power.[56] This asymmetry was hinted at earlier in the section on rights, where constitutional and human rights were cited as buffers against the excesses of systemic over-reach and processes of de-differentiation.[57]

In this sense it is not difficult to see the task law faces, not only to maintain its position at the international level but also to avoid any further erosion. One could query at this point whether or not such dangers can be understood as giving rise to a systemic crisis,[58] which can be said to occur when a system's operations and procedures are disturbed, but it would be hasty to jump automatically to this conclusion. Indeed, while there is an asymmetry of politics and law at the international level, with politics the ascendant, the reverse is arguably true at the EU level.[59] This is an uncomfortable situation under a societal horizontal order premised upon the condition that 'no

---

55 Teubner, 'The anonymous matrix'.

56 Neves, 62.

57 De-differentiation can be described as the encroachment by one system on to the territory of another; an overstepping of a system's own systemic bounds.

58 Kjaer *et al.*

59 For an in-depth discussion of the EU as a polity created by and through law, see Daniel Augenstein (ed.) *'Integration Through Law' Revisited: The Making of the European Polity* (Ashgate 2012).

system possesses a structural primacy vis-à-vis other systems'.[60] However, rather than shout 'crisis', it would more likely be a better idea to look beyond the trials of a single function system to the dual asymmetry that the *Kadi* case sheds light upon, and to query whether this is in fact symptomatic of a broader malaise.

60 Id., specifically the Introduction, xvi.

7 The intractably unknowable nature of law

Kadi, Kafka, and the law's competing claims to authority

Luke Mason

Introducing *Kadi*: a new production of Kafka's *The Trial*, starring Mr Kadi as Josef K.

The denouement of *Kadi II*[1] in the Grand Chamber of the Court of Justice might be read as the *Disneyfication* of Kafka's *The Trial*,[2] a happy ending for our downtrodden protagonist. In Kafka's famous tale, a man facing mysterious, seemingly *unknowable* accusations and a Byzantine legal system with no apparent means of redress or rectification is eventually executed with none of the accusations ever having become any clearer. In *Kadi II*, the Court's forceful reconfirmation and aggressive application of the principle of 'full review' laid down by the same judicial body in *Kadi I*[3] meant that Mr Kadi, originally facing similarly opaque accusations, was able to rely on his own 'trial' to *escape* this nightmarish scenario by having the Court strike down the measures applied to him. Indeed, the Court, in underlining the importance of the fundamental principle of *effective judicial protection*,[4] in particular in the face of complex questions of inter-systemic supremacy[5] between legal systems and the delicate nature of anti-terrorism measures, might be seen as casting as antithetical to the

---

1 Joined Cases C-584/10 P, C-593/10 P, and C-595/10 P, *Commission, Council and United Kingdom* v. *Kadi*, judgment of the Grand Chamber of the CJEU of 18 July 2013, NYR, hereinafter, *Kadi II*.
2 Franz Kafka, *The Trial* (David Wyllie tr, Echo Library, 2007).
3 Joined Cases C-402/05 P and C-415/05 P, *Kadi and Al Barakaat* [2008] ECR I-06351, hereinafter, *Kadi I*, at para. 326: 'the Community judicature must, in accordance with the powers conferred on it by the EC Treaty, ensure the review, in principle the full review, of the lawfulness of all Community acts.'
4 *Kadi II*, at paras. 133–4.
5 *Ibid*. The court, at para. 133, seems to be making the point that effective judicial protection must be guaranteed by the EU legal order due to the fact that the UN Security Council's procedures do not provide such protection. In this manner, the Security Council procedures seem to fail the Court's *solange* test. Much of the discussion of *Kadi I* focused on the *solange* aspects of the judgment and the competing claims for supremacy in the international legal order. See in particular N Türküler Isiksel, 'Fundamental rights in the EU after Kadi and Al Barakaat' (2010) 16 *European Law Journal* 551; Grainne De Burca, 'European Court of Justice and the international legal order after Kadi' (2010) 51 *Harvard International Law Journal* 1.

values of the European Union (EU) legal order the experience of law as unknowable and inaccessible which Kafka depicts so powerfully.

However, it would be hasty to focus solely on the happy outcome (for Kadi, our own K.) in this particular case in seeking to understand what *Kadi* might tell us about the law when understood in the light of Kafka's work. This chapter takes advantage of the striking similarities between the cases of Mr Kadi and Josef K., and indeed their contrasting conclusions, to delve into the insights of Franz Kafka's fictional depictions of the law. These focused heavily, among other themes, on the experience of law for those who are subject to the legal system's demands but who do not have, at that moment at least, privileged access to its inner workings. This vision of law, as experienced by non-lawyers in the real world, is one not always fully considered by legal theorists until they become apparent in cases such as *Kadi*. While *Kadi* demonstrates the law's innate ability to 'redeem' itself in such circumstances, the case should also bring home to us the inherent unknowability and inaccessibility of the law for those who are subject to it, regardless of its myriad virtues so often highlighted by legal theorists.

Rather, therefore, than contributing to the literature on *Kadi* which focuses on intra- and inter-systemic normative conundra, this chapter seeks to understand law as it is experienced as a social artefact which primarily serves and seeks to regulate the actions of people who are not lawyers. It highlights the complex *dual claim to authority* which law makes of those subject to it, an apparent paradox neglected by legal theorists because of the law's own apparent internal ability to dissolve it. Because the law seeks to regulate behaviour *ex ante* by laying down standards, while also attempting to judge behaviour *ex post* through adjudication, law is experienced much of the time in the manner depicted in Kafka's *The Trial* and brought out in the real-life case of *Kadi*. Legal systems are not blind to these dangers, however, and this Kafkaesque experience of law is often seen by courts as contrary to fundamental principles which legal systems seek to uphold.

However, while such cases might produce happy endings for those such as Mr Kadi, the dual claims to authority which the law makes are always present; they are the essence of legal systems as we know them. Finally, this chapter draws further on the *Kadi* saga to demonstrate that, beyond these conceptual concerns, certain empirically observable contemporary trends within the law are contributing additional complexity to this problem. Law is becoming more difficult to discover as we move from Kafka's already troubling *modernity* into a *postmodern* legal phase. The law's content seems to be fragmenting and growing in complexity as it becomes the tool of a technocratically driven world of *regulation*. At the same time, adjudication is also made more complex by a growing number of competing legal sources claiming entrenched or superior status. While these developments might carry the promise of better laws and better legal outcomes from a substantive perspective, they exacerbate the *unknowability* of law as it is experienced by people such as Kafka's Josef K. and our own Mr Kadi.

Kafka and the law

The similarity between the ordeal of Mr Kadi and that of Josef K., the protagonist of Kafka's *The Trial*, has been pointed out elsewhere.[6] Kafka's work, the meaning and significance of which are discussed in this section, was described by W.H. Auden as representing for the twentieth century that which the work of Shakespeare and Dante represented for their own.[7] The influence of Kafka's work has entered into mainstream Western culture to such an extent that the term 'Kafkaesque' is routinely used to describe situations of impenetrable bureaucracy and the more general feeling of hopelessness of the individual in the face of modernity and its intimidating institutions.

With this in mind, it would not be far-fetched to think that the Court in *Kadi* would also have apprehended the obvious Kafkaesque elements of Mr Kadi's now well documented predicament: his assets had been frozen by a *lex specialis*, yet he possessed no real knowledge of what he was accused of, nor a clear path for challenging the measures in question. The Kafkaesque nature of the scenario was seemingly complete when, following the judgment of the Grand Chamber in *Kadi I*, ostensibly in his favour following the ruling by the Court of Justice of the European Union (CJEU) that the measures in question were unlawful for failing to provide adequate reasons, the same sanctions were left in place with a view to simply redrafting them with scant additional detail.[8] As outlined in the other chapters in this collection, the second *Kadi* judgment of the Grand Chamber made good on its own promise in *Kadi I*. It was held that even the expanded reasons given for the freezing of his assets were insufficient to justify the measures against him under EU law, in particular in view of the importance of *effective judicial protection*. Appearing to adopt a *solange*-type approach, the Court felt that the United Nations (UN) Security Council Ombudsperson system was unable to provide such protection, and thus carried out its own substantive review of the provisions as they applied to Mr Kadi.

In its technical, *per curiam* judgments, the CJEU does not use such literary devices as references to Kafka or *The Trial* when delivering its opinions. Such references are however relatively frequent in the more expansive linguistic

---

6 Filippo Fontanelli, 'Kadi II, or the happy ending of K's trial' (*Diritti Comparati*, 29 July 2013) <http://www.dirritticomparati.it/2013/07/kadi-ii-or-the-happy-ending-of-ks-trial-court-of-justice-of-the-european-union-18-july-2013.html>; Robert Schuetze, 'Coda: Kafka, Kadi, Kant' (*SSRN*, 11 September 2013) <http://ssrn.com/abstract=2324574> accessed 25 September 2013.

7 W.H. Auden, 'The Wandering Jew' (1941) 104 *New Republic*.

8 On the 'Pyrrhic victory' in *Kadi I*, see Katja S Ziegler, 'Strengthening the rule of law, but fragmenting international law: the Kadi decision of the ECJ from the perspective of human rights' (2009) 9 *Human Rights Law Review* 288.

context of American[9] and English[10] judicial opinions. While of course such literary sources lack any binding legal authority, such references tend to operate as a *symbol* or *illustrative device* to describe unacceptably opaque or dense legal or bureaucratic procedures, standing in stark contrast to principles perceived as inherent to the law. Similar references to Kafka can also be found in several judgments of the European Court of Human Rights,[11] and even in a number of opinions of the Advocate General to the CJEU.[12] The most apposite example however is Zinn J's judgment in *Abdelrazik* v. *Canada*[13] before the Federal Court of Canada. This case concerned similar issues to *Kadi* regarding the legality, under Canadian law and international law, of the implementation of listings under UN Security Council Resolution 1267. Zinn J stated that 'for a listed person [such a situation is] not unlike that of Josef K. in Kafka's The Trial,'[14] this within a judgment which effectively declared Canada's implementation of the listing illegal.[15] One can see the CJEU's judgment in *Kadi II* as reflecting similar concerns, heeding the apparent warnings of Kafka's work. Legal systems seem therefore to see Kafka's work as a morality tale for courts themselves. In this light, *Kadi*, were it recast as fiction, would seem more akin to optimistic accounts of the law and its ability to produce just outcomes, such as in *The Merchant of Venice*,[16] or in the television series *Perry Mason*, where the courtroom is depicted as a forum in which a charismatic

---

9 For extremely detailed treatment of references to Kafka in American judicial opinions, see Brian Pinaire, 'Essential Kafka: definition, distention, and dilution in legal rhetoric' (2007) 46 *University of Louisville Law Review* 113; Parker B Potter Jr, 'Ordeal by trial: judicial references to the nightmare world of Franz Kafka' (2004) 3 *Pierce Law Review* 195; Scott Finet, 'Franz Kafka's trial as symbol in judicial opinions' (1988) 12 *Legal Studies Forum* 23.

10 A typical example can be found in the High Court decision in *Sepracor Inc* [1999] EWHC Patents 259, at para. 14, where Laddie J remarks dismissively: 'A less sensible system could not have been dreamt up by Kafka.'

11 Unsurprisingly these concern issues related to the rights of those under arrest under art 5 ECHR. References to Kafka can be found, for instance, in *Murray* v. *UK* (1995) 19 EHRR 193 and *Allen* v. *UK* App no 25424/09 (ECHR, 12 July 2013).

12 AG VerLoren Van Themaat included references to Kafka in two separate Opinions: Case 79/81 *Baccini* (1982) ECR 1063 and Case 33/82 *Murri Freres* v. *Commission* [1985] ECR 2759. Confusingly, in Case C-1/04 Susanne Staubitz-Schreiber [2006] ECR I-00701AG Ruiz-Jarabo Colomer referred to the Kafkaesque ('Kafkiano' in the original Spanish) nature of the developments of EU insolvency regulations because they had started off life within a treaty. Here the reference is of course to a famous transformation in another of Kafka's works!

13 *Abdelrazik* v. *Canada (Minister of Foreign Affairs)*, 2009 FC 580 (CanLII), [2010] 1 FCR 267.

14 *Ibid.*, para. 53.

15 The idea that *Abdelrazik* can be seen as representing an effective remedy for Josef K. along similar lines to the parallel drawn in the present chapter can be found in Antonios Tzanakopoulos, 'An effective remedy for Josef K: Canadian judge "defies" Security Council sanctions through interpretation' (*EJIL: Talk!*, 19 June 2009) <http://www.ejiltalk.org/an-effective-remedy-for-josef-k-canadian-judge-defies-security-council-sanctions-through-interpretation/> accessed 12 October 2013.

16 William Shakespeare, *The Merchant of Venice* (Wordsworth Classics, 2000). Of course, in *The Merchant of Venice*, the 'lawyer' in question is really Portia, a leading character in the play.

lawyer can utilize the procedures of the law to the benefit of someone facing false accusations or the application of unjust laws. Such a conclusion would however underestimate the depth of Kafka's critique of law and its relevance to understanding its particular characteristics highlighted in *Kadi*.

Beyond the superficial similarities between Mr Kadi and Josef K.'s cases therefore, let us consider Kafka's depiction of law and the way it is experienced in his fiction. Kafka's work dealing with law and authority, and those subject to it, stretches beyond *The Trial* itself to several other stories of varying length. Kafka himself worked within the legal system and much in his fictional portrayals of the operation of the law, dismissed by Posner as fantastical and having little to say about actual legal doctrine,[17] is based on his own experiences working for an insurance firm dealing with the special workers' injury compensation system within the Austro-Hungarian legal system.[18] Kafka was a law graduate, and indeed once formulated a detailed idea for reform of the workers' insurance system, and was therefore very much *au fait* with the procedures of the law and their potential to contribute to both just and unjust outcomes. However, his fiction does not present law from the perspective of someone who is working within the legal system, but rather from the perspective of those who are subject to its demands with no access to its inner workings.

Several recurring themes emerge therefore in Kafka's treatment of the law. In *The Trial* itself, Josef K. wakes one morning to find that he is under arrest, although the legal system which then proceeds to subject him to 'trial' is very alien to any lawyer reading the novel, as it is to the protagonist who had considered himself relatively familiar with the law. Josef K. never learns what he is accused of, and is allowed to continue with his job in a bank while his 'trial' continues. The proceedings are very unorthodox, and many of the characters whom K. meets turn out to be in the service of the court. While many people offer him help with his case, none is particularly helpful in reality. There seems to be no way for K. to control his own fate, the law offers no way out, and everything is against him. In the end, when he is led away, he accepts his fate, and is executed 'like a dog'.

Before the Law[19] is a short story both published separately during Kafka's lifetime but also told by a prison chaplain in *The Trial* as a 'story within a story'. The protagonist, a man from the country, wishes to gain access to 'the law'. The law lies through an open doorway, which is guarded by a doorkeeper who stands 'before the law'. The man attempts to gain access to the law,

17 Richard A. Posner, 'The ethical significance of free choice: a reply to Professor West' (1985) 99 *Harvard Law Review* 1431.

18 For an excellent examination of how such experiences might have influenced his fiction, see Douglas E. Litowitz, 'Franz Kafka's outsider jurisprudence' (2002) 27 *Law and Social Inquiry* 103, 108–12.

19 Franz Kafka, 'Before the law' in *The Complete Short Stories of Franz Kafka* (Minerva, 1992).

believing it open to everyone. He is denied entry by the doorkeeper, who continues to refuse him entry despite accepting bribes. The man maintains hope that he will one day gain admission, but eventually grows old and dies, never having gained entry to the law. Before he dies the man asks the door-keeper why no one else had sought to enter. The doorkeeper tells him that this door was only for him and that the door would now be closed.

In the very short story *The Problem of Our Laws*,[20] the narrator describes a legal system which is controlled and known only by an elite, 'the nobles', who keep the content of the law secret. There is uncertainty regarding whether there is any substance to these 'laws' or whether 'law' is simply a name given to whatever the nobles happen to decree. Despite their subjugation, the people subject to the law prefer to continue living in this manner, accepting its authority. There are also numerous other works[21] by Kafka in which powerful and seemingly irrational authority figures strongly, often with the full consent of those subject to it. Particularly noteworthy are *The Refusal*, where an authority figure who holds power for no apparent reason routinely rejects petitions by people who are ignorant of the law but accept the refusals despite their knowledge that they are inevitable, and *In the Penal Colony*, where an executioner operates a barbaric machine which kills the condemned by stitching words into their body. The executioner is so convinced of the justice of the machine and the sentences which it carries out that he executes himself using it.

Kafka's vision of law as experience: unknowable and inaccessible

Kafka's work has been subject to an extraordinary amount of analysis and commentary, not least by legal scholars. Although Posner maintains that it is not possible to draw any meaningful conclusions about the content of law from Kafka's stories, or indeed any depiction of law in literature,[22] this has certainly not prevented a large number legal theorists from seeking to develop themes from Kafka into more general theses about the law or its place in society. While Posner is right to insist that Kafka's work cannot be treated as a doctrinal exam-ination in the traditional sense, we should not therefore underestimate its value in seeking to engage with the experience of law for those who must live within a legal system. *The Trial* may not help us to understand the rules of criminal procedure in the Austro-Hungarian legal system, but it may tell us something about what it is like to be subject to such a procedure. The role of the legal theo-rist is to seek to make sense of this portrayal using his or her knowledge of law.

20 Franz Kafka, 'The problem with our laws' in *The Complete Short Stories of Franz Kafka* (Minerva, 1992).
21 Franz Kafka, *The Complete Short Stories of Franz Kafka* (Minerva, 1992).
22 Posner, 1356–9.

Looking solely at work which examines Kafka from the perspective of legal and political theory, there exist a plethora of attempts by influential scholars to make sense of what Kafka's depiction of law and authority might represent. These include an exploration of the search for a lost *Heimat* of community following a move from *Gemeinschaft* to *Gesellschaft*;[23] an illustration of the questionable moral status of consent, given that Kafka's protagonists acquiesce to manifestly abhorrent treatment, thus bringing into question theories of justice and law, such as *law and economics*, and liberalism more generally, which are founded on the moral importance of autonomy and upholding voluntary transactions;[24] an examination of Jewish understandings of divine justice and violence, and human imitations thereof;[25] and a demonstration of the necessary lie that upholds any legal system, based as it is on a mere fictional validity.[26]

These are all certainly themes which might fruitfully be explored in relation to both law and Kafka's work, yet none of them really seem to get to the crux of Kafka's depiction of law itself, which is instead characterized by its *unknowable* and *inaccessible* nature.[27] In Kafka's stories the law is present and people are subject to it, yet the content of the law is never revealed. In *The Trial*, the tension and absurdity of K.'s situation rest entirely on his ignorance of the charges and the workings of the trial which he feels powerless to influence. Similarly, in *The Problem of Our Laws*, people are subject to a legal system which is so secret they are not even sure if it exists. In *Before the Law* this is depicted most graphically, with the protagonist's access to the law physically blocked, despite appearing possible due to the open door. Because access is denied, we never gain any insight into the *content* of the law. As Derrida characteristically puts it 'la loi est l'interdit'.[28] Rather than proscribing behaviour, it is the law itself which is proscribed.

The law in Kafka's œuvre therefore appears to possess no content. This has unwisely led some authors to conclude that the law is, both in Kafka and in reality, empty, existing merely by virtue of its inner paradoxes,[29] or through

23 Reza Banakar, 'In search of Heimat: a note on Franz Kafka's concept of law' (2010) 22 *Law and Literature* 463.

24 Robin West, 'Authority, autonomy, and choice: the role of consent in the moral and political visions of Franz Kafka and Richard Posner' (2011) 99 *Harvard Law Review* 384.

25 Walter Benjamin, 'Some reflections on Kafka' in Hannah Arendt (ed.), *Illuminations: Essays and Reflections* (Schocken Books, 1999).

26 Jacques Derrida, 'Force of law: the mystical foundation of authority' in Drucilla Cornell (ed.), *Deconstruction and the Possibility of Justice* (Routledge, 1992).
Haakan Gustafsson, '"As if": behind before the law' (1996) 7 *Law and Critique* 99.

27 Dominique Gros, 'Le "gardien de la loi," selon Kafka' (2002) 14 *Law and Literature* 11; Patrick Glen, 'The deconstruction and reification of law in Franz Kafka's "Before the Law" and "The Trial"' (2007) 17 *Southern California Interdisciplinary Law Journal* 23. A similar observation regarding the law's 'hidden' nature in Kafka is made in Fabrizio Sciacca, 'La Legge Nascosta: Il Paradosso Di Kafka' (1993) 70 *Rivista Internazionale di Filosofia del Diritto* 222.

28 Jacques Derrida, 'Devant la loi' (1983) 16 *Royal Institute of Philosophy Supplements* 173, 183.

29 *Ibid.* and 'Force of law', 16.

a process of *reification*,[30] whereby something with no real form or content obtains a 'phantom objectivity' due to its advanced formalized and bureaucratized appearance. Alternatively, law is reductively seen merely as its outcomes in the form of judgments, having no content before the outcome is reached.[31] Such conclusions would not shed much light on the nature of law, in general or in Kafka: as lawyers, we know that law does indeed possess content. Understanding Kafka in this way would merely therefore add credence to Posner's position that literature can tell us nothing about law. Kafka of course knew that the law possessed content, as he worked within the legal system. Kafka is writing about law as it is experienced by those who are subject to it but *unaware* of its content.

Kafka's clever writing means that the reader also knows nothing of the law's content, and is thereby placed in the same position as the protagonists. It is perfectly conceivable that the law in these stories, were it to be revealed, would be a perfectly familiar legal system with familiar doctrines. US Supreme Court Judge Anthony Kennedy has also made this point, saying that all lawyers should read *The Trial* precisely to understand the law from the perspective of the client.[32] Litowitz has described this as an example of 'outsider jurisprudence',[33] that is the law as it appears to those who are not familiar with the workings of the legal system. He seeks to contrast this with more traditional forms of 'outsider jurisprudence' (such as feminist jurisprudence or critical race theory) which seek to draw a connection between other forms of social marginalization or minority status and the law.[34] He is right to reject such reductionism, as such perspectives, as *general theories of law*, are too simplistic to capture anything about the essence of law itself rather than the injustice of its content or application when these are subjected to critical analysis. Such theories thus recognize that law can play a significant part in wider forms of social exclusion, but they do not demonstrate how even those who are not marginalized in other ways can nonetheless suffer alienation at the hands of the law. Similarly, Banakar argues that Kafka's depiction of the law moves us past a vision of law as an instrument of social control towards the idea of law as a form of experience.[35] Kafka's insight is that the logic or rationality which appears evident to those within the workings of a legal system will not be apparent to those on the outside, to whom it appears illogical and irrational.[36] This sheds new light on the meaning

---

30 Glen, 50–63.
31 Gunther Teubner, 'The law before its law: Franz Kafka on the (im)possibility of law's self-reflection' (2013) 14 *German Law Journal* 405, 413.
32 Terry Carter, 'A justice who makes time to read, and thinks all lawyers should, too' (1993) *Chicago Daily Law Bulletin* (26 January); Glen also draws on this quote in his discussion of Kafka.
33 Litowitz.
34 *Ibid.* In particular, see Litowitz's discussion of 'situational' outsiders and the law, 107–9.
35 Banakar.
36 *Ibid.*, 482.

of Luhmann's celebrated analysis of legal systems as *normatively closed*.[37] As Teubner argues, while theorists such as Habermas and Alexy celebrate the rational discourse which is inherent to law and its production, one's experience of law might nonetheless be one of anxiety and a sense of oppression.[38] The role of the legal theorist is to ensure that such important perspectives are accounted for and properly explained within a theory of law. A consideration of *Kadi II*, where the law itself confronts these issues, might help us in this task.

Kadi in the light of Kafka's theory of law

In *Kadi* the 'accused' must have felt subject to a mysterious *calumnia* similar to that experienced by Josef K.[39] and possessed no apparent means of challenging it. However, the respective outcomes of *Kadi I* and *II* suggest that the opaque procedures which Kafka is often seen as depicting in his work can be averted by the operation of the law itself. Setting aside the myriad doctrinal and constitutional discussions concerning the pedigree of the norm which led to this outcome, and the relationship between different legal systems which caused many of the complexities in the case, the law would have appeared to have redeemed itself on this view. As literature, *The Trial* and *Before the Law* would be less powerful if Josef K.'s case were thrown out, or the doorkeeper eventually relented and allowed the man to enter. However, the foregoing discussions of Kafka's work have revealed a more complex depiction of law in Kafka than mere bureaucratic hurdles or infelicitous endings. If they depict something essential about the law, it should hold true regardless of the outcome of any particular case, happy or unhappy, such as that of *Kadi*.

In reality, the endings of Kafka's stories are not really part of Kafka's account of the law itself, but rather separate themes in Kafka's work concerning the willing acceptance of unjust authority by people who are subject to it, alongside a more general fatalism which infects his stories. In all his stories, those subject to the *unknowable* law seem to have it in their power to reject in some manner the course of events but choose not to. Mr Kadi evidently did not take this route, and the law itself offered him a just outcome. However, the law still put Mr Kadi through the same opaque and alienating experience which Josef K. had to endure. The experience of the law would have been identical, that is, an accusation which is difficult to understand, and a legal procedure which is equally opaque and threatening: imagine for a moment being the accused in a case where your lawyer informs you that the outcome hinges on a favourable reading of the relationship between competing claims to supremacy

37 See, for instance, Niklas Luhmann, 'The unity of the legal system' in Gunther Teubner (ed.), *Autopoietic Law: A New Approach to Law and Society* (Walter de Gruyter, 1988).
38 Teubner, 'Law before its law', 420.
39 The famous first line of *The Trial* reads: 'Someone must have slandered Josef K., for one morning, without having done anything truly wrong, he was arrested.'

in a pluralist international legal order! This is not to say that these are not valid and important questions upon which cases should indeed rest. It is instead to emphasize that they are *lawyers' questions*. The *experience* of law for those subject to it is bound to be less comprehensible precisely *because of* their intra-systemic importance. Here we begin to see how Kafka's fictional portrayal of the legal system is rooted firmly within the *reality* of people's experience of law even outside his fiction. What is it about law therefore, that most vaunted of social artefacts and the basis of the grand ideas of the *Rule of Law* and the *Rechtsstaat*, which produces this experience? Legal theory should not simply seek to make sense of law for lawyers. The following sections seek to sketch an account which makes sense of Kafka's vision of law and Mr Kadi's experience of the legal system and process.

Making sense of Kafka's theory of law: the law's dual claim to authority

As with Kafka's protagonists, Mr Kadi chose to put his *faith* in legal procedures which appeared hostile to him, but eventually found himself, and the law, redeemed.[40] Kafka's characters found no such redemption in the law. The experience of the legal system will have been similarly inaccessible and opaque to all of them however. *Kadi*'s case can help us to understand two things about law highlighted in Kafka's work as law as experience. The first is a *conceptual* one, applicable to all legal systems. The law, as it is experienced by those subject to it, inherently makes two competing claims to authority, rendering it unknowable and inaccessible. The second, examined in the following section, is a contemporary, empirically observable trend in *postmodern* legal systems, that is their increasing complexity and fragmentation, which promise the *potential* of better, more precise legal outcomes, but an equal potential for the law to be experienced as even more irrational and unknowable. Let us deal with these two aspects in turn.

The idea of *law as experience* takes seriously the place of law in the world, rather than simply as a self-referential normative system whose content rests on some imagined or assumed validity. Law seen in this way is something that makes a claim on you, or more precisely on your actions. That law makes a claim on those subject to it is a widely, although not universally, shared position in much contemporary legal theory,[41] yet the full complexity of these claims, and the relationship between them, are not generally appreciated. For those subject to the law, the law makes two claims to authority. On the one

---

40 Gardner has sought to show how legal validity and effectiveness can be explained by people's 'faith' therein: John Gardner, 'Law as a leap of faith' in Sionaidh Douglas-Scott *et al.* (eds), *Faith in Law* (Hart, 2000).

41 A survey of such positions can be found in John Gardner, 'How law claims, what law claims' in Matthias Klatt (ed.), *Institutionalized Reason: The Jurisprudence of Robert Alexy* (OUP, 2012).

hand, it claims authority by providing you with rules which attempt to *pre-empt* your own practical reasoning, that is, your decision-making process.[42] Accounts of law as a system of rules are prevalent in both contemporary positivist[43] and natural law theories[44] which stress the importance, either in fact or in ideal terms, of the *normative* form which law possesses. The basic point here is that law seeks to intervene in your reasoning process *ex ante*. The idea that law primarily takes this form, and makes this sort of claim, provides the basis for two of law's strongest redeeming features in moral and political theory, thus giving it the potential to transcend the simple status of hand-maiden of the all-powerful state. Firstly, theorists such as Fuller[45] explain how the law, taking this normative form, is able to provide a framework for action, enhancing the autonomy of those subject to it, by allowing them to predict the actions of others and of officials of the legal system. This in turn facilitates planning and the ability to direct one's own life. Secondly, also centring on the law's relationship with autonomy, Raz has stressed, using his service conception of authority, how the peremptory nature of law's claim to authority allows one to use law to better achieve one's own goals, relying on its likely better judgment where applicable.[46] On this view, the law's claims should not produce the anxiety which Kafka portrays in his work. However unjust the content of the law, it is presented in a way which permits planning and purports to perform a service for those subject to it.

However, the experience of law as unknowable and inaccessible stems primarily from its *competing* second claim to authority which exists contemporaneously and in concert with the first. This second claim can be seen in general theories of law which focus on the *adjudicatory* function of legal systems, as diverse as the legal realists[47] and Dworkinian interpretivism,[48] among others. As with *ex ante* authority visions of law, such theories can be seen as offering the law a form of redemption, in their case by promising a *just outcome* of some kind or another: regardless of the mistakes of the law-as-rules, a just judgment can be reached in court. What these law-as-adjudication theories have in common is their belief that law primarily consists in the passing of

---

42 This formulation is based on Raz's hugely influential account of rules as exclusionary reasons, first laid out in detail in Joseph Raz, *Practical Reason and Norms* (Hutchinson, 1975).

43 Classic examples are: H.L.A. Hart, *The Concept of Law* (Clarendon Press, 1997); Hans Kelsen, *General Theory of Law and State* (Harvard University Press, 1945); Joseph Raz, *The Concept of a Legal System* (Clarendon Press, 1980).

44 The centrality of law's normative character to the law's moral significance is present in both John Finnis, *Natural Law and Natural Rights* (Clarendon Press, 1982); Lon Fuller, *The Morality of Law* (Yale University Press, 1969).

45 Fuller, in particular ch. 2.

46 Joseph Raz, 'The obligation to obey: revision and tradition' (1984) 1 *Notre Dame Journal of Law, Ethics and Public Policy* 139.

47 Oliver Wendell Holmes, 'The path of the law' (1897) 10 *Harvard Law Review* 457.

48 Ronald Dworkin, *Law's Empire* (Hart, 1998).

judgment, that is that it is essential to law's nature that it claims the authority to pass judgment on the past actions of those subject to it and declare on
their legal status. This is an *ex post* claim to authority.

The insight of these latter theorists is perhaps somewhat lost on those who
insist that law is essentially a system of rules. For such law-as-rules theorists,
those rules constitute the legal framework which *establishes* both the form and
the content of any adjudication, and are therefore logically prior to it. These
theorists fail to apprehend the *non-lawyer's* experience of this second claim to
authority. For the lawyer, there is no dual claim to authority, as adjudication
proceeds according to legal rules which are analytically and intra-systemically
prior. Any apparent paradox of competing claims to authority is dissolved
therefore by the law itself. For someone merely *subject* to the law however, any
apparent guidance which rules provide *in advance* is offset to the law's parallel
claim to pass judgment on your actions *after the fact*. Legal theorists may engage
in fruitful debate about which of these claims is prior, more conceptually
central, or morally more significant, yet this misses the crucial fact that for
those outside the workings of the legal system, both claims to authority are
experienced with equal force.

This dual claim to authority is the basis of the truth in Kafka's depiction of
law as experience. The law makes contradictory claims on people's actions,
meaning that regardless of how clear or precise the original *ex ante* norms are,
or how reasonable, predictable, or transparent the *ex post* adjudication is, one
lives permanently in between these two stools of the law's competing claims to
authority. Law is, at once, an institution which claims to direct your behaviour
in advance and then also judge it in retrospect. That these two functions are
both necessary and desirable for numerous reasons, and linked in numerous
ways, does not take away from the fact that, for those who are simply subject
to the law's demands, this double claim to authority means that one can *never*
be sure of what the law is requiring of you. Even when one thinks that one
understands the law's *ex ante* requirements, the law reserves the right to come
to a different conclusion, *ex post*, for better or worse.

How does this relate to Mr Kadi and Josef K.? Their respective cases are so
powerful for lawyers because they bring home to those within the law what
it is to experience the *unknowability* and *inaccessibility* of an institution which
they usually experience and rationalize in terms of its inner logic, rationality,
openness, and myriad other virtues. The unknowability and inaccessibility in
Kadi and Kafka are self-evident due to their extremes. However, what this
section has sought to show is that law, through its dual claim to authority –
through its very nature – will *always* possess these alienating characteristics
for those subject to the law without access to its inner workings. Due to its
competing claims of authority one can *never* be sure what the law requires.
One can of course hope for a just outcome, or at least a favourable one, which
may well be forthcoming, but this does not remove the anxiety which one
experiences while awaiting it.

Kafka, *Kadi*, and the experience of law in postmodernity

If unknowability and inaccessibility are part of law's nature, therefore, how should one understand cases such as *Kadi*? One reading suggested above would see *Kadi II* as a happy ending to a Gothic tale, thus demonstrating the inherent goodness and redeeming potential of law in general, and the EU legal system in particular. On this view, Kafka's morality tales have been heeded as Mr Kadi has avoided the fate of Josef K., and the law has produced the just outcome which its adjudicatory system of authority promises. As the previous section concluded, however, the outcome of *The Trial* itself, or of any legal procedure is not the source of the unknowability and inaccessibility of the law and its workings. What *Kadi* represents is instead a case where these elements are brought to the attention of lawyers, for whom the law is, by definition, neither inaccessible nor unknowable. This is perhaps because the *Kadi* saga hinges on certain contemporary trends within the law and their tendency to *heighten* the level of unknowability and inaccessibility which lead to the alienating experience of law as depicted in Kafka. These trends take the form of the increasing complexity of both the *ex ante* claims to authority in the form of rules and the *ex post* claims to authority in the form of adjudication. While both of these trends contain the potential for better, more tailored laws and legal outcomes, they do this at the expense of any remaining *accessibility* or *knowability*. While Kafka's work is often understood as depicting the troubling aspects of *modernity*, the *Kadi* saga demonstrates particular developments in law's *postmodern* phase.

The first development is the increasing prevalence of technical regulatory-type laws and various forms of *lex specialis*, of which the targeted sanctions applied to Mr Kadi are an example. The increasing number and complexity of laws and their lack of generality can only add to the feeling of alienation of people seeking to plan their actions according to the law's commands or to use the law in their practical reasoning process. Laws are becoming more targeted towards specific problems, bringing the promise of more precisely engineered provisions, but also rendering the law more fragmented. In particular the use of *criminal* law and other sanctions to bolster the regulatory aims of government makes this problem particularly acute.[49]

The second development is equally evident in *Kadi*. This is the increasing complexity of sources of law to be taken into consideration in the adjudication phase, in particular that which appears to possess hierarchical superiority or constitutional force, which has become equally fragmented.[50] Much of the literature on the *Kadi* saga has focused on the problems of the relationship

---

49 On this issue, and the related *maxim ignorantia juris non excusat*, see Andrew Ashworth, 'Ignorance of the criminal law, and duties to avoid it' (2011) 74 *The Modern Law Review* 1.
50 Gunther Teubner, 'Global Bukowina' in Gunther Teubner (ed.), *Global Law without a State* (Ashgate, 1997).

between legal systems and their claims to supremacy, redolent of constitutional and legal *pluralism*. The tendency to seek to describe or advocate an 'integrated' inter-systemic approach to legal questions, drawing upon legal norms from a variety of competing sources which all claim hierarchical preeminence has become extremely prevalent. Even the *Kadi* judgments themselves, which are often seen[51] as representing a form of hermetically sealed *dualist* approach to international law, are ultimately grounded on principles which form part of the EU system by virtue of their status in *other*, i.e. national,[52] legal systems, and possibly also international law itself.[53] The great advantage, from the broader perspective of justice and the law's ability to furnish it, is that such approaches, in their sensibilities to varying concerns and willingness to find a balance between different substantive claims, offer the possibility that a *better* outcome will be reached: the court can find a combination of sources which produces the outcome which the case requires. However, as mentioned above, the reality of such adjudicatory considerations, when looked at from the perspective of those *subject* to the law is somewhat different. While they might hold out hope for a favourable outcome to their case, which may or may not arrive, this judicial balancing of a plurality of legal values of varying pedigree is far from accessible.

The fragmented and increasingly complex nature of modern legal systems and their interaction can only serve to exacerbate the impact of conflicting claims to authority of law which make Kafka's depiction of law as experience so powerful. Law has an *inherently* unknowable nature for those who are subject to it. However, this is always a question of degree. *Kadi* is an illustration that, beyond law's inescapable unknowability due to its competing claims on people who are subject to it, legal systems can contribute greatly to this alienating experience by making law *even less* knowable and its processes *even less* accessible. Douglas-Scott has recently and powerfully described this 'postmodern', post-systemic fragmented constellation of law – these new forms of legal pluralism – by drawing parallels with more general postmodern themes of chaos and fragmentation of meaning in literature and art, seeking to demonstrate the absurdities and alienation that such an explosion in competing signs brings.[54]

However, by considering Kafka's depiction of law as experience we are able to see the consequences of this fragmentation in terms of how people *relate* to law. While Douglas-Scott concludes her work with the argument that the

---

51 In relation to *Kadi*, see the literature cited above in note 5.

52 See, for instance, the discussion regarding the place and pedigree of general principles and fundamental rights in EU law in Case 11/70 *Internationale Handelsgesellschaft* [1970] ECR 1125, para. 4.

53 This is the general idea of *solange*-type controls representing a dialectic whereby values inherent within the legal system being scrutinized are the very basis for review. An argument of a similar type can be found in Tom Eijsbouts, Leonard Besselink, '"The law of laws" – overcoming pluralism' (2008) 4 *European Constitutional Law Review* 395.

54 Sionaidh Douglas-Scott, *Law After Modernity* (Hart, 2013) in particular ch. 4.

standards of justice which inform the law might still prevail within such a complex system, *pace Kadi II*, such a view risks neglecting the place that an accessible and comprehensible legal system *itself* has in a just society, regardless of the justness of discrete instances of adjudication. What the judgment in *Kadi II* shows is that these inaccessible legal processes are capable of comprehending the danger of their own incomprehensibility. While the inner workings of the law are indeed inaccessible to those subject to it, thus making the law inherently unknowable, the law contains not only the promise of redemption in terms of just outcomes to cases before it, but also redemption in the form of some relief from the extremes of law's own inaccessibility. To prevent more people from enduring Josef K.'s plight, the law must *present itself* as something which is both accessible and knowable. If people subject to the law *perceive* it as rational and comprehensible they are spared the anxiety of both Mr Kadi and Josef K. This however would require the law to pull back from its current fragmentation, with the consequent danger of less suitable, even less just, laws and judgments. The UN Security Council, the original source of Mr Kadi's woes, has already begun to make its sanctions less targeted in nature in response to the rulings of the CJEU and other courts. It is far from evident that this is a better solution. Here it is the law itself, rather than those subject to it, which finds itself in a double-bind.

Part 3

The public international law perspective

8 The *Kadi II* judgment of the Court of Justice of the European Union

Implications for judicial review of UN Security Council resolutions

Arman Sarvarian

The judgment of the Court of Justice of the European Union (CJEU) in *Kadi II*[1] concludes a lengthy set of litigation[2] concerning the freezing of assets belonging to the applicant by the European Union (EU), acting pursuant to the 'targeted sanctions' mechanism prescribed by the United Nations (UN) Security Council. The jurisprudence, which has been of considerable interest to the international law community, has the potential to alter the dynamics of UN Security Council operations not only where they engage individual human rights but in other spheres as well. The implications for the responsibility of UN member states and other international organizations, such as the EU, for infringements of human rights make this study all the more timely.

This chapter examines the potential implications of *Kadi II* judgment of the CJEU for the principle of judicial review of EU legislation enacted in support

---

1 Joined Cases C-584/10 P, C-593/10 P, and C-595/10 P *Commission, Council and United Kingdom* v. *Kadi* (European Court of Justice), Judgment of 18 July 2013. See also Joined Cases C-584/10 P, C-593/10 P, and C-595/10 P *Commission, Council and United Kingdom* v. *Kadi*, Opinion of AG Bot (19 March 2013).

2 Case T-315/01 *Kadi* v. *Council and Commission* [2005] ECR II-3649 (CFI); Case T-306/01 *Yusuf and Al Barakaat International Foundation* v. *Council and Commission* [2005] ECR II-3353 (CFI); Joined Cases C-402/05 P and 415/05 P *Kadi and Al Barakaat International Foundation* v. *Council and Commission* [2008] ECR I-6351 (ECJ); Case T-85/09 *Kadi* v. *Commission* [2010] ECR I-0000 (General Court). See also, e.g., Annalisa Ciampi, 'Security Council targeted sanctions and human rights' in Bardo Fassbender (ed.), *Securing Human Rights? Achievements and Challenges of the UN Security Council* (OUP, 2011), 98–140, 122–3; Erika de Wet, 'Human rights considerations and the enforcement of targeted sanctions in Europe: the emergence of core standards of judicial protection' in Bardo Fassbender, *Securing Human Rights? Achievements and Challenges of the UN Security Council* (OUP, 2011), 141–71, 143–63; Paul James Cardwell *et al.*, 'Case comment: Kadi v. Council of the European Union (C-402/05 P)' (2009) 58(1) *International and Comparative Law Quarterly* 229–40; Stefan Griller, 'Case comment: international law, human rights and the European Community's autonomous legal order: notes on the European Court of Justice decision in Kadi' (2008) 4(3) *European Constitutional Law Review* 528–53; P. Takis Tridimas, 'Terrorism and the ECJ: empowerment and democracy in the EC legal order' (2009) 34(1) *European Law Review* 103–26; Simon Chesterman, '"I'll take Manhattan": the international rule of law and the United Nations Security Council' (2009) 1(1) *Hague Journal on the Rule of Law* 67–73.

of UN Security Council resolutions. It focuses upon three strands of the judgment: 1) the applicable standard of review; 2) the requisite threshold of evidentiary substantiation for compliance with the right to a fair trial; and 3) the implications of the judgment for future judicial review, particularly in light of the previous judgments in the proceedings and the judgment of the European Court of Human Rights in *Nada*.[3] The chapter appraises the consequences of the judgment for the long-running debate between the General Court of the EU, the CJEU, and certain EU member states concerning judicial review by the EU judiciary.

While the complexity of the proceedings necessarily inhibits prediction, this chapter suggests that the terms of judicial review set by the CJEU paradoxically may reduce the likelihood of future cases of review. In laying down a standard of full or *de novo* review of EU legislation, the Court has made it incumbent upon the European Commission to exact substantiating evidence from the Sanctions Committee of the UN Security Council for the enactment of targeted sanctions by the Union. The robustness of this approach will reduce the likelihood of judicial challenge by compelling the Union organs to secure the fundamental rights of individuals facing targeted sanctions. By serving notice to the EU organs (and, by extension, to the UN Security Council) that human rights must be respected, the CJEU may prompt those institutions to adopt stricter standards of procedure and substantiation in the future.

However, even as the judgment closes the *Kadi* saga, it does not end the debate concerning the lawfulness of judicial review according to the reasoning of the CJEU in its judgment in *Kadi I*. In the light of the controversial nature of the proceedings and the views of the General Court and AG Bot, a future challenge by the EU organs or member states to the principle of judicial review is also likely. Although a full reprisal of the *Kadi I* arguments may not be heard, it is probable that there will be calls for a more restricted standard of review and for laxer requirements of substantiation for listings.

Standard of review

A critical issue in the *Kadi II* proceedings was the standard of review to be applied by the EU judicature. In its judgment in *Kadi I*, the CJEU affirmed that judicial review was to be:

> in principle, the full review, of the lawfulness of all Community acts in the light of the fundamental rights forming an integral part of the general principles of Community law, including review of Community measures which... are designed to give effect to the resolutions adopted

---

3 *Nada* v. *Switzerland* (App. No. 10593/08), Judgment of 12 September 2012. See Fabbrini and Larik, ch. 11 this volume.

by the Security Council under Chapter VII of the Charter of the United Nations.[4]

The issue in *Kadi II* was the meaning to be construed from the phrase 'full review', namely, the exact standard to be applied under art. 263 of the Treaty on the Functioning of the European Union (TFEU).

Before the General Court, the applicant had argued that an 'intensive and anxious review' should be conducted, whereas the Commission, EU Council, and member states proposed a 'fair balance' test between respect for fundamental rights and the need to combat international terrorism.[5] In particular, the Commission argued for a standard of 'restricted review', entailing an assessment of the procedure and criteria employed to evaluate the evidence but not an evaluation of its merits.[6] In this respect, it is noteworthy that the standard of review is necessarily developed through judicial doctrine in the absence of express provision in the EU treaties and that the applicable standard can be drawn at a number of points, including procedural irregularity, illegality, irrationality, and/or full merits review.[7]

In addition, the outcome of the *Kadi I* proceedings cannot be bulkheaded from those of *Kadi II* in that, notwithstanding the decision of the CJEU to endorse the principle of judicial review of EU legislation designed to give effect to UN Security Council resolutions, arguments predicated upon the normative supremacy of the UN Charter continued to be employed by the Commission and member states in *Kadi II* to restrict the standard of review.[8] In particular, the Commission and member states sought to preclude a review of the merits of the listing decision on the ground that the international legal order demands that the evaluation of the Sanctions Committee be upheld without scrutiny of the evidence. Thus, the determination of the standard of review carried as much practical importance for the dynamics of the UN and EU legal orders as the principle of review itself.[9]

In its judgment, the General Court rejected the submissions of the Commission and member states. It held:

> If the intensity and extent of judicial review were limited in the way advocated by the Commission and the intervening governments (see [86]–[101] above) and by the Council (see [102]–[111] above), there would be no effective judicial review of the kind required by the Court

---

4 *Kadi and Al Barakaat International* (ECJ), para. 326.
5 *Kadi* v. *Commission* (General Court), paras. 82–5.
6 *Ibid.*, paras. 86–8.
7 For an overview of the possible standards, see Fontanelli, ch. 2 this volume.
8 *Kadi* v. *Commission* (General Court), paras. 92–111.
9 In its judgment, the General Court expressed its disquiet with the decision of the CJEU in *Kadi I* – overturning its own, very different, decision in that case – but chose, as a matter of appellate principle, to refrain from re-examining the merits of that decision – *ibid.*, paras. 112–22.

of Justice in *Kadi* [2008] 3 C.M.L.R. 41 but rather a simulacrum thereof. That would amount, in fact, to following the same approach as that taken by this Court in its own judgment in *Kadi* [2008] 3 C.M.L.R. 41, which was held by the Court of Justice on appeal to be vitiated by an error of law. The General Court considers that in principle it falls not to it but to the Court of Justice to reverse precedent in that way, if it were to consider this to be justified in light, in particular, of the serious difficulties to which the institutions and intervening governments have referred.[10]

The General Court concluded that its task was to apply full review 'without affording the regulation any immunity from jurisdiction on the ground that it gives effect to resolutions adopted by the Security Council under Chapter VII of the Charter of the United Nations'.[11] It held that this could only be achieved by undertaking a substantive merits review and not the restricted review advocated by the Commission[12] and that this standard of review applied in the *OMPI* case[13] had been upheld by the CJEU.[14] Furthermore, it found that this standard of review was justified by the profound effects of the targeted sanctions regime upon human rights.[15]

In his Opinion of 19 March 2013, AG Bot opined, in contrast to the findings of the General Court, that:

> Whatever the case, as regards the implementation of restrictive measures decided by the Sanctions Committee, there are several reasons against a judicial review as thorough as that undertaken by the General Court in the judgment under appeal, with reference to its judgment in OMPI. Those reasons relate to the preventative nature of the measures in question, the international context of the contested act, the need to balance the requirements of combating terrorism and the requirements of protection of fundamental rights, the political nature of the assessments made by the Sanctions Committee in deciding to list a person or an entity, and the improvements in the procedure before that body in recent years and, in particular, since the judgment of the Court of Justice in *Kadi*.[16]

---

10 *Ibid.*, para. 123.
11 *Ibid.*, para. 126.
12 *Ibid.*, para. 129.
13 [2007] 1 C.M.L.R. 34.
14 *Kadi* v. *Commission* (General Court), para. 138. See also Hayley Hooper, 'Liberty before security: Case T-85/09 *Yassin Abdullah Kadi* v. *Commission (No. 2)* [2010] ECR 00000 (30 September 2010)' (2012) 18(3) *European Public Law* 457–70. See also Cases T-35/10 and T-7/11 *Bank Melli Iran* v. *Council of the European Union*, Judgment of the General Court (Fourth Chamber) of 6 September 2013, paras. 86–106.
15 *Kadi* v. *Commission* (General Court), paras. 150–2.
16 *Ibid.*, para. 67.

In particular, the AG argued that such an intensive judicial review

> such as advocated by the General Court in the judgment under appeal,
> cannot be performed without encroaching on the prerogatives of the
> Security Council in defining what constitutes a threat to international
> peace and security and the measures necessary to eradicate that threat.
> Since it is for the Sanctions Committee to decide to include a person or
> an entity on the list, the judicial review conducted within the EU must
> be commensurate with the limited discretion enjoyed by the EU institu-
> tions. In other words, the primary responsibility held by the Security
> Council in the area in question must not be undermined and the Union
> must not be made a forum for appeals against or reviews of decisions
> taken by the Sanctions Committee.[17]

In proposing a limited standard of review that does not question the merits
of the listing, the Advocate General argued that the applicant's procedural
rights were respected and called for the 'end [of] the saga of *Kadi* cases'.[18]

In its judgment of 18 July 2013, the CJEU held that the General Court had
committed errors of law in its judgment but that those errors did not 'affect
the validity of that judgment, given that its operative part, which annuls the
contested regulation in so far as it concerns Mr Kadi, is well founded on legal
grounds'.[19] The Court found that the General Court had erred by: 1) basing
its finding on the failure of the Commission to disclose to Mr Kadi and the
General Court the information underpinning his listing; and 2) basing its
finding of infringement on the fact that the allegations made in the summary
of reasons provided by the Sanctions Committee were vague.[20] The Court
affirmed the principle of judicial review of contested EU legislation concerning human rights, specifically the duty of the EU judicature to require the
competent authorities to produce the requisite information to enable it to
carry out that review.[21] Thus, the judgment primarily addresses the standard
of review with the Court declining the invitation from the appellants to
reverse its decision on the principle of review in *Kadi I*.[22]

However, as before the General Court, the theme of *Kadi I* of the relationship between the EU legal order and the wider international legal order of
which it forms part indirectly featured in the argumentation concerning the
standard of review. The crux of the appellants' arguments was the assertion
that the deference to be afforded to the UN Security Council obliges the EU

---

17 *Ibid.*, para. 71.
18 *Ibid.*, paras. 105–23.
19 *Commission, Council and United Kingdom* v. *Kadi* (ECJ), para. 164.
20 *Ibid.*, paras. 138–49.
21 *Ibid.*, paras. 117–34.
22 *Ibid.*, paras. 59–69.

judicature to adopt a restricted, rather than full, standard of review.[23] The CJEU rejected this argument, holding that the effectiveness of the judicial review guaranteed by art. 47 ('Right to an effective remedy and to a fair trial') of the Charter of Fundamental Rights[24] demands that the EU judicature verify the allegations underpinning the summary of reasons provided by the UN Sanctions Committee:

> with the consequence that judicial review cannot be restricted to an assessment of the abstract cogency in the abstract of the reasons relied on, but must concern whether those reasons, or, at the very least, one of those reasons, deemed sufficient in itself to support that decision, is substantiated.[25]

Thus, the Court laid down not only a requirement for EU bodies to furnish to the judicature evidence underpinning a listing decision but also a duty for the judicature to carry out a *de novo* review of the evidence to satisfy itself of its probative value.[26]

Although the Court relied upon the second paragraph of art. 275 TFEU at the outset of its analysis,[27] that provision – while providing a legal basis for judicial review – does not address the standard of review. While the logic of the Court that the right to an effective remedy guaranteed by art. 47 of the Charter requires intensive review is attractive, there is similarly no jurisprudence of the European Court of Human Rights[28] suggesting that judicial review must take the form of full merits review to ensure that the right to an effective remedy is secured. Consequently, it is suggested that the standard of full review laid down by the Court is essentially judicial doctrine based upon policy considerations rather than a Treaty obligation.

The Court distinguished between general information or material concerning an individual subject to listing – which may carry confidentiality

---

23 *Ibid.*, para. 74.
24 'Everyone whose rights and freedoms guaranteed by the law of the Union are violated has the right to an effective remedy before a tribunal in compliance with the conditions laid down in this Article.'
25 *Commission, Council and United Kingdom* v. *Kadi* (ECJ), para. 119.
26 *Ibid.*, para. 120.
27 'The Court of Justice of the European Union shall not have jurisdiction with respect to the provisions relating to the common foreign and security policy nor with respect to acts adopted on the basis of those provisions. However, the Court shall have jurisdiction to monitor compliance with Article 40 of the Treaty on European Union and to rule on proceedings, brought in accordance with the conditions laid down in the fourth paragraph of Article 263 of this Treaty, reviewing the legality of decisions providing for restrictive measures against natural or legal persons adopted by the Council on the basis of Chapter 2 of Title V of the Treaty on European Union.'
28 The doctrine of 'anxious scrutiny' has some common law support but it has not been applied consistently – R. Clayton and H. Tomlinson, *The Law of Human Rights* (OUP, 2009, vol. I), 36 (para. 1.35).

concerns – and the specific evidence underpinning the allegations against that individual.[29] This distinction is persuasive in pinpointing the essence of the obligation, namely, to substantiate those allegations underpinning the listing rather than to disclose all information in its possession concerning an individual. This strengthens its finding that the confidentiality concerns asserted by EU bodies based upon international peace and security cannot displace the duty to substantiate allegations underpinning an interference with the human right to, inter alia, peaceful enjoyment of possessions.

The Court's careful articulation of the principles by which the EU judicature is to carry out its review of EU implementing targeted sanctions legislation thus decouples international peace and security from human rights. It achieves this by removing the dichotomy whereby the upholding of human rights should be subject to the overarching need to protect international peace and security, so that the two policies are set in opposition. By acknowledging the importance of international peace and security yet requiring human rights standards to be upheld in its pursuit, the Court sidestepped the dichotomy by avoiding a pronouncement to the effect of 'it is more important to uphold human rights than to maintain international peace and security'. Although the two concepts cannot be fully divorced from each other, the Court's approach successfully rebuts the prioritization of the international security argument while avoiding a policy prioritization paradigm.

In addition to the *Kadi I* decisions and the *Kadi II* judgment of the General Court, the *Kadi II* judgment of the CJEU adds to the growing body of juris-prudence in various courts with human rights remits.[30] Having circumvented (though not broken through) the impenetrable barrier of judicial review of UN Security Council resolutions, the articulation of a standard of review by the CJEU in *Kadi II* breaks new ground in threading the camel through the eye of the needle. In necessarily innovating new doctrine in the absence of express legislative principles, the Court plumbed for the most robust standard of review available to it.

While this approach may be challenged in future for setting the bar need-lessly high when lower standards could arguably achieve the legal duty of realizing the human right to an effective remedy and a fair trial, the Court skilfully justified its approach by nullifying the oft-invoked justification of security concerns for a failure to substantiate targeted sanctions listings. This approach provides a model for the potential exercise of judicial review by

---

29 *Commission, Council and United Kingdom* v. *Kadi* (ECJ), paras. 125–7.
30 No. 1472/2006 *Sayadi and Vinck* v. *Belgium* (UN Human Rights Committee, Communication of 29 December 2008); Joined Cases C-399/06 P and C-403/06 P *Hassan and Ayadi* v. *Council and Commission* [2009] ECR I-11393; Case C-548/09 P *Bank Melli Iran* v. *Council* [2011] ECR I-0000; app. no. 10593/08 *Nada* v. *Switzerland* (European Court of Human Rights, Grand Chamber, Judgment of 12 September 2012); no. 1472/2006 *Sayadi and Vinck* v. *Belgium* (UN Human Rights Committee, Communication of 29 December 2008).

other courts. In this respect, the battleground in future litigation may narrow to focus upon the element of full merits review of the evidence with proponents of greater deference to executive bodies likely to argue that a lower standard of requiring the production of sufficient evidence, without a qualitative assessment of it, would be a preferable approach in the interests of systemic efficiency by limiting the scope for excessive second-guessing.

Evidentiary substantiation

The second main issue arising out of the *Kadi II* judgment and pertaining to judicial review is the evidentiary substantiation required to sustain the denial of the human right to peaceful enjoyment of possessions to an individual by the EU through targeted sanctions. In an analysis reminiscent of the approach of the European Court of Human Rights (ECtHR), the CJEU declared that a 'fair balance' must be struck between the priorities of maintaining international peace and security and protecting human rights[31] and that, in principle, only one of the reasons asserted by the UN Sanctions Committee to the EU needed to be substantiated for the listing to be upheld by the EU judicature.[32] In this context, the Court held that the EU is obliged to: 1) disclose to the affected individual the summary of reasons provided by the Sanctions Committee as the basis for their listing by the EU; 2) permit the affected individual to make observations upon that subject; and 3) examine, carefully and impartially, whether the reasons alleged are well founded in the light of the observations and any exculpatory evidence produced by the individual.[33] These principles expressly underpinned the Court's finding that the EU judicature is to review the merits of the listing, including such evidence as is disclosed to substantiate or rebut it.[34]

In finding that the General Court erred in law by holding that the failure by the European Commission to disclose to Mr Kadi and to that Court the evidence underpinning his listing, the CJEU distinguished between that omission and a failure to adequately substantiate the reasons asserted for the listing.[35] Whereas the procedural failure to disclose such evidence is legally insufficient to constitute, as such, a violation of the rights to effective judicial protection and fair trial, the failure to support the reasons underpinning the listing can legally do so. While this may appear to be a sophistic distinction to the observer, it has an important practical bearing upon the decision due to the fact that the European Commission did not have in its custody the evidence concerning Mr Kadi.[36]

---

31 *Commission, Council and United Kingdom* v. *Kadi* (ECJ), para. 131.
32 *Ibid.*, para. 130.
33 *Ibid.*, para. 135.
34 *Ibid.*, para. 136.
35 *Ibid.*, paras. 137–9.
36 *Ibid.*, para. 138.

Thus, the violation by the Commission was not the failure to disclose as such but rather the listing of Mr Kadi in the absence of adequate supporting evidence that it could disclose to him and to the EU courts. The absence of such supporting evidence fatally undermined the listing decision in the Court's merits review, which found that all of the four reasons asserted by the UN Sanctions Committee for the listing of Mr Kadi were not adequately substantiated.[37] Ironically, the lack of inculpatory evidence necessarily obliged the Court to assess the exculpatory evidence adduced by Mr Kadi and the Commission's observations upon that evidence.

Concluding its merits review, the Court held that the lack of substantiation proffered by the Commission, coupled with the rebuttal evidence submitted by Mr Kadi, failed to justify the adoption at EU level of targeted sanctions against the latter.[38] Furthermore, it ruled in light of this finding that the aforementioned errors of law in the judgment of the General Court were insufficiently grave to invalidate its validity.[39] In so doing, the CJEU was essentially laying down parameters for the future conduct of judicial review by the EU judicature of targeted sanctions legislation inspired by UN Security Council actions.

It is respectfully suggested that the finding of the Court that the errors of law committed by the General Court were insufficient as to obviate the judgment is correct. Although the errors identified carry implications for future cases in which the factual circumstances differ (e.g. where the Commission is furnished by the Sanctions Committee with the evidence underpinning a listing decision), in the instant case they do not produce a different outcome in the light of the uncontested lack of substantiation by the Commission for the particular listing of Mr Kadi. In this respect, the judgment provides an important clarification concerning the scope of judicial review in the light of the principles discussed above.

In this respect, an important factor in the Court's analysis was the sufficiency of the summary of reasons furnished by the Commission in the absence of additional information. Contrary to the approach of the General Court, the CJEU found that most of the allegations against Mr Kadi were on their face sufficient to uphold his listing. However, the submission of exculpatory evidence by Mr Kadi and the lack of an adequate response by the Commission made the difference. Here, it is suggested that the imprecision of the weighing exercise is a weak link in the analysis: even had Mr Kadi failed to produce the exculpatory evidence that he did, the summary of reasons should not be sufficient to uphold his listing unless buttressed by inculpatory evidence. In this respect, although the CJEU was correct to conduct the detailed analysis that it did with respect to the summary of reasons, ironically the more general approach of the General Court produced the better substantive result.

---

37 *Ibid.*, paras. 153, 156, 159, 162–3.
38 *Ibid.*, para. 163.
39 *Ibid.*, para. 164.

However, an important issue remains as to whether full merits review is, as the Court asserted, necessary to ensure respect for the human rights to an effective judicial remedy and to a fair trial. It is respectfully suggested that that conclusion is not fully borne out in the factual context of the case, in that the Court may well have reached an identical outcome through the application of a more restricted standard of review. In particular, the failure to produce supporting evidence for the summary of reasons or rebuttal evidence against Mr Kadi and, in itself, should as a matter of law constitute a violation of the aforementioned rights. Consequently, it is arguable that a full merits review entailing a re-examination of the strength of the evidence is superfluous. Although it is not necessarily so that a full merits review would cause systemic inefficiency through excessive judicial scrutiny and it could be argued as a matter of policy that the human rights problems arising out of the *Kadi* case and others in relation to the targeted sanctions regimes require a robust standard of review, these considerations are not addressed in the judgment.

Moreover, an analytical weakness in the judgment is the absence of a standard of proof[40] concerning the merits review. This is of especial importance in the light of the full merits review standard laid down by the Court, in that the EU judicature will need guidance concerning the appropriate measure to be applied in assessing the evidence. This lack of guidance is compounded by the added complexity of the balance between international peace and security on the one hand and human rights considerations on the other hand set out by the Court as justification for the necessity of judicial review.[41] To strike that balance – particularly in the light of the robust standard of review laid down by the Court – it is essential that the judicial scrutiny endorsed at the EU level be accompanied by a more precise analytical framework in the assessment of evidence. This is all the more necessary due to the relative rarity of evidentiary assessment in the EU courts and the need to provide guidance, at one remove, to the European Commission and, at two removes, to the Sanctions Committee as to the weighing exercise expected by the EU judicature.

Implications for judicial review

While the ECJ decision in *Kadi I* has been described as a breakthrough concerning human rights protection for the UN Security Council targeted sanctions regime, on closer inspection its implications are limited and its Eurocentric analytical approach problematic.[42] The Court did not purport to

---

40 This common law concept of objectivity should be read as a qualified criticism in light of its absence in Franco-Germanic systems, wherein a subjective concept of *conviction intime* applies. Nevertheless, it is suggested that the criticism has value concerning the need for predictability for administrative organs (namely, the UN Security Council and European Commission) of CJEU standards on listing.

41 *Ibid.*, paras. 131–4.

42 Cardwell *et al.*, 239–40; Cuyvers, 489, 496–506.

assert jurisdiction to review the lawfulness of the background resolution but only that of the implementing EU legislation. This follows the pattern of national and international courts shying away from directly challenging the lawfulness of Security Council resolutions:

> A more active engagement by domestic and regional courts with these questions could contribute significantly to the international debate. Although interpretations of international law made by these courts are not binding on the UN, they do carry significant judicial authority and also shape the debate at the international level. The reluctance of domestic and regional courts to engage in this debate may inter alia relate to their understandable desire to avoid an open conflict with the Security Council. However, the approach carries with it the risk of devaluing and marginalizing international law. In addition, it fuels the perception that an irreconcilable normative conflict exists between the UN legal regime and domestic or regional regimes that value the protection of human rights – a conflict which could only be resolved by protecting either one of the regimes at the expense of the other.[43]

The *Kadi II* judgments concerning standard of review did not address the legal problems concerning the formula for judicial review identified in *Kadi I*, including the problem of the CJEU constitutionalist approach for the relationship of the EU with the wider international legal order and the difficult distinction between reviewing EU targeted sanctions legislation while refusing to review the background UN Security Council resolution that directly prompts it. Although the net result is to invalidate EU legislation implementing UN Security Council resolutions found by the EU judicature to infringe human rights at the EU level, it does not constitute direct 'bottom up' judicial review of the background resolutions themselves. Until the Security Council is compelled by pressure from the member states, regional courts, and/or other UN organs to respect international human rights standards in its activities pursuant to its own Charter duty, this distinction is likely to perpetuate these tensions.

However, the *Kadi II* judgment of the CJEU is ground-breaking in transcending the debate concerning the possibility of review, instead addressing its mechanics. While the EU Council sought to re-argue the principle of immunity from review before the General Court and the CJEU and the Opinion of AG Bot (itself ignored in the CJEU judgment) endorsed a restricted standard of review in order to support the fight against international terrorism,[44] the CJEU has confirmed the principle of review and, to a considerable degree, defined its parameters. Although, as argued above, open

43 De Wet, 171.
44 See note 1, paras. 85–7.

issues remain concerning the standard of review and the weighing of evidence, the judgment does advance the debate concerning judicial review beyond the principle of review in *Kadi I*. This keeps the door ajar for future actions seeking to annul EU-targeted sanctions listings and, almost certainly, featuring attempts to reverse or restrict the *Kadi* judgments.

As indicated above, the repeated failure to win immunity from review for listings emanating from the UN Security Council and the robust standard of review laid down by the Court may reduce the possibility of future actions. This is due to the possibility of the European Commission refusing to initiate listings at the EU level without evidentiary substantiation and procedural guarantees conforming to EU human rights standards. A consequential effect may be fewer EU listings, should the Sanctions Committee refuse to conform to those standards, or reform at the UN level of the targeted sanctions regime to attempt to harmonize the regimes. As noted above, despite the principles laid down in the *Kadi II* judgment, a potential complexity in the latter possibility is the lack of guidelines concerning the weighing of evidence.

In the event of fewer EU listings inspired by the UN Security Council-targeted sanctions regimes due to human rights concerns, an important consequence would be differentiation between the UN and EU regimes. In the absence of an implementing EU framework, this leaves the possibility of challenges to the national implementation of UN Security Council sanctions on grounds of incompatibility with EU human rights standards. According to the *Kadi* approach, this would potentially annul not only sanctions implemented by the Union but also by member states. The potential impotence of UN Security Council-targeted sanctions in the largest free-trade zone in the world provides an important incentive for the Security Council to bring its procedures into harmony with EU standards. This could, on the other hand, invite more litigation through attempts by member states to partially or fully reverse the *Kadi* decisions.

Another variant is the refusal of the Sanctions Committee and the EU organs to change the system to bring it into line with the judgments but rather to seek, in the event of future judicial challenge, to successfully reverse them or win important limitations that would demand no more than token or cosmetic changes. Should arguments concerning the principle of review grounded in 'damaged international cooperation' fail to persuade the EU judicature to concede, an important battleground in the future is likely to be the standard of review. Should reforms be instituted to the targeted sanctions regime, it is not inconceivable that a refinement of the standard of review be instituted to lower it. A precondition for this would be architectural changes at the UN level such as would persuade the EU judicature of the trustworthiness of its procedural guarantees for human rights.[45]

45 See Tzanakopoulos, ch. 10 this volume.

Thus, the *Kadi* proceedings may be the cornerstone for a new approach towards UN Security Council activities that places a higher emphasis upon human rights guarantees. Although they may well produce substantial changes in the targeted sanctions regime, at least insofar as it pertains to the EU, the judgments may prove to be less revolutionary than they appear to be. The constitutionalist approach upon which the principle of review is grounded – itself problematic – and the power of the EU legal order and its judiciary do not make it likely that the *Kadi* approach can be replicated in other jurisdictions. In particular, the status of the EU as a non-member of the UN places it in a unique position, which national jurisdictions cannot legally attempt to duplicate in the light of art. 103 of the UN Charter.

Ironically, should a breakthrough in the principle of judicial review be reached for national jurisdictions through a different approach, the *Kadi II* judgment could well prove to be more influential in the long term than that of *Kadi I*. The limitations of the constitutionalist premise of *Kadi I* for national jurisdictions and the uniqueness of the EU as an international organization with powerful supranationalism – in addition to the legal and political contro- versies associated with that judgment – makes it unlikely to be duplicated elsewhere. However, it is possible that national jurisdictions will directly challenge the implementation of targeted sanctions through review of the lawfulness of the UN Security Council resolution concerned – an approach that has seemingly been taken by the Federal Assembly of Switzerland in the *Nada* case.[46] In the event of a breakthrough of this kind, the mechanics of such review (likely to be exercise by courts) will need to be determined and applied. The *Kadi II* judgment of the CJEU provides a leading light for future courts to follow in the stormy seas of challenging the UN Security Council.

---

46 See further Arman Sarvarian, 'The attribution of conduct in the law of international responsibility, the European Union and the European Court of Human Rights' (2013) 1(4) *European Journal of Human Rights*, 654–77.

9 *Kadi II*

Backtracking from *Kadi I?*

Nikos Lavranos and Mihail Vatsov

Introduction

The *Kadi I* judgment of the Court of Justice of the European Union (CJEU) is without doubt one of the most important constitutionally relevant judgments in the history of the Union. Indeed, *Kadi I* instantly obtained a top place in the 'hall of fame' of European Court of Justice (ECJ) judgments – similar to *Van Gend & Loos, Costa* v. *Enel, Simmenthal* and *Francovich.* Having the history of the *Kadi* saga discussed at length in this book,[1] the main point of interest will be *Kadi II* and how the CJEU dealt with it in the end. Among the legal community the initial reactions to the *Kadi II* judgment of the CJEU were quite strong in their criticisms and even led to some poetic outbursts in The Hague. One can say that they were quite natural having in mind that the ground was set for something else.

At the United Nations (UN) level the Security Council understood that it had to improve the listing and de-listing system, otherwise more states would follow the example of refusing to automatically implement UN Security Council Resolutions, which it did by incrementally introducing new elements such as the 'focal point' and more recently by the establishment of the Ombudsperson.[2] Also, new requirements were imposed on the UN members regarding the evidence that must be shown to justify the 'blacklisting' of individuals and organizations that are suspected of terrorism or associated with supporting and/or financing terrorist activities. Last but not least, Mr Kadi was actually, finally, delisted as a result of all the changes.

At the European Union (EU) level the Commission and the Council, which are responsible for the implementation at the Union level of the lists managed by the various UN Sanctions Committees, were required to inform persons

---

1 See chs. 2–4.
2 See, e.g., M. Cremona, F. Francioni, S. Poli (eds.), *Challenging the EU Counter-terrorism Measures through the Courts, EUI Working Papers,* AEL 2009/10, in particular the contribution by Scheinin (available at <http://cadmus.eui.eu/handle/1814/12879> accessed 18 October 2013); J. Kokott, Ch. Sobotta, 'The Kadi case – constitutional core values and international law – finding the balance?', (2012) 23 *European Journal of International Law* 1015–24.

and organizations that are to be listed more extensively – and if possible in an earlier stage – and to provide them with the possibility to ask for a review of the listing. Also, Advocate General (AG) Bot delivered his Opinion and argued quite strongly for an interpretation of the words 'in principle full review' that will lower the intensity of review of the EU measures.[3] Since the AG Opinion did make a difference in *Kadi I* this was also expected to happen in *Kadi II*. Moreover, the Lisbon Treaty came into force with the changes that it contained and it was not unthinkable to expect the CJEU to give different interpretations.[4]

At the European Court of Human Rights (ECtHR) the *Al-Jedda* and *Nada* judgments were delivered where the ECrtHR used interpretative methods in order to avoid the problem of conflicting obligations and introduced a much more flexible test than the one of the General Court (GC) in *Kadi II* when dealing with measures implementing targeted sanctions by the Security Council.

In short, the level of expectation that was built up towards the CJEU to tear apart *Kadi I* and overturn the GC in *Kadi II* was so big that anything short of that would not have brought satisfaction to the interested legal quarters. However, the chances of this really happening were not that high. How can it be expected that after Lisbon – where the Charter of Fundamental Rights was actually given a status of equality with the Treaties, where fundamental rights were made an EU policy, and where the EU shall accede to the European Convention of Human Rights (ECHR) – the CJEU will all of a sudden feel compelled to change its mind completely?

That being said, the CJEU did not turn a blind eye to the consequences of its judgment in *Kadi I*. Admittedly, it did not go as far as it was expected to go by some but it did not ignore those expectations altogether. Whereas the GC tried its best to follow the *Kadi I* judgment by the letter in its *Kadi II* ruling,[5] the CJEU has gotten second thoughts about the impact of its *Kadi I* judgment. As is discussed in more detail in this contribution, in *Kadi II*[6] the CJEU is backtracking from its *Kadi I* judgment, albeit within important limits. Thus, it corrected the GC, again, this time for overly close reading of the *Kadi I* judgment. Accordingly, this contribution discusses exactly how the CJEU backtracked and distanced itself from the GC's reading of *Kadi I*. However, it must be clear at the outset that it will neither be argued that the CJEU backtracked from its position on the *sui generis* nature of the EU legal

---

3 Joined Cases C-584/10 P, C-593/10 P, and C-595/10 P *Commission* v. *Kadi*, Opinion of Advocate General Bot of 19 March, nyr.

4 See Case C-414/11, *Daiichi Sankyo Co. Ltd, Sanofi-Aventis Deutschland GmbH* v. *DEMO Anonimos Viomikhaniki kai Emporiki Etairia Farmakon*, nyr which was decided on the very same day as *Kadi II* and where the CJEU threw out of the window perfectly good old case law on the count of Treaty changes.

5 Case T-85/09 *Yassin Abdullah Kadi* v. *Commission* [2010] ECR II-5177.

6 Joined Cases C-584/10 P, C-593/10 P, and C-595/10 P, *Commission, Council and United Kingdom* v. *Kadi*, Judgment of 18 July 2013 (Grand Chamber), nyr (hereinafter: *Kadi II*).

order nor will it be argued that the CJEU redefined the relationship between the EU and UN. Those topics are yet to be explored and discussed by the authors after the new judgment.

The backtracking in this contribution is examined in regard to two main points. The first relates to the improvements of the procedural guarantees at the UN level. In particular, attention is given to what the CJEU 'expects' those improvements to be. The second point relates to how the CJEU views what is necessary for the listing of an individual. The support for this point is further divided into two parts. The first part clarifies the difference between the reasons for listing an individual and the evidence to support those reasons. Having in mind that difference, the second part shows the CJEU's backtracking. The chapter then examines the paragraphs of *Kadi I* from which the CJEU backtracked in *Kadi II* and then how the CJEU actually backtracked. Furthermore, this contribution points out briefly one other case where the backtracking of the CJEU can be seen. Finally, two complementary factors that induced the CJEU to backtrack are examined.

Backtracking as regards the improvements at UN level

The basis for the possibility of backtracking, as regards the improvements of the procedural safeguards at the UN level, can be already found in the *Kadi I* judgment. Indeed, the Commission raised the argument that 'so long as under that system of sanctions the individuals or entities concerned have an *acceptable opportunity* to be heard through a mechanism of administrative review forming part of the United Nations legal system, the *Court must not intervene in any way whatsoever*'.[7]

In the light of the far-reaching statements concerning the right to full and effective judicial review against UN Security Council Resolutions and Sanctions Committee decisions, which the ECJ repeatedly made in its *Kadi I* judgment, it is interesting to note that the ECJ did not flatly reject this argument but showed some sympathy to it. The ECJ explicitly noted in several paragraphs the incremental improvements, which have been introduced over time with regard to the listing and delisting procedures.[8] The ECJ seemed to recognize those improvements to a certain extent, while at the end it concluded that they cannot give rise to generalized immunity from the ECJ's review jurisdiction.[9] Moreover, the ECJ noted that clearly the re-examination procedure 'does not offer the guarantees of judicial protection'.[10] Consequently,

---

7 Joined Cases C-402/05P and C-415/05P *Yassin Abdullah Kadi and Al Barakaat International Foundation* v. *Council and Commission* (Grand Chamber) [2008] ECR I-6351 para. 319 (emphasis added).
8 *Ibid.*, paras. 320–1, 323–5.
9 *Ibid.*, para. 321.
10 *Ibid.*, para. 322.

the European courts must ensure 'the review, in principle the full review' of the legality of all EC acts in the light of fundamental rights.[11]

These paragraphs in the ECJ's *Kadi I* judgment seem to suggest that if the UN review procedures for the blacklisting are improved to a level that is comparable to the full judicial review offered by the European courts, such a review would not be needed anymore.[12] In other words, the ECJ left the possibility open to rescind its jurisdiction to provide for judicial review from the moment the UN establishes a review system that offers equivalent judicial protection. *De facto* this amounted to the application of the *Solange*-approach,[13] which the ECtHR has been applying vis-à-vis the ECJ[14] and which originates from the German *Bundesverfassungsgericht* approach vis-à-vis the ECJ.[15]

The CJEU continued this line of reasoning in *Kadi II* where it emphasized again the importance of a judicial review in the light of the existing gaps at the UN level. In particular, the CJEU pointed out the still inadequate effective judicial protection at the UN level.[16] The CJEU even referred, in support, to the recent ECrtHR judgment in *Nada*,[17] which contained the same observation but, it should be noted, had a quite different reasoning from the CJEU's.[18] The CJEU made it very clear that in order for backtracking to take place in the light of improvements at the UN level those improvements must be such as to provide for a court which can annul by a declaratory judgment a contested measure *ex tunc*.[19]

Admittedly, the CJEU did not backtrack in this case. However, it is important for this contribution that the CJEU explicitly stated what it considers ultimately necessary in order to backtrack. Failing this, the CJEU was left only with the possibility to backtrack when it comes to the required information for listing that respects fundamental rights.

---

11 *Ibid.*, para. 326.

12 This is indeed suggested by Kokott and Sobotta.

13 R. Schütze, *Coda: Kafka, Kadi, Kant* (11 September 2013), available at <http://ssrn.com/abstract=2324574 or http://dx.doi.org/10.2139/ssrn.2324574> (accessed 18 October 2013).

14 *Bosphorus Hava Yolları Turizm ve Ticaret Anonim irketi* v. *Ireland* Application no. 45036/98, Eur. Ct. H. R. [GC], Judgment of 30 June 2005, para. 155.

15 See for an extensive analysis of the *Solange*-approach N. Lavranos, 'The *Solange*-method as a tool for regulating competing jurisdictions among international courts and tribunals' (2008) 30 *Loyola of Los Angeles International and Comparative Law Review* 275–334; see also Tzanakopoulos, ch. 10 this volume.

16 *Kadi II* (CJEU), para. 133.

17 *Nada* v. *Switzerland*, Application no. 10593/08, Eur. Ct. H. R. [GC], Judgment of 12 September 2012 (hereinafter: *Nada* v. *Switzerland*).

18 E. de Wet, 'From Kadi to Nada: judicial techniques favoring human rights over United Nations Security Council sanctions' (2013) 12 *Chinese Journal of International Law* 19 *et seq.*

19 *Kadi II* (CJEU), para. 134.

Backtracking as regards the requirements for listing

The important line between reasons and evidence to support them

The difference between what the CJEU referred to as reasons, on the one hand, and evidence and information to support those reasons, on the other hand, is of crucial importance for understanding how the CJEU actually backtracked. On first reading one can be misled to think that the CJEU uses those terms interchangeably. However, this is not the case. The CJEU clearly showed the distinction between the two in *Kadi II*, while it had distinguished them already, in a more subtle way, in *Kadi I*.

The CJEU did that in *Kadi II* when it examined the errors of law affecting the judgment under appeal. In particular, the CJEU first discussed whether the five reasons, given for the listing Mr Kadi, were sufficiently detailed and specific. Only after concluding that one of the reasons was 'insufficiently detailed and specific'[20] while the other four were indeed sufficiently detailed and specific[21] did the CJEU consider the evidence supporting those reasons. The discussion on the evidence was even put under a separate heading of the judgment concerning the unlawfulness of the contested regulation. There the CJEU found that the information or evidence which was supposed to substantiate the sufficiently detailed reasons was not enough, especially in the face of the detailed rebuttals submitted by Mr Kadi.[22] As such, there are two main points of distinction between the reasons and the evidence that can be identified from the attitude of the CJEU.

The first one is the consequences of the unavailability of the reasons as opposed to the consequences of the unavailability of the evidence supporting those reasons. The CJEU has stated clearly that the availability of the reasons for listing is the absolute minimum in order to have the rights of the defence and the right to effective judicial protection respected.[23] However, when it comes to the evidence supporting those reasons the CJEU refuted the GC and held that the unavailability of information or evidence to Mr Kadi or the EU Courts does not as such mean that the rights of the defence or the right to effective judicial protection are infringed.[24]

The second one is the different threshold that the CJEU applies for accepting, on the one hand, the reasons and, on the other hand, the supporting evidence. A particular example of this is the fourth reason that the CJEU examined, which related to the use of Depositna Banka for planning attacks against a United

20 *Ibid.*, para. 141.
21 *Ibid.*, paras. 143–9.
22 *Ibid.*, para. 163.
23 *Ibid.*, para. 111.
24 *Ibid.*, para. 139.

States facility in Saudi Arabia. The CJEU accepted as sufficiently detailed and specific that reason and held notably:

> The circumstance that the indication that it was in that institution that planning sessions for that *alleged* project took place *is expressed as a possibility* is not incompatible with the essential requirements of the duty to state reasons, since the reasons for listing on a European Union list may be based on suspicions of involvement in terrorist activities, without prejudice to the determination of whether those suspicions are justified (emphasis added).[25]

However, when it came to examining the support for this reason the CJEU, after looking at the explanations provided by Mr Kadi and the Commission's answer to them, held that:

> [S]ince no information or evidence has been produced to support the claim that planning sessions might have taken place in the premises of Depozitna Banka for terrorist acts in association with Al-Qaeda or Usama bin Laden, the indications relating to the association of Mr Kadi with that bank are insufficient to sustain the adoption, at European Union level, of restrictive measures against him.[26]

Thus, it can be seen that while the CJEU is willing to be lenient for the reasons the situation is different as regards the information or evidence to support them.

In *Kadi I* the ECJ distinguished in a more subtle way the difference between reasons and evidence. This can be seen when the ECJ referred to the guidelines of the Sanctions Committee which did not require it to communicate 'the reasons and evidence justifying [the applicant's] appearance in the summary list'.[27] Next, the ECJ held that there is an obligation on the Community authority to communicate the 'grounds' on which the person concerned was listed. Observance of that obligation was held necessary for the protection of that person's rights.[28] At this juncture, it must be mentioned that the ECJ used 'reasons' and 'grounds' interchangeably and used the term 'grounds' more often in *Kadi I*. This can safely be concluded because when the CJEU held, in *Kadi II*, that the absolute minimum was to provide the reasons given by the Sanctions Committee, it cited exactly the same paragraphs in *Kadi I* discussed above where it used the term 'grounds'. The ECJ discussed the evidence separately in several paragraphs and held that, since the evidence used

---

25 *Ibid.*, para. 149.
26 *Ibid.*, para. 169.
27 *Kadi I* (ECJ), para. 325.
28 *Ibid.*, paras. 336–7.

against the appellants to justify the restrictive measures imposed on them was not provided, fundamental rights were breached.[29]

The conclusion as to the distinction between the two notions is further supported by the statement of the CJEU in the *Bank Melli* case, which was referred to in the *Kadi II* judgment. In particular the CJEU held that: 'The issue of *the grounds* for the contested decision is *different*, however, from that of *the evidence* of the conduct of which the appellant is accused...' (emphasis added).[30] This statement was made while discussing the ground of appeal alleging an infringement of the obligation to state the grounds for a measure, of the rights of the defence, and of the principle of effective legal protection. That is, a discussion on mostly the same rights as those discussed in *Kadi II*.

Actual backtracking

Although, as stated in the beginning, *Kadi I* has been explained at length in this book, it is crucial for the main argument to examine a few paragraphs of the *Kadi I* judgment by the ECJ. This is needed, in particular, in order to show what the CJEU backtracked from in its *Kadi II* judgment.

In *Kadi I* the ECJ focused strongly on the issue of evidence and the unavailability of such evidence in that case. First, it pointed to the lack of procedure for communicating evidence to the listed persons.[31] Secondly, the Council did not inform the appellants of the evidence against them,[32] which the Council obviously did not have since the Sanctions Committee did not provide it. Thirdly, the ECJ notably held that it was precisely '[b]ecause the Council neither communicated to the appellants the evidence used against them to justify the restrictive measures imposed on them nor afforded them the right to be informed of that evidence within a reasonable period after those measures were enacted...' that the appellants' rights of defence were not respected.[33] Fourthly, given that failure of the Council, the appellants were also unable to defend their right before the Community judicature and as a result their right to an effective legal remedy was also infringed.[34] Finally, the ECJ observed that that infringement was not remedied in the course of those actions.

In its judgment in *Kadi II* the GC picked right up on that clear statement by the ECJ and held that the lack of evidence supporting the reasons for listing is as such a violation of Mr Kadi's fundamental rights even though the Commission was not in possession of any such evidence. Of course, by saying this, the GC wanted the impossible from the Commission but this was no different from

29 *Ibid.*, paras. 345–50.
30 Case C-548/09 P *Bank Melli Iran* v. *Council of the European Union* [2011] ECR I-11381 para. 88.
31 *Kadi I* (ECJ), para. 345.
32 *Ibid.*, para. 346.
33 *Ibid.*, para. 348.
34 *Ibid.*, para. 349.

what the ECJ wanted in *Kadi I* because the Council was also not in possession of such evidence. The GC basically followed what the higher Court said.

However, in *Kadi II* the CJEU had something different in mind by holding that the GC was wrong, again.[35] Then, the CJEU provided new reasoning with the effect of backtracking. It started by listing three main requirements that need to be satisfied by the Union organs in order for the rights of the defence and the right to effective judicial protection to be considered respected.[36] First, the Union organs must disclose the Sanctions Committee's summary of reasons which served as a basis for initial listing or maintaining of it. Secondly, the Union organs must enable the person concerned to make their observations known effectively. Thirdly, the Union organs must carefully and impartially examine the reasons alleged and how well-founded they are, having regard to the explanations provided by that person as well as to any exculpatory evidence thus provided. Additionally, the CJEU included a somewhat fourth element, which was, however, addressed to the Courts of the European Union.[37] This element concerns the respect for the rights of effective defence and effective judicial protection. It implies that in the event of a challenge of a listing, both the CJEU and the GC are to review, among others, whether the reasons in the Sanctions Committee's summary were 'sufficiently detailed and specific' as well as whether the reason in question relates to facts with established accuracy.

The emphasis on providing the supporting evidence was completely different. Only in the last requirement did the CJEU come close to the supporting evidence where it talked about facts with established accuracy. This is much less than what was required in *Kadi I*. Moreover, when the CJEU held that the GC was wrong in saying that fundamental rights were breached when the Commission did not provide evidence that it did not even have, it *de facto* re-interpreted the paragraphs in *Kadi I* discussing the importance of providing evidence. This is because the CJEU identified paras. 181, 183, and 184 of the GC judgment which in turn referred exactly to paras. 349–52 which concluded the evidence discussion of the ECJ which was explained above.

Furthermore, the CJEU noted that there is no obligation on the Sanctions Committee to provide to the EU any other material than the summary of reasons. Consequently, the Commission was not in a position to have extra information regarding Mr Kadi when listing him. In addition, the EU bodies may need to ask the Sanctions Committee for assistance in the light of art. 220 of the Treaty on the Functioning of the European Union (TFEU). When assessing the decision of the Commission, the CJEU can request the Commission to provide all the relevant information, although there is no requirement that all the information and evidence is submitted to the CJEU.[38]

---

35 *Kadi II* (CJEU), para.138.
36 *Ibid.*, para. 135.
37 *Ibid.*, para. 136.
38 See E. de Wet, 10.

The CJEU even showed understanding that in certain circumstances disclosure of information is for security reasons not possible, meaning that the summary information of the Sanctions Committee is considered sufficient to undertake a judicial review. This contradicts *Kadi I* where the ECJ said that, due to the lack of evidence, it was 'not able to undertake the review of the lawfulness of the contested regulation'.

Earlier signs of backtracking

Although *Kadi* is the case that always hits the legal headlines, the CJEU had to deal with many more targeted sanctions cases in the last few years. Admittedly, they were not identical to *Kadi* and analogies must be made carefully. Nevertheless, points for analogies do exist. As regards backtracking in relation to what are the minimum requirements for listing, signs can be seen in the *Parliament* v. *Council* case, delivered exactly a year before *Kadi II*.

In the case of *Parliament* v. *Council*, the European Parliament challenged the legal basis for Regulation 881/2002. This Regulation is one of the instruments which the Council used to implement Security Council targeted sanctions. In particular, Mr Kadi was initially listed in Annex I of Regulation 881/2002 and, after *Kadi I*, he continued to be listed there by one of the Commission Regulations amending the Annex.[39] The CJEU, in the relevant paragraph stated that 'a measure, such as the contested Regulation, *containing safeguards for the respect of the fundamental rights* of the persons whose names appear in the list, may be adopted on the basis of Article 215(2) TFEU' (emphasis added).[40] In this quotation the CJEU in an *obiter dictum* held that the Regulation that Mr Kadi was effectively challenging did contain safeguards for the respect of the fundamental rights of listed persons. This was an important indication of the view of the CJEU on the protection of fundamental rights as it sat in Grand Chamber in that case.

Supplementary reasons for backtracking

As was observed in the introduction, a lot of things have changed since *Kadi I* and the bold judgment did not fit nicely with those developments. In this section, two factors are examined, both of which are not binding upon the CJEU but have authoritative status for the CJEU's judgments in general. Those are the ECtHR decision in *Nada*[41] and the Opinion of AG Bot. Although the CJEU did not as such follow either of the two, they are important to mention

---

39 Commission Regulation (EC) 1190/2008 of 28 November 2008 amending for the 101st time Council Regulation (EC) No 881/2002 imposing certain specific restrictive measures directed against certain persons and entities associated with Usama bin Laden, the Al-Qaida network and the Taliban [2008] OJ L322/25.

40 Case C-130/10 *Parliament* v. *Council*, nyr, para. 84.

41 For the factual background of the *Nada* case, see Fabbrini and Larik, ch. 11 this volume.

because of two reasons. First, both of them present ways which the CJEU can use to backtrack. Secondly, having the authoritative status that they have before the CJEU it is easily foreseeable that the CJEU was influenced by the general call for backtracking.

In *Nada* the ECrtHR held that the *Al-Jedda* presumption[42] was rebutted in this case.[43] It referred to *Kadi I* and found that Switzerland enjoyed 'limited, but nevertheless real' latitude for implementation. Then the ECtHR went on to discuss the factual peculiarities of the case and concluded that Switzerland 'could not validly confine itself to relying on the binding nature of UN Security Council Resolutions, but should have persuaded the Court that it had taken – or at least had attempted to take – all possible measures to adapt the sanctions regime to the applicant's individual situation'.[44] This is an important finding because by saying 'could not validly confine' the ECtHR introduces a twofold test for the proportionality of measures for sanctions regimes. First, there must be a binding UN Security Council Resolution and, secondly, to take or at least to attempt to take all possible measures for tailor-made sanctions. This is a completely different approach from the backtracking of the CJEU.

In his Opinion AG Bot adopted an international law approach but within limits. He differentiated between the applicable intensity of review for external and internal lawfulness of the EU measures. In particular, he argued for a 'normal review' for the former and a limited review for the latter.[45] Five reasons were put forward in support of this: (1) the preventative nature of the measures; (2) the context of the EU measure; (3) the need to balance the requirements of combating terrorism and the requirements of protection of fundamental rights; (4) the political nature of the assessments made by the Sanctions Committee in deciding to list a person or an entity; and (5) the procedural improvements at the Sanctions Committee.[46]

On the preventative nature of the measures,[47] AG Bot highlighted, by referring to ECJ's case law, that freezing measures constitute temporary precautionary measures which do not deprive of property and the funds are not being confiscated. Furthermore, the measures are neither criminal sanctions, nor do they imply criminal accusations. In addition, although the sanctions may be of long duration, AG Bot points to the fact that the measure and its duration could be reviewed.

---

42 The presumption is that 'the UN Security Council does not intend to impose any obligation on Member States to breach fundamental principles of human rights'. *Al-Jedda* v. *UK*, Application no. 27021/08, Eur. Ct. H. R. [GC], Judgment of 7 July 2011, paras. 102 and 105.
43 *Nada* v. *Switzerland*, para. 172.
44 *Ibid.,* para. 196.
45 AG Bot, para. 10.
46 *Ibid.*, para. 67.
47 *Ibid.*, para. 68.

Regarding the context of the EU measure,[48] AG Bot referred to the ECJ's statement that international law must be observed by the EU. Then AG Bot pointed to the primary responsibility of the UN Security Council and opined that the review of implementing measures must correspond to the margin of the EU institutions in implementing and that the EU must not be a forum to review Sanctions Committee's decisions. For further support AG Bot referred to arts. 3 (5), 21 (1), and 21 (2) (c) TEU as well as Declaration no. 13.[49] AG Bot argued that, in order to truly take into consideration the context of the EU measures, cooperation between the EU and the UN must be developed, as envisaged in art. 220 TFEU. To that extent he referred to the recent *Parliament* v. *Council* judgment[50] where the ECJ held the EU implementing measures to have established a 'system of interaction between the UN Security Council and the Union'.

On the need to balance the requirements of combating terrorism and the requirements of protection of fundamental rights,[51] AG Bot simply referred to the pronouncement of the ECJ that the Union Courts must use appropriate techniques which balance the security concerns with the need for procedural safeguards, while undertaking a review of implementing measures.

On the political nature of the assessments made by the Sanctions Committee in deciding to list a person or an entity,[52] AG Bot referred to the view of the Commission and the intervening governments which emphasized that the decision to list does not lie with them. Furthermore, he referred to the strategic and geopolitical interests involved in such a decision. He concluded, on that point, that the political dimension of the sanctions regime is something that calls for less strict review. Otherwise it will amount to second-guessing of the political decisions.

On the procedural improvements at the Sanctions Committee,[53] AG Bot referred to the various improvements including the focal point and the Ombudsperson and how the ECJ's stance in *Kadi I* is considered to have been a driving force behind some of them.[54]

It can be seen that the Opinion of AG Bot supports the view that a special status of UN Charter obligations must be recognized and as a consequence of

---

48 *Ibid.*, paras. 69–76.
49 Declaration 13 Concerning the Common Foreign and Security Policy. In its relevant part it provides: '[The Conference] stresses that *the European Union* and its Member States *will remain bound* by the provisions of the Charter of the United Nations and, in particular, by the primary responsibility of the Security Council and of its Members for the maintenance of international peace and security' (emphasis added).
50 *Parliament v Council*, n 40 *supra*, para. 71.
51 AG Bot, para. 77.
52 *Ibid.*, paras. 78–80.
53 *Ibid.*, paras. 81–90.
54 For a succinct discussion on the improvements, see E. de Wet, 2–4.

such a special status, a lower intensity of judicial review was proposed. As such AG Bot sided to some extent with the ECtHR in *Nada*.[55]

Conclusion

So, what is the bottom-line of the CJEU's *Kadi II* judgment? What is the GC supposed to do next time it is faced with an EU Regulation, which is challenged by an individual who is blacklisted by the UN Security Council and the Sanctions Committee?

The beauty of the ECJ's *Kadi I* judgment was its clarity, boldness, and ultimate simplicity (or as some would say one-sidedness), which *prima facie* left no doubt that the European legal order and European fundamental rights and principles are supreme and that full judicial review must be provided by European courts in all cases and as long as the deficiencies of judicial protection continue to exist at the UN level. No law, no institution – not even the powerful UN Security Council – could affect the 'very foundations of the European legal order' – or so it seemed.[56]

But now we see – as this contribution has demonstrated – that even the CJEU as the final, ultimate guardian of the European legal order has started to crumble under the political pressure by lowering the threshold for the evidence necessary to be provided for blacklisting thereby giving significant margin of appreciation back to the Commission, Council, and, ultimately, to the UN Security Council.

The backtracking of the CJEU from its bold *Kadi I* approach is particularly humiliating for the GC. While the GC in its *Kadi I* judgment was overly leaning towards giving full effect to UN Security Council Resolutions without sufficient consideration of fundamental EU law rights and principles, it fully corrected that mistake in its *Kadi II* judgment only to be told now by the CJEU that it was not completely wrong in giving a certain margin of appreciation to the Union bodies and the UN Security Council that is beyond its judicial review.

Next time the GC has to deliver a judgment on this matter, it will have to explain in detail why it cannot uphold its *Kadi II* approach any longer. Or the GC may simply state that if 'some interested quarters' wish that it continues to stick to its *Kadi II* approach, they need to appeal to the CJEU or ask the Union organs to change their policy and procedures. Either way, the GC will lose face and may induce it to become more careful in the future. This is – of course – the fate of all first-instance courts that have to live with an appeal court above them, which from time to time corrects the lower court for reasons other than purely legal ones.

---

55 See Fabbrini and Larik, ch. 11 this volume.
56 See more generally on this point N. Lavranos, 'Protecting European law from international law' (2010) 15 *European Foreign Affairs Review* 265–82.

For the CJEU the *Kadi* saga, which ultimately resulted in backtracking from its bold and sweeping statements made in *Kadi I*, may be a lesson to refrain in future from delivering such clear and bold judgments as it did in *Kadi I*. Clearly, this would be a very sad effect because without bold judgments of the CJEU, which effectively protect the fundamental rights of individuals and provide some element of control over the actions of Union bodies, the Union will continue to lose credibility when it comes to the effective protection of fundamental rights.

10 The *Solange* argument as a justification for disobeying the Security Council in the *Kadi* judgments

Antonios Tzanakopoulos

Introduction

The *Kadi* judgments of the courts of the European Union (EU) have received enormous scholarly attention and have had significant practical impact. And reasonably so: they are landmark decisions, with numerous implications for several crucial issues, from the relationship between different legal orders to the primacy of Security Council decisions, from the required level of protection of fundamental human rights in the application of coercive measures against individuals to the competence of the EU, and so forth. This brief study focuses on one particular aspect of the *Kadi* decisions: their employment of the *Solange* argument as a justification for disobeying the Security Council by not implementing its binding decisions.[1]

The first substantive section aims to dispel the pretension to some extent put forward by the Court of Justice of the European Union (CJEU) in *Kadi I*, and maintained by the EU courts throughout the *Kadi* saga, that review of EU measures implementing Security Council decisions in the context of the 1267/1989 sanctions regime does not actually constitute review of the Security Council measures themselves. The disassociation/disengagement of the 'domestic' implementing measure from the international measure that conditions it is what allows the EU courts to review the implementing measures for compliance with EU 'domestic' law, while pretending not to affect the international measure. But this pretension is belied by the employment by EU courts of the *Solange* argument to justify the significant impact their decisions have on the international measures. The second section introduces

---

1 In that this contribution is based on a number of blog posts regarding the *Kadi* cases published by the author in *EJIL: Talk!*, the blog of the *European Journal of International Law*, available at www.ejiltalk.org. It also draws on arguments previously presented in Antonios Tzanakopoulos, 'Domestic court reactions to UN Security Council sanctions' in August Reinisch (ed.), *Challenging Acts of International Organizations before National Courts* (OUP, 2010) 54; and in Antonios Tzanakopoulos, 'Judicial dialogue in multi-level governance: the impact of the *Solange* argument' in Ole Kristian Fauchald, André Nollkaemper (eds.), *The Practice of International and National Courts and the (De-)Fragmentation of International Law* (Hart, 2012) 185–216.

the *Solange* argument by putting it in the context of multi-level governance. The next section traces the employment of the *Solange* argument in the *Kadi* cases. The penultimate section translates the *Solange* argument into a meaningful justification for disobedience under general international law. The final section concludes.

In what follows, the Court of First Instance, renamed 'General Court of the EU' after Lisbon, is abbreviated 'GCEU', even if it was called 'CFI' when it rendered its decision. *Kadi I* and *Kadi II* refer to the two sets of proceedings, i.e. 2005–2008 and 2009–2012 respectively, on both first instance and on appeal. Reference is only to the 'EU' throughout.

The pretension of obedience: dualism or disassociation?

In order to be able to strike down 'domestic' implementing measures, in effect the EU Regulation requiring the application of sanctions against Kadi, the EU courts, that is the CJEU in *Kadi I*, followed by the GCEU in *Kadi II*, and reiterated by the CJEU on appeal in *Kadi II*, had to formally disassociate the EU measures from the United Nations (UN) measures, and were thus criticized for adopting a strictly dualist approach. The 'charge' may be true, depending on what one understands under the term 'dualism'. If that is a strict separation of legal orders so that legal acts in one legal order may not produce effects in the other legal order, then the charge of dualism has some merit. The CJEU in *Kadi I* did indeed stress the 'autonomy' of the EU legal order and went on to assert that all EU legal acts must fully comply with EU primary law, including respect for fundamental rights. It also argued that this review has no formal impact on the relevant Security Council Resolutions: review of the domestic measure does not also subject the international measure to review; neither does it challenge its primacy in international law.[2]

This is formally correct, but the latter part of the reasoning merely reflects the fact that the CJEU has no competence to pronounce with binding force on decisions of the Security Council. Indeed no court, whether domestic or international, not even the International Court of Justice (ICJ) – the principal judicial organ of the UN – has such competence. The latter fact indicates, however, that the argument of no formal effect of the court's decision on Security Council (SC) measures is not necessarily a dualist argument of acts in one legal order being unable to produce effects in another legal order. Rather, it can be seen as a simple argument of lack of competence to affect the legal position of a particular measure irrespective of separation of legal orders. This argument is equally applicable to the ICJ, which cannot decide with binding legal effect on the legal consequences of an SC decision: it can

2 See Joined Cases C-402/05 P and C-415/05 P, *Yassin Abdullah Kadi and Al Barakaat International Foundation* v. *Council of the European Union and Commission of the European Communities* [2008] ECJ I-6351, paras. 286 and 288 (hereinafter CJEU *Kadi I*).

opine on the matter if asked by a competent UN organ, but without legal effect; or it can deal with the question incidentally in a contentious proceeding between states, still being incapable to formally affect the legal consequences of the SC decision except between the parties to the dispute before it.

The charge of dualism completely breaks down when considering the justification for the lack of formal effect of its decision on the SC measures provided by the CJEU itself. The disassociation is justified by the Court not on the basis that the two legal orders are separate, but rather on the basis that

> the Charter of the United Nations *does not impose the choice of a particular model* for the implementation of resolutions [of] the Security Council under Chapter VII…, since they are to be given effect in accordance with the *procedure* applicable in that respect in the domestic legal order of each Member…[3]

'It follows from all those considerations', continues the CJEU,

> that *it is not a consequence of the principles governing the international legal order under the United Nations that any judicial review of the internal lawfulness of the contested regulation in the light of fundamental freedoms is excluded by virtue of the fact that that measure is intended to give effect to a resolution of the Security Council* adopted under Chapter VII of the Charter of the United Nations.[4]

Effectively the Court disengages the domestic from the international measure. It claims: we have an international obligation, but we have freedom (granted by the international legal order, no less) to comply with that obligation in the fashion that our domestic law prescribes. We are reviewing here the manner in which we complied (and find it lacking). The rule being invoked here is not one of strict *separation* of legal orders, but rather one of their mutual *accommodation*.

What the CJEU in *Kadi I* ignores, however, is that the international obligation imposed under the 1267/1989 regime is one of result, as it were, which allows no discretion in its implementation. The obligation is to freeze the assets of Kadi. If, in the end, Kadi's assets are not frozen, for whatever reason under domestic law that may be, the international obligation (of member states to comply with SC decisions under art. 25 of the UN Charter) is breached. The GCEU had previously clearly drawn the distinction between 'strict' obligations (of result) allowing no discretion, and other obligations allowing for some discretion in their implementation, in *OMPI*.[5] There the GCEU said

---

3 *Ibid.*, para. 298 (emphasis added).
4 *Ibid.*, para. 299 (emphasis added).
5 Case T-228/02, *Organisation des Modjahedines du peuple d'Iran* v. *Council of the European Union* [2006] ECR II-4665, paras. 100–2.

that unlike the 1267/1989 regime, which imposed the obligation to take measures against *specific* persons *designated by the UN*, the 1373 regime (which was being discussed in that case) imposed an obligation to take measures against a *category* of persons, who were however not individually designated. Thus, the 1373 regime allows the member states discretion as to how to comply (i.e. discretion as to whom to designate). On the contrary the 1267/1989 regime allows none. In circumstances where member states retain a measure of discretion as to compliance, the domestic court can review the exercise of that discretion under domestic law. Where no discretion is allowed, there is no such possibility: review of the domestic measure means 'review' of the international measure at the same time. And such review could not take place on the basis of 'domestic' EU law, to which the SC and its measures are not subject. Hence the only conceivable means to proceed is to review on the basis of a 'lowest common denominator', i.e. of law binding (also) the SC (or more precisely the UN, of which the SC is an organ), which the GCEU did in *Kadi I*, determining that 'lowest common denominator' to be *jus cogens*.

The CJEU in *Kadi I* obliterated this distinction between international obligations allowing for no discretion as to the manner of compliance (strict obligations), and those allowing for some. As such, it was able to claim that the international legal order 'accommodates' the domestic legal order in that, effectively, the EU member states have still (after annulment) the possibility to comply with the international obligation in a manner compliant with EU law.

In *Kadi II* the General Court 'grudgingly' applied CJEU *Kadi I*:[6] it is apparent throughout the judgment that the General Court was not completely comfortable with the CJEU's reasoning in *Kadi I*. For example, while the GCEU acknowledged the different scope of the international obligations imposed on member states of the UN under the 1267/1989 and 1373 sanctions regimes discussed above and in its own previous decision in *OMPI*,[7] it accepted the CJEU's obliteration of this distinction later on in its judgment.[8] That it did so without being fully convinced is implicit in the language used by the Court,[9] and explicit when the General Court lists the significant criticisms leveled by scholarship with respect to CJEU *Kadi I*.[10] The GCEU

---

6 For the term and further comment, see Tim Stahlberg, 'Case T-85/09, Kadi II', CourtofJustice. EU, 26 October 2010, available at http://courtofjustice.blogspot.com/2010/10/case-t-8509-kadi-ii.html.

7 Case T-85/09, *Yassin Abdullah Kadi* v. *European Commission* [2010] ECR II-5177, paras. 32–3 (hereinafter GCEU *Kadi II*).

8 *Ibid.*, paras. 138–9.

9 For example, *ibid.*, para. 41: 'Notwithstanding Articles 25 and 103 of the Charter of the United Nations…, and although it observed… that observance [*sic*] of the undertakings given in the context of the United Nations was required when the Community gave effect to resolutions adopted by the Security Council under Chapter VII of the Charter, the Court of Justice asserted…'

10 *Ibid.*, paras. 113–20.

went on to acknowledge 'that those criticisms are not entirely without foundation'.[11] But given that the *Kadi I* decision was rendered by the CJEU in Grand Chamber formation, i.e. with the intent of setting down certain principles,[12] 'in principle it falls not to [the General Court] but to the Court of Justice to reverse the precedent'.[13]

In appealing the decision of the GCEU in *Kadi II*, the appellants (and interveners) sought to achieve precisely that: to have the CJEU reverse the precedent set in its *Kadi I* decision with regard to the 'disassociation' of the domestic EU measures from the international measures adopted by the SC under the 1267/1989 regime. In essence the first ground of appeal was a direct challenge to *Kadi I*, the Council and Ireland going as far as to formally request the CJEU to revisit its reasoning.[14] The appellants again raised the issue that the effect of CJEU *Kadi I* was the (indirect) review by EU courts of measures imposed by the SC, in the implementation of which the EU had no discretion. The CJEU dismissed those arguments in a handful of short paragraphs and found that the GCEU had not erred in law in applying the CJEU's (now reaffirmed) reasoning in *Kadi I*.[15]

The disassociation/accommodation claim, and the obliteration of the distinction between obligations allowing no discretion and those allowing some discretion in their implementation, permits the CJEU to view the 'domestic' EU measures as autonomous, as always subject to the discretion of the implementing entity, and to subject them to review for compliance with 'domestic' EU law. This results in the EU courts not purporting to exercise any competence that may be open to question, such as that of indirectly reviewing SC action for compliance with EU-guaranteed fundamental rights. As such, it does not purport to force member states to disobey the SC: it merely asks them (and the institutions adopting EU implementing measures) to implement the SC measures while also complying with relevant EU law. But the accommodation/disassociation claim is clearly wrong, and so the pretension of obedience, such as it is, is false. Under the 1267/1989 regime, the EU and the member states have no discretion whatsoever. When the SC demands the listing of Kadi and the freezing of his assets etc., all the EU and the member states can do is to list Kadi and freeze his assets etc. Should the EU afford Kadi any meaningful opportunity to challenge the listing, the challenge, if successful, will lead to the member states disobeying the SC in breach of their international obligations under art. 25 of the UN Charter. How could such an extreme result be justified?

---

11 *Ibid.*, para. 121.
12 *Ibid.*
13 *Ibid.*, para. 123.
14 See Joined Cases C-584/10 P, C-593/10 P, and C-595/10 P, *European Commission and Others* v. *Yassin Abdullah Kadi* [2013] ECR I-0000, para. 60 (hereinafter CJEU *Kadi II*).
15 See *ibid.*, paras. 65–9.

The CJEU in both *Kadi I* and *II* does offer an implicit justification for the disobedience it knows it is forcing upon member states, all the while having pretended not to do so. Strictly speaking, because the CJEU maintains that the UN/international legal order affords member states (and thus the EU) discretion in implementing SC decisions in all circumstances, it does not need to offer any justification for disobedience: there is no disobedience to justify. But at the same time it is clear that the Court knows that the effect of its decisions in *Kadi I* and *II* is to force member states to disobey the SC, unless they adopt their own implementing measures complying with the SC decisions on the matter – a power that is questionable at any rate,[16] but which space does not permit consideration of here. This is evident when the CJEU suspends, in *Kadi I*, the effect of its annulment decision, giving the EU time to adopt implementing measures that are compliant with its decision[17] (which the EU sought to do, and which then gave rise to the second set of proceedings with respect to Kadi). These significant effects of the decision, while implicit, do call for justification. And one is, implicitly, offered, in the guise of the *Solange* argument. In order to explain the justification of disobedience offered by means of the *Solange* argument, it is first required that this argument be set out. This is done in the next section.

The *Solange* argument and multi-level governance

In situations where binding ('sovereign' or 'governmental') decisions on a particular matter can be made at various levels of governance (international, regional, domestic), there is significant potential for conflict between those various levels (and the partial legal orders that these various levels represent). This is the case, in particular, when the power to impose certain restrictive measures on individuals has been conferred (whether delegated or transferred[18]) from one level to another, without safeguards equivalent to those which existed at the original level of exercise of the power being also imposed at the new *locus* (level) of exercise of the power.

When a relevant case comes before the court of the legal order that has conferred the relevant power, a reaction is to be expected, if not for any other reason, then at least because the court finds itself at first sight unable to control the exercise of a power that it originally had the competence to review. This reaction has so far generally taken the shape of the '*Solange* argument', enunciated by the German Federal Constitutional Court when attempting to

---

16 See generally Takis Tridimas, Jose A Gutierrez-Fons, 'EU law, international law, and economic sanctions against terrorism: the judiciary in distress?' (2008) 32 *Fordham International Law Journal* 660.

17 See CJEU *Kadi I*, paras. 373–5.

18 See generally Dan Sarooshi, *International Organizations and their Exercise of Sovereign Powers* (OUP, 2005).

define the relationship between German constitutional law and acts of the EU, first in the 1970s (*Solange I*)[19] and then in the 1980s (*Solange II*).[20]

A (much simplified) version of the argument runs thus: for as long as the exercise of the conferred powers on the (different or higher) level of governance takes place without safeguards equivalent to those to which it was subject before the conferral, when it was still exercised at the (lower) level, the court of the (lower) level will review the act of the (higher) level for compliance with the safeguards at the (lower) level (*Solange I*). When equivalent safeguards are adopted at the (higher) level, the court at the (lower) level will desist, presuming conformity (*Solange II*).

The *Solange* argument seeks to establish that the exercise of 'sovereign' powers cannot be freed from judicial control simply by being conferred on an actor that escapes the controlling court's jurisdiction. It could be seen as an implementation of the maxim *nemo plus juris transferre potest quam ipse habet*. One may not circumvent limitations on the exercise of a power by conferring that power to someone else who can now exercise it without similar limitations. As employed by the German Federal Constitutional Court in the homonymous cases, the EU courts in *Kadi*, and other courts, the *Solange* argument requires that the exercise of 'sovereign' power be subject (a) to control offering guarantees of judicial protection (b) for compliance with certain fundamental rights. So in effect, reference is made to a catalogue of substantive rights that must be protected, as well as to a right to meaningfully challenge the exercise of power for compliance with this catalogue of rights. The latter, a right in and of itself, is established as the pinnacle of all other rights, as an enabling right allowing all other rights to be effective because effectively protected.

The *Solange* argument requires *equivalence* on both these points: (a) equivalence as to the rights to be protected; and (b) equivalence as to the mechanics of their protection. This requirement of mere equivalence (or adequacy) allows for *flexibility* on both fronts: as to the catalogue and substantive content of the rights to be protected, these need not be *identical* at the different levels of exercise of the 'sovereign' power. The rights sought to be protected may be drawn from the 'local' level and projected on to the current (non-local) level of the exercise of the 'sovereign' power, but they are in reality only core rights – or core aspects of rights – that are *also* protected on the current (non-local) level of exercise of power. To put this simply, the rights that the German Federal Constitutional Court sought to 'impose' on the EEC (as it then was) were not rights peculiar to the German Basic Law; they were drawn from the Universal Declaration of Human Rights, and indeed the Court in *Solange II* was satisfied with EU protection of rights 'drawn from the common constitutional traditions of the Member States and inspired by the ECHR'. There is a fundamental feedback loop between rights protected at various international

19 37 BVerfGE 271.
20 73 BVerfGE 339.

and domestic levels: domestic constitutional protection across various states influenced the catalogue of rights to be internationally protected through multifarious regional and global instruments. These instruments have in turn shaped, through their domestic implementation, the subsequent evolution of the content of constitutionally protected rights. It is thus meaningless to try and establish primacy between the local/domestic and non-local/international in these circumstances: the rights are 'consubstantial', i.e. in their core aspects they have the same 'substantive' content.[21]

Equivalence also refers to the method, or mechanics, of protection: this protection need not be, strictly speaking, judicial protection. Rather, it must offer guarantees of judicial protection. What is established here is the right to challenge the exercise of 'sovereign' powers before an instance that offers such guarantees, i.e. an *independent* and *impartial* instance with the power to make *binding* determinations at the very least.[22]

The *Solange* argument thus seeks to achieve, through its pattern of defiance (*Solange I*) and deferral (*Solange II*), equivalent protection of certain fundamental rights at various levels of exercise of sovereign powers. It acts as an equalizer, subjecting all exercises of sovereign power to similar, 'adequate', limitations, with a view to avoiding circumvention.

The *Solange* argument has been employed by the European Court of Human Rights (ECtHR), in its *Solange II* incarnation (through the immediate acceptance of existence of equivalent protection which thus allows for a presumption of conformity with the requirements at the 'local' level[23]), and in a number of cases, such as *Waite and Kennedy*[24] and *Bosphorus*.[25] It has also been employed, this time as *Solange I*, by the UK Supreme Court in *HM Treasury* v. *Ahmed and ors*,[26] as well as by other courts.[27] Most interesting for present purposes,

---

21 For the term 'consubstantial' see Antonios Tzanakopoulos, 'Domestic courts in international law: the international judicial function of national courts' (2011) 34 *Loyola of Los Angeles International and Comparative Law Review* 133, 163–4. Regarding the terms 'fundamental rights' and 'human rights' see further Tzanakopoulos, 'The impact of the *Solange* argument'.

22 See Antonios Tzanakopoulos, 'Falling short: UN Security Council delisting procedural reforms before European courts', *Sanctions and Security Research Program*, Report 2013, available at http://sanctionsandsecurity.nd.edu/assets/110262/falling_short.pdf.

23 In this respect one should be cautious and mention that the *Solange* argument cuts both ways, as it may serve not as a tool for resistance – as *Solange I* – but also as a method to water down human rights protection – as *Solange II*. Also, according to some, the *Solange* argument presumes autonomous (if only so self-proclaimed) legal orders, while the ECtHR has not proclaimed the ECHR to constitute such an autonomous legal order. On these points see generally Marko Milanović, 'Norm conflict in international law: whither human rights?' (2009) 20 *Duke Journal of Comparative and International Law* 69.

24 *Waite and Kennedy* v. *Germany*, App no. 26083/94.

25 *Bosphorus Hava Yolları Turizm ve Ticaret Anonim Şirketi* v. *Ireland*, App no. 45036/98.

26 *HM Treasury* v. *Mohammed Jabar Ahmed and ors (FC); HM Treasury* v. *Mohammed al-Ghabra (FC); R (on the application of Hani El Sayed Sabaei Youssef) v HM Treasury* [2010] UKSC 2.

27 See the case-law cited in Tzanakopoulos, 'The impact of the *Solange* argument'.

however, is the employment of the *Solange* argument, in its *Solange I* incarnation, by the EU courts in both *Kadi* cases. To this the next section now turns.

The *Solange* argument in the *Kadi* cases

One cannot fail to notice the irony inherent in EU courts employing, when dealing with the relationship between the UN and the EU in the *Kadi* cases, the very same argument employed against them by the German Federal Constitutional Court in the *Solange* cases. It was the CJEU that first made a *Solange* argument in *Kadi I*, striking down EU measures implementing SC decisions under the 1267/1989 regime. Even though the CJEU purported not to be reviewing the Council measures, it must have considered that it did in fact do so to some extent, because it clearly stated that the re-examination procedure within the UN system could not give rise to 'generalised immunity from jurisdiction' within the legal order of the EU.[28] This was because said re-examination procedure at UN level 'does not offer guarantees of judicial protection'.[29] 'From that follows', continued the CJEU, 'that the Community judicature must ensure full review' of the implementing measures.[30] What this implies is that if the re-examination procedure at UN level were to be reformed so as to offer such guarantees of judicial protection, EU courts would defer to that procedure and abstain from review, or at least from 'full review' of the domestic implementing measures.

In *Kadi II* the General Court was as explicit regarding this matter as it could be: it stated that it must ensure the 'full review' of the domestic implementing measure for compliance with fundamental rights (guaranteed under EU law), 'without affording [the measure] any immunity from jurisdiction on the ground that it gives effect to resolutions adopted by the SC under Chapter VII of the Charter of the United Nations'.[31] 'That must remain the case', the Court continued, 'at the very least, as long as (i.e. *Solange*) the re-examination procedure operated by the Sanctions Committee clearly fails to offer guarantees of effective judicial protection'.[32] In effect, the EU institutions and intervening member states, having lost the battle regarding review of the measures per se, sought to challenge the applicable standard of review: they tried to re-introduce the argument regarding lack of discretion at the point of implementation as a justification for adopting a more lax standard of review (or rather for interpreting the 'full review' requirement of CJEU more laxly). But the CJEU would have none of it, relying as it did on the *Solange* argument.

28 CJEU *Kadi I*, para 321.
29 *Ibid.*, para. 322.
30 *Ibid.*, para. 326.
31 GCEU *Kadi II*, para. 126.
32 *Ibid.*, para. 127.

Then the GCEU had to deal with whether the safeguards adopted at EU level were inadequate to fulfill the requirements for the protection of fundamental rights under EU law. This led the Court further to engage with the regulation of multi-level governance. In response to the EU institutions' argument that they have adopted with respect to *Kadi* the very same safeguards that the EU courts had found adequate in the *OMPI* line of cases,[33] the General Court drew a distinction between the two regimes of multi-level governance: the *OMPI* regime (i.e. the 1373 sanctions regime) is structured in two tiers, one national and one regional (EU): the provision of safeguards at the national levels relieves EU institutions from the obligation to impose fresh safeguards relating to the same subject-matter on EU level.[34] Conversely, the *Kadi* regime (i.e. the 1267/1989 sanctions regime) is structured in two tiers as well, but here one is international (UN) and the other regional (EU): for as long as there are no safeguards on the UN level, the EU will have to provide them.[35]

There is surely something to be said about the General Court accepting – however half-heartedly – the obliteration of the distinction between the two sanctions regimes in order to allow review of EU implementing measures and to confirm and elaborate on the strict standard of review pronounced by the CJEU in *Kadi I* ('full review'), and then re-introducing it, albeit in another guise, when considering the merits of the claim for the violation of the right to effective judicial protection. Obviously the only reason that safeguards can be adopted at any level under the 1373 regime is because the identification of those to be subjected to restrictive measures is left to the discretion of member states, unlike in the case of the 1267/1989 regime, where the targets of the measures are designated by the SC, leaving member states or the EU no room for manoeuver.

Be that as it may, the decision of the GCEU in *Kadi II* confirmed that the EU courts have adopted the medicine they were served by the German Federal Constitutional Court in *Solange I* in their relationship with the UN. This was indeed further reiterated in the final instance of the *Kadi* cases, the CJEU decision in *Kadi II*. There, as before the GCEU, the main argument centered around the question of the standard of review to be applied by the EU courts when reviewing EU measures implementing SC decisions, and around the actual merits of the claim that fundamental rights had been violated. In essence, the appellants and interveners tried to mitigate the impact of EU judicial review of (in effect) SC measures, by arguing again in favor of a rather lax standard of review, taking into account the 'international context' of adoption of the measure,[36] and the fact that EU institutions have no discretion under the 1267/1989 regime.[37]

---

33 *Ibid.*, para. 185.
34 *Ibid.*, para. 186.
35 *Ibid.*, para. 187.
36 CJEU *Kadi II*, para. 72.
37 *Ibid.*, para. 73.

The appellants were again hoping that the same argument that failed on formal grounds in securing immunity of the impugned measures from EU judicial scrutiny would now succeed in at least limiting that scrutiny as much as possible. Effectively, they were seeking to move the argument to a *Solange II* position, asking for marginal review also in view of the significant improvements introduced at UN level in the listing and, especially, delisting procedures by SC Resolutions 1904 (2009) and 1989 (2011): this should earn the UN-level process deferral on the part of EU courts, not by making the measures immune from review, but by limiting the intensity of that review. In that argument, the appellants were joined by Advocate General Bot, who argued in favor of a (rebuttable) 'presumption of justification' of measures adopted in accordance with the reformed procedure at UN level.[38]

The CJEU did not accept that the time was ripe for a move from *Solange I* to *Solange II*. One of the main arguments of the appellants in *Kadi II* was that the EU institutions did transmit to Kadi all the evidence in their possession, *in casu* the summary of reasons for listing. This was all they had, so that they could not meaningfully be required to adduce evidence they were not in possession of. The Court accepted as much,[39] but went on to clarify that this does not discharge the obligations of the institutions under EU law: it is the obligation of the competent authority to seek cooperation on the part of the UN and its member states if it appears that further information is required to allow the authority to discharge its duty of stating the specific and concrete reasons which justify subjection to restrictive measures.[40] As such, the standard of review applied by EU courts will not only cover the procedural aspects of EU obligations, i.e. the obligation to transmit reasons for listing and to allow the targeted individual an opportunity to be heard, but will also extend to a substantive review of the reasons offered, i.e. whether these are sufficiently detailed and specific, whether they rest on a solid factual basis, and generally whether the reasons offered, or at least one of them, is substantiated.[41] If the EU institutions cannot adduce additional evidence, then review will take place on the evidence at hand – since it is for Union to prove that the reasons are well-founded, not for the individual to prove that they are not.[42] If even one of the reasons stated, albeit in summary form, is substantiated, then the CJEU will not annul the listing.[43]

This rather stringent (level of) review is required, according to the Court, not just because it is 'indispensable to ensure a fair balance between the maintenance of international peace and security and the protection of fundamental rights and freedoms, those being shared values of the UN and the EU',[44] but

---

38 See the Opinion of AG Bot in CJEU *Kadi II*, paras. 81–8.
39 CJEU *Kadi II*, para. 111.
40 *Ibid.*, paras. 114–16.
41 *Ibid.*, paras. 118–19.
42 *Ibid.*, paras. 120–4.
43 *Ibid.*, para. 130.
44 *Ibid.*

'*all the more*' so because, 'despite the improvements added' by Resolutions 1904 and 1989, the procedures at UN level, including the Office of the Ombudsperson, still do not provide the guarantees of 'effective judicial protection'.[45] In this assessment, the CJEU not only explicitly endorsed the ECtHR's decision in *Nada*,[46] but also reiterated its *Solange* approach by intimating that it may tone down its intensity of review should even more robust procedures be adopted at UN level. But it also went on to tell the UN what the essence of that concept of 'judicial protection' must be: not *ex officio* review, not Ombudspersons, no half-baked measures:

> The essence of effective judicial protection must be that it should enable the person concerned *to obtain a declaration from a court, by means of a judgment ordering annulment whereby the contested measure is retroactively erased from the legal order* and is deemed never to have existed, that the listing of his name, or the continued listing of his name, on the list concerned was vitiated by illegality, *the recognition of which may re-establish the reputation of that person or constitute for him a form of reparation for the non-material harm he has suffered.*[47]

The inadequacy of the *Solange* argument as a justification for disobedience

The employment of the *Solange* argument by the EU courts in its *Solange I* incarnation, and their denial to accord *Solange II* deference to the UN level despite the reform of the relevant UN-level procedures, confirms the ability of that argument to furnish a powerful tool of resistance, and potentially a powerful incentive, for the regulation of the relationship between different levels of governance. But it also attests to the perils that the argument may bring if it is pushed too far. It can hardly be doubted that the serious improvements at UN level in the listing and delisting procedures of the 1267/1989 sanctions regime are to a significant degree due to the pressure applied by the EU courts in their *Kadi* judgments, coupled with the consequent disobedience of SC decisions by a significant number of states. At the same time, despite these significant improvements at UN level, the CJEU in *Kadi II* continues to push, equating the requirement for 'guarantees of judicial protection' with the introduction of a court procedure resulting in a judgment (rather than the possibility of recourse to an independent and impartial third party with the power to make binding decisions, indicated in the section above). This may be a step too far, and is further dealt with in the conclusion.

---

45 *Ibid.*, para. 133 (emphasis added).
46 *Nada* v. *Switzerland*, App no. 10593/08.
47 CJEU *Kadi II*, para. 134 (emphasis added).

However, the most important aspect of the *Solange* argument from an inter-national law perspective, that of the legal characterization of such a reaction, remains to be broached. This is because from the perspective of the international legal order the *Solange* argument employed by the EU courts in the *Kadi* cases is quite without formal significance or impact. It cannot, in and of itself legally 'justify' disobedience of SC decisions, even if it may well explain it. The *Solange* argument thus needs to be translated into a cognizable international legal argu-ment if it is to offer any meaningful legal justification for disobeying the SC.

The possibility for such a meaningful translation is inherent in the *Solange* argument, however. As indicated above, the *Solange* argument posits review of measures adopted at one (non-local) level by a court at another (local) level, in accordance with the latter level's (local) laws. However, in the way that it has been employed, whether by the German Federal Constitutional Court or by the EU courts in *Kadi*, the *Solange* argument does not in fact posit such review with respect to any local law: it is limited to positing review with certain funda-mental human rights which exist simultaneously at the local (domestic) and non-local (international) level. The overlapping content of these fundamental human rights, guaranteed simultaneously at both levels of governance (or, to put it another way, in both partial legal orders) allows for a translation of the *Solange* argument into an argument under public international law. The fundamental human rights sought to be protected, being guaranteed at the international level, including under customary international law, as well as at the 'domestic' one, can be argued to be binding on the UN and on the SC as its organ. If so, the violation by the UN (through the SC) of these international obligations incumbent upon the organization engage the UN's responsibility. Member states then are entitled to invoke this responsibility and seek to imple-ment it, including through – in the last instance – the taking of countermeas-ures. These may take the form of disobedience of SC decisions (a violation of art. 25 of the UN Charter) in response to the UN's violation of its own obligations toward the member states. In that, the countermeasure may only seek to induce the UN's compliance with its obligations – which indeed it does by demanding 'equivalent protection' of fundamental human rights at UN level. This is a complicated argument to make, and it has been made in full elsewhere.[48] Here, it only seeks to demonstrate that the *Solange* argument may be meaningfully translated into an international legal justification for disobeying the SC.

Conclusion

The disobedience of SC decisions, whether on the basis of the *Solange* argument, or on the basis of countermeasures against the UN in response to a previous breach by the organization of its own obligations, is no doubt dangerous and

---

48 See generally Antonios Tzanakopoulos, *Disobeying the Security Council: Countermeasures against Wrongful Sanctions* (OUP, 2011).

hugely destabilizing. Both the *Solange* argument and the circumstance precluding wrongfulness that is countermeasures acknowledge and anticipate that, and present themselves as interim solutions,[49] pending accommodation of the dispute. They can both, however, be pushed too far. Indeed the CJEU can be seen to have raised the bar extremely high for the UN and its SC in *Kadi II*: it seems that nothing short of a full-blown court procedure will be enough to solicit the EU courts' deference to review at UN level. No doubt the establishment of an international court to deal with issues of delisting of individuals targeted by SC sanctions would be a welcome, if rather unrealistic, development. It seems however that all this pressure, after procuring some progress, is now sending the SC into regression and may end up being counterproductive. Indeed, in order to avoid challenges in domestic and other courts, the SC has started to make its sanctions regimes less and less targeted: in blunting the identification of those targeted, the SC makes it more difficult for those affected to challenge the measures in domestic or regional international fora. The Council re-situates the game on the intergovernmental level, where it is much stronger, no less so on account of art. 103 UN Charter. The essence of the *Solange* argument is seizing the momentum for passing from the defiance of *Solange I* to the deference of *Solange II*. EU courts may, in their zeal, have overshot that target. Whether that is indeed the case, only time will tell.

---

49 See generally James Crawford, 'Counter-measures as interim measures' (1994) 5 *European Journal of International Law* 65.

Part 4

The constitutional law perspective

11 Global counter-terrorism sanctions and European due process rules

The dialogue between the CJEU and the ECtHR

Federico Fabbrini and Joris Larik

Introduction: from *Kadi* to *Nada* and back again

The *Kadi* case law has been at the crossroads of many scholarly analyses. Academics have investigated the question of the powers of the United Nations (UN) Security Council and the autonomy of the European Union (EU) legal order vis-à-vis international law.[1] At the same time, an issue that has increasingly attracted attention concerns the standard of proof, and the use of secret evidence, in proceedings affecting the civil liberties of individuals in the context of global counter-terrorism.[2] In this chapter, we examine the *Kadi* case from the perspective of judicial dialogue.[3] A growing body of literature has researched the interaction between courts in the transnational context, and explained how judges in the field of national security may benefit from mutual engagement with their peers.[4] In this chapter, we focus

---

1 See with regard to the 2005 decision of the Court of First Instance and the 2008 decision of the Court of Justice, Sara Poli, Maria Tzanou, 'The *Kadi* rulings: a survey of the literature' (2009) 28 *Yearbook of European Law* 533, 535–44 as well as the collection of references in Rudolf Streinz, 'Does the European Court of Justice keep the balance individual and community interest in Kadi?' in Ulrich Fastenrath *et al.* (eds), *From Bilateralism to Community Interest: Essays in Honour of Bruno Simma* (OUP, 2011), 1118–31, 1121 (footnote 21), as well as Joris Larik, 'Two ships in the night or in the same boat together: how the ECJ squared the circle and foreshadowed Lisbon in its Kadi judgment' (2010) 13 *Yearbook of Polish European Studies* 149.

2 See e.g. Federico Fabbrini, 'Global sanctions, state secrets and supranational review: seeking due process in an interconnected world', in David Cole *et al.* (eds), *Secrecy, National Security and the Vindication of Constitutional Law* (Elgar, 2013), 284–301 (discussing in comparative perspective the use of confidential evidence in counter-terrorism proceedings before the EU courts).

3 On judicial dialogue in general, see Anne-Marie Slaughter, 'A global community of courts' (2003) 44 *Harvard International Law Journal* 191 and Filippo Fontanelli, Giuseppe Martinico, 'Alla ricerca della coerenza: le tecniche del "dialogo nascosto" fra i giudici nell'ordinamento costituzionale multi-livello' (2008) *Rivista Trimestrale di Diritto Pubblico* 37.

4 See e.g. Eyal Benvenisti, 'Reclaiming democracy: the strategic use of foreign and international law by national courts' (2008) 102 *American Journal of International Law* 241 and Aharon Barak, *The Judge in a Democracy* (Princeton University Press, 2006).

on the relationship between the Court of Justice of the European Union (CJEU) and the European Court of Human Rights (ECtHR) and explain how the dialogue between 'two of Europe's most powerful and prestigious courts'[5] has contributed to striking a better balance between due process rights and national security in the global fight against terrorism.[6]

In its September 2012 decision in *Nada* v. *Switzerland*, the Grand Chamber of the ECtHR addressed the legality of measures implementing targeted sanctions stemming from the UN Security Council and, relying on the *Kadi* decision of the CJEU, found a violation of the rights enshrined in the European Convention on Human Rights (ECHR).[7] More recently, in the *Kadi II* judgment of July 2013, the CJEU in turn cited the ECtHR and reaffirmed its previous conclusion that Mr Kadi had been deprived of due process rights in being subject to UN sanctions within the EU. Based on this recent case law, in this chapter we argue that the CJEU and the ECtHR have been influencing each other, and that their interaction, under the looming accession of the EU to the ECHR, has been instrumental to ensure the effectiveness of the protection of due process standards in the European multilevel human rights architecture.

Recasting the Luxembourg–New York standoff as a Strasbourg–Luxembourg–New York triangle reveals an interactive process. Firstly, the *Kadi* case law of the CJEU has left its mark on human rights protection within the framework of the ECHR with regard to the implementation of Security Council resolutions. Secondly, instead of seeing the CJEU as the sole pacemaker in this regard, the *Kadi II* judgment can be understood as having been influenced, on its part, by the ECtHR. To elaborate on these points, the chapter is structured as follows. In the next two sections we sketch out the changing international context in which the *Kadi II* judgment took place and outline the prospects of the upcoming accession of the EU to the ECHR and its implications for the relationship between the CJEU and the ECtHR. In the next section we briefly describe the *Nada* case of the ECtHR. In the following two sections we consider how the CJEU influenced the ECtHR in *Nada* and subsequently we discuss the impact of *Nada* on the CJEU in *Kadi II*. In the conclusion we summarize our findings and highlight the implications for the protection

---

5 Erika de Wet, 'From Kadi to Nada: judicial techniques favouring human rights over United Nations Security Council sanctions' (2013) 12 *Chinese Journal of International Law* 787, 790.

6 On the dialogue between the CJEU and the ECtHR, see Francis Jacobs, 'Judicial dialogues and the cross-fertilization of the legal systems: the European Court of Justice' (2003) 38 *Texas International Law Journal* 547; Sionaidh Douglas-Scott, 'A tale of two courts: Luxembourg, Strasbourg and the growing European human rights *acquis*' (2006) 43 *Common Market Law Review* 629.

7 *Nada* v. *Switzerland*, Application no. 10593/08, Eur. Ct. H. R. [GC], judgment of 12 September 2012 (hereinafter: *Nada* v. *Switzerland*).

of fundamental rights in the European multilevel human rights architecture of the dialogue between Luxembourg and Strasbourg.

The changing international context: UN reforms

The decision of the CJEU in *Kadi II* took place in a changing context marked by two principal developments. The first occurred at the international level, having to do with the evolution of the UN Security Council's 'blacklisting' regime. An essential feature of the *Kadi* saga was the question to which extent human rights, in particular procedural guarantees, can be observed in the implementation of sanctions imposed by the UN Security Council on persons suspected of being involved in the financing of terrorism. As it is well known, after 9/11 the UN Security Council began to draw a list of individuals and entities suspected of involvement in terrorism activities. Given that the Security Council adopts these measures under ch. VII of the UN Charter, the UN members are obliged to comply with them, even in the face of opposing international treaty obligations (art. 103 UN Charter). This led to the adoption of domestic laws and regulations to implement the sanctions on a global scale over the past decade.[8]

This form of targeted sanctions originated from Resolution 1267/1999 in the context of measures taken against the Taliban regime in Afghanistan in the late 1990s.[9] These included the setting up of a designated committee of the Security Council to manage the 'blacklists' of targeted individuals and entities. Shortly after its inception, the scope of the regime was extended beyond targets linked to the Taliban or Afghanistan to cover 'funds and other financial assets of Usama bin Laden and individuals and entities associated with him as designated by the Committee, including those in the Al-Qaida organization'.[10]

The original sanctions regime received fierce criticism from scholars,[11] as well as judicial challenges given the lack of due process from the point of view of the listed individuals. Mr Kadi's complaints of the measures adopted against him by the EU are but one of these challenges. However, the *Kadi* litigation

8 See, for example, UN Security Council, letter dated 23 August 2004 from the Chairman of the Security Council Committee established pursuant to resolutions 1267 (1999) and 1989 (2011), first report of the Monitoring Team, S/2004/679 (reporting on the implementation of sanctions by states worldwide).

9 UN Security Council Resolution 1267 (15 October 1999).

10 UN Security Council Resolution 1333 (19 December 2000), para. 8 (c); UN Security Council Resolution 1390 (16 January 2002). See further Larissa van den Herik, 'The Security Council's targeted sanctions regimes: in need of better protection of the individual' (2007) 20 *Leiden Journal of International Law* 797, 800.

11 See e.g. Iain Cameron, *The European Convention on Human Rights, Due Process and United Nations Security Council Counter-Terrorism Sanctions*, report commissioned by the Council of Europe, 6 February 2006.

was followed particularly closely by the Monitoring Team of the '1267 Committee',[12] and arguably the most vocal judicial criticism of the regime was issued by Advocate General (AG) Poiares Maduro in his opinion preceding the 2008 judgment.[13]

The Security Council, on its part, was not entirely unresponsive to these criticisms. In the course of the years, it endeavoured to make the regime friendlier to human rights concerns. This includes above all the regulation of information of the target to be provided by the country requesting its listing,[14] and the establishment of a focal point responsible for managing individual de-listing requests,[15] which would eventually be replaced by a so-called Office of the Ombudsperson.[16] At the same time, the saga continued before the EU courts, with several appeals from the various parties challenging the superseding implementing measures adopted in the wake of the 2008 judgment. From the point of view of the EU courts, the sanctions regime represented a moving target.

At the time of the first *Kadi* judgment of the Court of First Instance (CFI) in 2005, no procedure existed for individual de-listing as blacklisted persons had to rely on the diplomatic protection of their countries of nationality or residence to this effect, based on a set of guidelines adopted by the '1267 Committee'. Nonetheless, the CFI ruled that 'the Security Council intended to take account, so far as possible, of the fundamental rights of the persons entered in the Sanctions Committee's list, and in particular their right to be heard'.[17]

This ruling, framed by the controversial *jus cogens* standard, was resoundingly overturned on appeal three years later. The CJEU rejected the adaptations made

12 See, for instance, letter dated 13 May 2008 from the Chairman of the Security Council Committee established pursuant to Resolution 1267 (1999), eighth report of the Monitoring Team, S/2008/324, 14 May 2008, 16–17. In its report of December 2012, the Monitoring Team still referred to the *Kadi* case as one of the 'outside factors [which] might upset' the 'stable, if temporary, equilibrium with respect to due process issues' which the sanction regime was said to have reached after its latest reforms, UN Security Council, letter dated 31 December 2012 from the Chairman of the Security Council Committee established pursuant to Resolutions 1267 (1999) and 1989 (2011), thirteenth report of the Monitoring Team, S/2012/968, 31 December 2012, 9 (para. 17).

13 Joined Cases C-402/05 P and C-415/05 P, *Kadi and Al Barakaat*, Opinion of Advocate General Poiares Maduro [2008] ECR I-06351.

14 UN Security Council Resolution 1735 (22 December 2006) and subsequently UN Security Council Resolution 1822 (30 June 2008).

15 UN Security Council Resolution 1730 (19 December 2006).

16 UN Security Council Resolution 1904 (17 December 2009). See also the summary of these development provided in Joined Cases C-584/10 P, C-593/10 P, and C-595/10 P, *Commission, Council and United Kingdom* v. *Kadi*, Judgment of 18 July 2013, nyr, paras. 9–12 (hereinafter: *Kadi II*); and Lisa Ginsborg, Martin Scheinin, 'You can't always get what you want: the Kadi II conundrum and the Security Council 1267 terrorist sanctions regime' (2011) 8 *Essex Human Rights Review* 7, 10–13.

17 Case T-315/01 *Kadi* v. *Council and Commission* [2005] ECR II-03649, para. 265.

to the UN blacklisting regime (at that point in time the 'focal point') as insufficient, admonishing that 'the fact remains that the procedure before [the "1267 Committee"] is still in essence diplomatic and intergovernmental, the persons or entities concerned having no real opportunity of asserting their rights and that committee taking its decisions by consensus, each of its members having a right of veto'.[18] The CJEU hence famously held that it needed to 'ensure the review, in principle the full review, of the lawfulness of all Community acts in the light of the fundamental rights forming an integral part of the general principles of Community law', which explicitly included 'review of Community measures which, like the contested regulation, are designed to give effect to the resolutions adopted by the Security Council under Chapter VII of the Charter of the United Nations'.[19]

The General Court (as the CFI was renamed by virtue of the Lisbon Treaty) acquiesced in this standard in its 2010 judgment.[20] At the same time, it acknowledged the changes that had been effected at the UN level in the meantime, including the establishment of the Office of the Ombudsperson.[21] However, it noted that judicial review at EU level must be exercised 'at the very least, so long as the re-examination procedure operated by the Sanctions Committee clearly fails to offer guarantees of effective judicial protection'.[22]

In his March 2013 Opinion in *Kadi II*, however, AG Bot put a stronger emphasis of the need to pursue international security, suggesting a more deferential approach towards the Security Council, aimed more towards compliance with international law.[23] The AG avowed himself more sympathetic to the sanctions regime and the work of the Ombudsperson, noting that in 'view of the important role played by the Ombudsperson in the decisions taken by the Sanctions Committee, [he considered] that the procedure before it can no longer be regarded as purely diplomatic and intergovernmental' and that the 'improvements to the procedure before the Sanctions Committee thus help to guarantee that listings are based on sufficiently serious evidence and are evaluated on an on-going basis'.[24] Consequently, instead of a rigorous review, he advised that 'the EU courts should not adopt a standard of review which would require the EU institutions to examine systematically and intensively the merits of the decisions taken by the Sanctions Committee, on the basis of evidence or information available to that body, before giving effect to them'.[25]

18 Joined Cases C-402/05 P and C-415/05 P, *Kadi and Al Barakaat* [2008] ECR I-06351, para. 323.
19 *Ibid.*, para. 326.
20 Case T-85/09 *Kadi* v. *Commission* [2010] ECR II-05177, para. 126.
21 *Ibid.*, paras. 15–29.
22 *Ibid.*, para. 127. On the *Solange* aspect of this reasoning, see Tzanakopoulos, ch. 10 this volume.
23 *Kadi II*, Opinion of Advocate General Bot of 19 March, nyr.
24 *Ibid.*, para. 82.
25 *Ibid.*, para. 86.

In its July 2013 appeals judgment in *Kadi II*, at last, the CJEU upheld the requirement of a full review,[26] but also added more detailed language on the duty incumbent on the Union institutions to acquire information to justify their measures and on the treatment of such confidential and sensitive information by courts.[27] In the words of the CJEU, judicial review conducted along these lines 'is indispensable to ensure a fair balance between the maintenance of international peace and security and the protection of the fundamental rights and freedoms of the person concerned'.[28]

Hence, the relationship between the Security Council and the CJEU can been cast as a dialogue about the balance of human rights and the public interest for (inter)national security. More precisely, it is about weighing the need to effectively combat global terrorism, including the use of confidential information to that end, against the requirements of due process at various levels of governance. Over time, this balance was tipped in favour of human rights by the EU courts.

The changing European context: the accession of the EU to the ECHR

Besides interacting with the UN, the CJEU has also been dialoguing with the ECtHR on matters of due process and the right balance between security and fundamental rights. This dialogue was structurally conditioned by the looming accession of the EU to the ECHR, and helped to tip the balance in favour of due process in both courts.

In the *Kadi* case law, we can observe a changing appreciation of the rights enshrined in the ECHR, moving from dismissal to increased referencing to the ECHR and the ECtHR's case law. Unsurprisingly, Mr Kadi has relied from the outset on the ECHR, stressing the long-standing case law of the CJEU that the ECHR represents a special source of inspiration for the rights forming part of the Union legal order.[29] The CFI in 2005 was as forgiving to the UN as it was dismissive towards the ECHR. It noted that as a matter of international law, 'the obligations of the Member States of the United Nations under the Charter of the United Nations clearly prevail over every other obligation of domestic law or of international treaty law' including both the ECHR and the EU Treaties.[30] By contrast, in its 2008 judgment, in preparing the ground for its 'full review' stance, the CJEU acknowledged the

---

26 *Kadi II*, para. 97.
27 *Ibid.*, paras. 107 et seq.
28 *Ibid.*, para. 131.
29 Case T-315/01 *Kadi* v. *Council and Commission* [2005] ECR II-03649, para. 138, referring to Case 4/73 *Nold* v. *Commission* [1974] ECR 491, para. 13.
30 Case T-315/01 *Kadi* v. *Council and Commission* [2005] ECR II-03649, para. 181.

'special significance'[31] of the ECHR in inspiring the rights which act as a condition for the lawfulness of secondary Union law. Moreover, it explicitly referred to the ECtHR decisions in *Bosphorus*, as well as *Behrami* and *Saramati* in arriving at the conclusion that the contested measures did not benefit from immunity from jurisdiction due to attribution to the UN.[32] In finding the violations of fundamental rights, the CJEU again referred to the ECHR as a source of support.[33] In the 2010 judgment, having aligned with the CJEU, the General Court looked more favourably upon the ECHR. For instance, it explicitly referred to the ECHR and Strasbourg case law when it ruled that the need for confidentiality in the quest for (inter)national security does not exempt judicial review altogether,[34] and subsequently that the information provided to justify the contested measures was deemed insufficiently specific.[35]

This alignment can be best explained by a second grand development that has unfolded prior to the *Kadi II* judgment – the Draft Agreement on the accession of the EU to the ECHR.[36] After earlier attempts for accession failed, either for political[37] or judicial reasons[38], with the entry into force of the Lisbon Treaty and the necessary amendments of the ECHR, the road is now open for the accession of the EU to the ECHR. Pursuant to the new art. 6 (2) TEU – as well as the new art. 59 (2) ECHR, as modified by the 14th Additional Protocol to the ECHR – the negotiating process for the accession

---

31 Joined Cases C-402/05 P and C-415/05 P, *Kadi and Al Barakaat* [2008] ECR I-06351, para. 283.

32 *Ibid.*, paras. 311–13 referring to *Bosphorus* v. *Ireland*, Application no. 45036/98, Eur. Ct. H. R. [GC], Judgment of 30 June 2005; *Behrami & Behrami* v. *France*, Application no. 71412/01, Eur. Ct. H. R. [GC], Judgment of 2 May 2007; and *Saramati* v. *France, Germany and Norway*, Application no. 78166/01 Eur. Ct. H. R. [GC], Judgment of 2 May 2007.

33 Joined Cases C-402/05 P and C-415/05 P, *Kadi and Al Barakaat* [2008] ECR I-06351, para. 335 (effective judicial protection, arts. 6 and 13 ECHR) and para. 356 (right to respect for property, art. 1 of the First Additional Protocol to the ECHR).

34 Case T-85/09 *Kadi* v. *Commission* [2010] ECR II-05177, para. 146, referring to *Chahal* v. *United Kingdom*, Application no. 22414/93, Eur. Ct. H. R. [GC], Judgment of 15 November 1996, para. 131.

35 Case T-85/09 *Kadi* v. *Commission* [2010] ECR II-05177, para. 176, on procedural fairness (art. 5 (4) ECHR), referring to *A. and Others* v. *United* Kingdom, Application no. 3455/05, Eur. Ct. H. R. [GC], Judgment of 19 February 2009 (note that this finding was partially overruled in *Kadi II*, para. 148).

36 See on this Federico Fabbrini, Joris Larik, 'The accession of the EU to the ECHR and its effects: inter-jurisdictional dynamics and the constitutionalization of the European Court of Human Rights' (2014) 32 *Yearbook of European Law* (forthcoming).

37 Gráinne de Búrca, 'The road not taken: the European Union as a global human rights actor' (2011) 105 *American Journal of International Law* 649 (elaborating on the early failures to link the European Communities to the ECHR).

38 Opinion 2/94, *Re the Accession of the EU to the ECHR* [1996] ECR I-1759 (ruling that the EU lacked the competence to join the ECHR and its institutional structures).

of the EU to the ECHR has reached an advanced stage and may soon conclude with a formal accession document.[39]

The Draft Agreement on the accession of the EU to the ECHR modifies the Convention in such a way as to accommodate 'the specific situation of the EU as a non-State entity with an autonomous legal system that is becoming a Party to the Convention alongside its own member States'.[40] This includes, most notably for the relationship between the two courts, the so-called 'co-respondent mechanism' and, as a part thereof, the prior involvement of the CJEU.[41] The former means that where either member states are implementing EU law or where primary EU law is at stake with regard to alleged violations of Convention rights, the EU and the member states can respond to the complaint jointly.[42] The latter provides the CJEU with the power to review the compatibility of Union legislation with the ECHR preceding a decision by the ECtHR.[43] This applies whenever member state courts fail to request a preliminary reference from the CJEU, meaning that the case arrives at the ECtHR without the EU courts having had the opportunity to review it. This grants the CJEU a privilege that no other court of a ECHR contracting party enjoys. This mechanism, as we argued elsewhere, represents the most powerful link between the two courts and harbours the greatest potential in intensifying their relationship.[44] Before the ECtHR can rule, the CJEU will always have the opportunity to set the tone. But if the former does not want to fall behind, it will have to align itself, and go beyond, the standards set by the CJEU.[45]

In the light of this, the fact that the EU courts, after the rejection of the CFI judgment of 2005, started heavily referencing the ECHR and the case law of the ECtHR, to the point of claiming to employ 'criteria identical to those used by the European Court of Human Rights'[46] in determining rights violations,

39 The negotiation process on the accession of the EU to the ECHR has been currently finalized in a Draft Accession Agreement. We refer here to the Draft Accession Agreement as annexed to the Final Report to the CDDH (*Comité directeur pour les droits de l'Homme*), Strasbourg, 5 April 2013, 47+1(2013)008, 4–12. See also Council of the European Union, 6–7 June 2013, Doc. 10461/13, 15 (indicating that once the CJEU has had the opportunity to give an opinion on the agreement, the Commission will come forward with a Council decision authorizing the signature of the agreement). See further Tobias Lock, 'End of an epic? The Draft Agreement on the EU's accession to the ECHR' (2012) 31 *Yearbook of European Law* 162.

40 Final Report to the CDDH, 22, point 38.

41 See on all aspects of the EU's accession Jean-Paul Jacqué, 'The accession of the European Union to the European Convention on Human Rights and Fundamental Freedoms' (2011) 48 *Common Market Law Review* 995, 995 and Robert Uerpmann-Wittzack, 'Rechtsfragen und Rechtsfolgendes Beitritts der Europäischen Union zur EMRK' (2012) *Europarecht (Beiheft 2)* 167.

42 Art. 3 Draft Accession Agreement.

43 *Ibid.*, art. 3 (6).

44 Fabbrini and Larik, 'The accession of the EU to the ECHR and its effects'.

45 *Ibid.*

46 Case T-85/09 *Kadi* v. *Commission* [2010] ECR II-05177, para. 177.

suggests that the EU courts recognize that they will be held accountable after accession for breaches of the ECHR which they failed to remedy. *Nada* made this hypothesis even more likely.

The decision of the ECtHR in *Nada*

The *Nada* case originated from an application against Switzerland lodged with the ECtHR by an Italian/Egyptian national, Mr Youssef Moustafa Nada. The latter had been living since the 1970s in Campione d'Italia, a small Italian exclave surrounded by Swiss territory. On 9 November 2001, at the request of the United States, his name was added to the UN blacklist run by the 1267 Sanctions Committee. Within days the Swiss government added Mr Nada to the domestic blacklist implementing the above-mentioned UN resolutions resulting in the freezing of all his funds. Moreover, pursuant to a 2003 request of the Monitoring Group of the UN Sanctions Committee, Switzerland subjected Mr Nada to a travel ban. Given the peculiar geographical situation of Campione d'Italia, the impossibility to enter into, and transfer through, Switzerland effectively confined him to this small strip of land. Mr Nada brought proceedings in Swiss courts against the measures. On 14 November 2007, the Swiss Federal Court heard the case but, following the same stand adopted by the CFI in *Kadi*, rejected Mr Nada's complaint ruling that it lacked a general power to review a national measure implementing a UN Security Council resolution listing suspected terrorist and freezing his assets except for conformity with *jus cogens*.[47]

Having exhausted the domestic avenues of recourse, in February 2008, Mr Nada brought proceedings before the ECtHR claiming that the addition of his name to the blacklist had breached his right to liberty (art. 5 ECHR), his right to respect for private and family life (art. 8 ECHR), and his right to an effective remedy (art. 13 ECHR). He complained that the travel ban was tantamount to ill-treatment within the meaning of art. 3 ECHR and in breach of his freedom to manifest his religion or beliefs (art. 9 ECHR). On 23 September 2009, while the case was pending, the UN Security Council decided to delete Mr Nada's name from the sanctions list, thus terminating the travel ban against him. Nevertheless, the ECtHR found that this decision did not modify the status of the applicant as a 'victim' within the meaning of art. 34 ECHR. According to the ECtHR,

> the lifting of sanctions… has not deprived the applicant of his status as victim of the restrictions from which he suffered from the time his name was added, in November 2001, to the Sanctions Committee's list… Moreover, it was not followed by any redress within the meaning of [its] case-law.[48]

47 Swiss Federal Court, ATF 1A.45/2007/daa, *Nada* v. *SECO*, Judgment of 14 November 2007.
48 *Nada* v. *Switzerland*, para. 129.

In doing so, the ECtHR discarded the argument by the Swiss government that Mr Nada did not have standing.[49]

In addition, the ECtHR resolved the other preliminary objection raised by the respondent government regarding the lack of jurisdiction in the present case in favour of Mr Nada. Whereas Switzerland had argued that the case was incompatible *ratione personae* with the ECHR, because the action taken against Mr Nada was ultimately to be attributed to the UN, the ECtHR found that the alleged violations of the ECHR were committed by Switzerland and that it was therefore competent to adjudicate the case. The ECtHR distinguished the present case from *Behrami and Behrami*.[50] The ECtHR noted that in *Behrami and Behrami*:

> the impugned acts and omissions of KFOR, whose powers had been validly delegated to it by the Security Council under Chapter VII of the Charter, and those of UNMIK, a subsidiary organ of the UN set up under the same Chapter, were directly attributable to the UN, an organisation of universal jurisdiction fulfilling its imperative collective security objective... In the present case, by contrast, the relevant Security Council resolutions, ... required States to act in their own names and to implement them at national level.[51]

In this way, the ECtHR squarely established it jurisdiction to review the case, and moved to assess Mr Nada's claim on the merits.

On the substance, the ECtHR decided to address Mr Nada's complaint primarily under art. 8 ECHR. As the ECtHR clarified, '"private life" is a broad term not susceptible to exhaustive definition', which encompasses the right to personal development and to establish and develop relationships with other human beings and the outside world in general.[52] The ECtHR found that the applicant's complaint fell within the scope of application of art. 8 ECHR and therefore moved to examine, following its conventional approach to proportionality analysis: first, whether there had been an interference with Mr Nada's right; and second, whether the interference was justified.

On the first question, the ECtHR took the view that 'the measure preventing the applicant from leaving the very confined area of Campione d'Italia for at least six years was likely to make it more difficult for him to exercise his right to maintain contact with others – in particular his friends and family'.[53] This thus amounted to an interference with art. 8 (1) ECHR by the Swiss government.[54]

---

49 *Ibid.*, para. 130.
50 See *Behrami & Behrami* v. *France*, Application no. 71412/01, Eur. Ct. H. R. [GC], Judgment of 2 May 2007.
51 *Nada* v. *Switzerland*, para. 120.
52 *Ibid.*, para. 150.
53 *Ibid.*, para. 165.
54 *Ibid.*, para. 166.

To address the second question, i.e. whether the interference of Mr Nada's right was justified, the ECtHR outlined at the outset the general principles which would guide its reasoning. On the one hand, the ECtHR restated its consolidated case law, epitomized by *Bosphorus*, according to which 'a Contracting Party is responsible under Article 1 ECHR for all acts and omissions of its organs regardless of whether the act or omission in question was a consequence of domestic law or of the necessity to comply with international legal obligations'.[55] On the other hand, the ECtHR expressed its concern for the phenomenon of the fragmentation of international law, and stated that '[w]here a number of apparently contradictory instruments are simultaneously applicable, international case-law and academic opinion endeavour to construe them in such a way as to coordinate their effects and avoid any opposition between them'.[56] In this light, the ECtHR re-called its decision in *Al-Jedda*,[57] introducing a presumption of compatibility between the resolutions of the UN and the ECHR. However, 'having regard to the clear and explicit language [of UN resolution 1390 (2002)], imposing an obligation to take measures capable of breaching human rights',[58] the ECtHR rebutted the presumption of compatibility between the ECHR and UN law.

Yet, the ECtHR refrained from following the previous statement to its logical conclusions.[59] Rather, after stating that the interference with Mr Nada's right found a legal basis in a Swiss law[60] and pursued the legitimate aim of protecting national security,[61] it began inquiring whether the relevant UN resolutions 'left States any freedom in their implementation and, in particular, whether they allowed the authorities to take into account the very specific nature of the applicant's situation and therefore to meet the requirements of art. 8 ECHR'.[62] In this regard, the ECtHR argued that the UN Charter 'd[id] not impose on States a particular model for the implementation of the resolutions adopted by the Security Council under Chapter VII'.[63] Moreover, the ECtHR sought to interpret the text of Resolution 1390 (2002) as 'affording the national authorities a certain flexibility in the mode of implementation'.[64] In view of the foregoing, the ECtHR found that 'Switzerland enjoyed some latitude, which was admittedly limited but nevertheless real, in implementing the relevant binding resolutions of the UN Security Council'.[65]

55 *Ibid.*, para. 168.
56 *Ibid.*, para. 170.
57 See *Al-Jedda* v. *United Kingdom*, Application no. 27021/08, Eur. Ct. H. R. [GC], Judgment of 7 July 2011.
58 *Nada* v. *Switzerland*, para. 172.
59 See further on this Fabbrini and Larik, 'The accession of the EU to the ECHR and its effects'.
60 *Nada* v. *Switzerland*, para. 173.
61 *Ibid.*, para. 174.
62 *Ibid.*, para. 175.
63 *Ibid.*, para. 176.
64 *Ibid.*, para. 178.
65 *Ibid.*, para. 180.

By arguing that Switzerland was endowed with some autonomy in the implementation of the UN resolution – a statement criticized in two separate opinions[66] – the ECtHR was able to avoid the thorny question 'of the hierarchy between the obligations of the States Parties to the ECHR under that instrument, on the one hand, and those arising from the UN Charter, on the other'.[67] The ECtHR examined whether Switzerland had 'the possibility of recourse to an alternative measure that would cause less damage to the fundamental right [of Mr Nada] whilst fulfilling the same aim [of protecting national security]'.[68] The ECtHR showed its awareness that 'the threat of terrorism was particularly serious at the time of the adoption, between 1999 and 2002, of the resolutions prescribing those sanctions'.[69] Nevertheless, on the basis of a plurality of factors, the ECtHR concluded that Switzerland had violated art. 8 ECHR. To begin with, the ECtHR noted with surprise that Switzerland, for more than four years, had failed to inform the UN Sanctions Committee that the domestic investigations against Mr Nada had been discontinued for lack of evidence of his involvement in terrorism-related activities.[70] Secondly, the ECtHR underlined how, despite the peculiar facts of the case, Mr Nada had been *tout court* prohibited from leaving an Italian enclave in Swiss territory.[71] Finally, the ECtHR criticized Switzerland for failing to comply with its positive obligations to act before the competent UN organs to seek his delisting.[72] Recalling its longstanding principle that the ECHR protects rights that are not theoretical or illusory but practical and effective,[73] the ECtHR therefore concluded that Switzerland 'could not validly confine itself to relying on the binding nature of Security Council resolutions, but should have persuaded the Court that it had taken – or at least had attempted to take – all possible measures to adapt the sanctions regime to the applicant's individual situation'.[74] Hence, the ECtHR condemned Switzerland for imposing a restriction

> on the applicant's freedom of movement for a considerable period of time [which] did not strike a fair balance between his right to the protection of his private and family life, on the one hand, and the legitimate aims of the prevention of crime and the protection of... national security and public safety, on the other.[75]

---

66 See *ibid.*, Joint Concurring Opinion of Judges Bratza, Nicolau, and Yudkivska and Concurring Opinion of Judge Malinverni. For a comment see Fabbrini and Larik, 'The accession of the EU to the ECHR and its effects'.
67 *Nada* v. *Switzerland*, para. 197.
68 *Ibid.*, para. 183.
69 *Ibid.*, para. 186.
70 *Ibid.*, para. 188.
71 *Ibid.*, paras. 190–1.
72 *Ibid.*, para. 194.
73 *Artico* v. *Italy*, Application no. 6694/74, Eur. Ct. H. R., Judgment of 13 May 1980, para. 33.
74 *Nada* v. *Switzerland*, para. 196.
75 *Ibid.*, para. 198.

Having found a breach of art. 8 ECHR for a violation of Mr Nada's right to private and family life, the ECtHR briefly considered Mr Nada's complaint under art. 13 ECHR. Here, the ECtHR drew extensively from the ruling of the CJEU in *Kadi*, according to which the requirement for judicial review is not removed by the fact that contested measures are implementing UN Security Council resolutions.[76] Applying *mutatis mutandis* the same reasoning to the present case, the ECtHR held that 'there was nothing in the Security Council resolutions to prevent the Swiss authorities from introducing mechanisms to verify the measures taken at national level pursuant to those resolutions',[77] and ruled that Switzerland had violated art. 13 ECHR.[78]

Speaking to Strasbourg: how *Kadi I* influenced *Nada*

The references made by the ECtHR in *Nada* to the 2008 *Kadi* judgment of the CJEU reveal the latter's influence on the Strasbourg Court. As we have argued elsewhere,[79] the ECtHR in *Nada* broke with its previous jurisprudence of deference vis-à-vis the UN and upheld a vanguard protection of rights due to the influence of the case law of the CJEU and the prospect of accession of the EU. Given the two main developments described above, the *Nada* case and its discussion on due process rights in targeted sanctions cases is particularly interesting as it represents a site where three constitutional claims from non-state entities met: firstly, this evoked the role of the ECHR 'as a "constitutional instrument of European public order" in the field of human rights'.[80] In order to make their case and bolster their constitutional credentials, both the ECtHR and the CJEU can be seen to assert the autonomy of their respective legal instruments from international law, including the UN.[81] Secondly, the case equally evoked the particular role of the UN Charter and its supremacy, according to its art. 103, over any other international agreement, which for some authors make it a sort of a global constitution.[82] Thirdly, the explicit reference to *Kadi* also recalled the constitutional principles of the EU legal order, which as the CJEU in *Kadi* ruled cannot be upset by any requirements under international law, even if stemming from the UN Charter.

---

76 Joined Cases C-402/05 P and C-415/05 P, *Kadi and Al Barakaat* [2008] ECR I-06351, para. 299.
77 *Nada* v. *Switzerland*, para. 212.
78 *Ibid.*, para. 214. The ECtHR, on the contrary, did not find a violation of art. 5 ECHR (*ibid.*, para. 230), and summarily rejected Mr Nada's complaint on arts. 3 and 9 ECHR (*ibid.*, para. 236).
79 Fabbrini and Larik, 'The accession of the EU to the ECHR and its effects'.
80 *Bosphorus* v. *Ireland*, Application no. 45036/98, Eur. Ct. H. R. [GC], Judgment of 30 June 2005, para. 156, quoting from *Loizidou* v. *Turkey*, Application no. 1538/89, Eur. Ct. H. R., preliminary objection, Judgment of 23 March 1995, para. 75.
81 Fabbrini and Larik, 'The accession of the EU to the ECHR and its effects'.
82 See e.g. Bardo Fassbender, 'Rediscovering a forgotten constitution: notes on the place of the UN Charter in the international legal order', in Jeffrey Dunoff, Joel Trachtman (eds), *Ruling the World? Constitutionalism, International Law and Global Governance* (CUP, 2009), 133–48.

This put the ECtHR in a very difficult position, forcing it to choose between accepting the supremacy of the UN, and thus falling far behind the CJEU as a human rights stronghold post-*Kadi I*, or competing with the CJEU in the quest for becoming the 'ultimate bulwark'[83] for the protection of human rights in Europe. In the former case the ECtHR would subjugate itself to the UN, thereby putting into question its own constitutional credentials. In the latter case, it would have to face the Luxembourg Court as the other powerful transnational judicial body in the 'European legal space'.[84]

In our view, the fact that the ECtHR upheld Convention rights even in the face of Security Council resolutions can only be properly understood in view of the *Kadi* case law combined with the accession of the EU to the ECHR. In order not be side-lined by the CJEU and instead to assert itself also in the future as the trailblazer for human rights in Europe, the ECtHR is all the more incentivized to maintain protection standards at least as high as those existing at the EU level. Given the accession of the EU to the ECHR and the mechanisms put in place, it is clear that for the future there will be no choice but to communicate with the CJEU and ensuring that its decisions conform with all obligations flowing from the ECHR. This difficult position is well captured in the *Nada* judgment, where the ECtHR, while avoiding an overt clash with the UN Security Council, makes sure not to fall behind the CJEU and its human rights standards.

In the past, the ECtHR accorded a certain margin of discretion to ECHR contracting parties when acting under a mandate of the Security Council.[85] In *Nada*, however, the ECtHR rebutted the *Al-Jedda* presumption in view of the 'clear and explicit language,' imposing an obligation to take measures capable of breaching human rights' [86] contained in the Security Council resolution at issue.[87] Nonetheless, instead of delving into the implication that the Security Council was potentially obliging states to act in violation of the ECHR, the Court focused exclusively on the manner in which Switzerland

83 *Nada* v. *Switzerland*, Concurring Opinion of Judge Malinverni, para. 15, citing in turn Josiane Auvret-Finck, 'Le contrôle des décisions du Conseil de sécurité par la Cour européenne des droits de l'homme' in Constance Grewe *et al.* (eds.), *Sanctions ciblées et protections juridictionnelles des droits fondamentaux dans l'Union européenne. Equilibres et déséquilibres de la balance* (Bruylant, 2010), 213–43, 214.

84 See on the concept Christopher Harding, 'The identity of European law: mapping out the European Legal Space' (2002) 6 *European Law Journal* 128.

85 See *Bosphorus* v. *Ireland*, Application no. 45036/98, Eur. Ct. H. R. [GC], Judgment of 30 June 2005 or *Behrami & Behrami* v. *France*, Application no. 71412/01, Eur. Ct. H. R. [GC], Judgment of 2 May 2007; note also the French reliance on these cases in order to argue as a third party in *Nada* that Switzerland had no jurisdiction over these measures (*Nada* v. *Switzerland*, paras. 107–9). The Court rejected this argument, however, in the case at hand (*ibid.*, paras. 116–25).

86 *Ibid.*, para. 172.

87 See also Inger Osterdahl, *Defer and Rule: The Relationship between the EU, the European Convention on Human Rights and the UN*, Uppsala Faculty of Law Working Paper no. 5 (2012).

had implemented the UN resolutions. In employing the same argumentative device as the CJEU in *Kadi*, the ECtHR managed to circumvent the discussion of art. 103 UN Charter – a controversial feature of its judgment.[88] Referring to *Kadi I*, the ECtHR held that 'the Charter in principle leaves to UN member States a free choice among the various possible models for transposition of those resolutions into their domestic legal order'.[89] In view of this 'latitude, which was admittedly limited but nevertheless real',[90] the ECtHR managed to conclude that Switzerland had breached Mr Nada's right to private and family life, combined with a failure of providing an effective remedy.

The factual differences between *Kadi* and *Nada* notwithstanding, a central issue in both cases concerned the lack of legal protection, at home and at the UN level, against the targeted sanctions. If such a satisfactory mechanism existed in New York, arguably either European court could have deferred to the international level.[91] As to what consequences such a lack of protection entailed, the ECtHR employed a lengthy quote from the CJEU's *Kadi* judgment of 2008 concerning art. 13 ECHR on the right to an effective remedy:

> The Court would further refer to the finding of the CJEC that 'it is not a consequence of the principles governing the international legal order under the United Nations that any judicial review of the internal lawfulness of the contested regulation in the light of fundamental freedoms is excluded by virtue of the fact that that measure is intended to give effect to a resolution of the Security Council adopted under Chapter VII of the Charter of the United Nations' (see the *Kadi* judgment of the CJEC, § 299...). The Court is of the opinion that the same reasoning must be applied, *mutatis mutandis*, to the present case, more specifically to the review by the Swiss authorities of the conformity of the Taliban Ordinance with the Convention. It further finds that there was nothing in the Security Council resolutions to prevent the Swiss authorities from introducing mechanisms to verify the measures taken at national level pursuant to those resolutions.[92]

In doing so, the ECtHR subscribed to the view of the CJEU in terms of the requirement of effective judicial review of the restrictive measures adopted by the UN Security Council. Given that the Swiss had failed to provide such protection, the ECtHR had to step in and uphold this right, thus re-asserting

---

88 See in particular *Nada* v. *Switzerland*, Concurring Opinion of Judge Malinverni.
89 *Ibid.*, referring to Joined Cases C-402/05 P and C-415/05 P, *Kadi and Al Barakaat* [2008] ECR I-06351, para. 298.
90 *Nada* v. *Switzerland*, para. 180.
91 On the *Solange* aspect of the *Kadi* case law, see Tzanakopoulos, ch. 10 this volume.
92 *Nada* v. *Switzerland*, para. 212.

the position of the ECHR as the 'constitutional instrument of European public order'.[93]

At the same time, the *Nada* judgment can even be seen to push protection standards further than the CJEU in its 2008 *Kadi* judgment, as the ECtHR tries to reclaim the vanguard from the CJEU. The Court put a particular emphasis on the positive obligations it deemed incumbent upon Switzerland under the ECHR. The ECtHR admonished Switzerland for having failed to convince the Court 'that it had taken – or at least had attempted to take – all possible measures to adapt the sanctions regime to the applicant's individual situation'.[94] Such measures included, according to the ECtHR, informing more promptly the UN Sanctions Committee of the results of the investigations against Mr Nada in Switzerland, which did not yield any proof that he was associated with terrorist groups.[95] Furthermore, the Swiss government should have made use of the exemptions granted under the sanctions regime more fully, and ought to have encouraged Mr Nada to this effect as well.[96] The ECtHR thus requires the signatories of the ECHR to be actively involved in preventing possible human rights violations flowing from the international level, also by minimizing the adverse consequences of the people affected.

Luxembourg is listening: how *Nada* influenced *Kadi II*

In the previous section, we argued that the judgment of the CJEU in *Kadi* influenced the decision of the ECtHR in *Nada*. Did *Nada*, in turn, hold sway over *Kadi II*? In its judgment of 18 July 2013, the Grand Chamber of the CJEU rejected the appeals against the decision of the General Court of 30 September 2010,[97] and confirmed the annulment of the Commission regulation re-listing Mr Kadi[98] for violation of due process standards. In its ruling, the CJEU cited the decision of the ECtHR in *Nada* only once – to confirm its argument that, despite the improvements in the UN machinery for listing and delisting suspected terrorists, the UN Security Council still did not provide to blacklisted persons 'the guarantee of effective judicial protection'.[99]

Nevertheless, the reference to *Nada* is the sole reference the CJEU actually made to a judgment by a court outside the EU. This suggests full awareness by the Luxembourg Court of the fact that an advanced standard of protection of human rights in counter-terrorism had been recently recognized and protected in the framework of the ECHR. In our view, therefore, it is plausible

---

93 *Loizidou* v. *Turkey*, Application no. 1538/89, Eur. Ct. H. R., preliminary objection, Judgment of 23 March 1995, para. 75.
94 *Nada* v. *Switzerland*, para. 196.
95 *Ibid.*, para. 188.
96 *Ibid.*, para. 193.
97 Case T-85/09 *Kadi* v. *Commission* [2010] ECR II-05177.
98 Commission Regulation (EC) no. 1190/2008 of 28 November 2008 [2008] OJ L 322/25.
99 *Kadi II*, para. 133.

to maintain that *Nada* influenced the CJEU, encouraging it to keep a vanguard degree of human rights protection for suspected terrorists, the need to fight global terrorism notwithstanding.

The explanation for the influence that *Nada* may have exerted on the CJEU is to be found in the prospect of the accession of the EU to the ECHR. In the absence of a formal link between the EU and the ECHR, the relationship between two institutions was regulated by the case law of the ECtHR, which had excluded the possibility to review acts by the EU institutions,[100] save for the EU Treaties, which could not be subject to the scrutiny of the CJEU.[101] In *Bosphorus*,[102] in particular, the ECtHR affirmed that it would review EU measures through the national implementing acts only as an *ultima ratio*, if the overall EU system of human rights protection suddenly falls below the ECHR standard[103] and if 'in the circumstances of a particular case, it is considered that the protection of ECHR rights was manifestly deficient [at the EU level]'.[104] Under this test, Annalisa Ciampi had plausibly argued that a decision such as the one of the CFI in *Kadi* would not obtain a remedy before the ECtHR.[105]

After the accession of the EU to the ECHR, however, a major institutional change will take place in the relationship between the EU and the ECHR and their respective courts.[106] Since the EU will be a contracting party to the ECHR, there would be no reason for the ECtHR to preserve a deferential approach in reviewing action by the EU institutions, including the CJEU.[107] Rather, it seems likely that the ECtHR will adopt vis-à-vis the EU the same full standard of review it employs vis-à-vis the other contracting parties to the ECHR.

---

100 See *Confédération Française Démocratique du Travail* v. *EEC (CFDT)*, Application no. 8030/77, Eur. Comm. H. R, Decision of 10 July 1978.

101 *Matthews* v. *UK*, Application no. 24833/94, Eur. Ct. H. R. [GC], Judgment of 18 February 1999.

102 *Bosphorus* v. *Ireland*, Application no. 45036/98, Eur. Ct. H. R. [GC], Judgment of 30 June 2005.

103 See Steve Peers, 'Limited responsibility of European Union member states for action within the scope of Community law. Case note to *Bosphorus Airways* v. *Ireland*' (2006) 2 *European Constitutional Law Review* 443, 452 (arguing that 'the concept of conditional review as developed by the [ECtHR] is fraught with ambiguities and uncertainties and runs the risk that human rights will not be sufficiently guaranteed in certain cases').

104 *Bosphorus* v. *Ireland*, Application no. 45036/98, Eur. Ct. H. R. [GC], Judgment of 30 June 2005, para. 156.

105 Annalisa Ciampi, 'L'Union Européenne et le respect des droits de l'homme dans la mise en œuvre des sanctions devant la Cour Européenne des droits de l'homme' (2006) *Revue générale de droit international public* 85.

106 See Tobias Lock, 'The ECJ and the ECtHR: the future relationship between the two European courts' (2009) 8 *The Law and Practice of International Courts and Tribunals* 375.

107 But see the cautionary remarks of Olivier De Schutter, *The Two Lives of* Bosphorus: *Redefining the Relationship between the European Court of Human Rights and the Parties to the Convention*, CRIDHO Working Paper 2013/6.

As a result, any lowering of the standard of protection in the EU legal order would come under the scrutiny of the ECtHR.

Given that strong pressures continue to be exerted from the EU political branches, and a handful of EU member states, to maintain wide discretionary powers in the struggle against terrorism,[108] the risks of a possible watering-down of the EU standards of due process protection for suspected terrorists are quite real. In fact, this was made plain by the Opinion of AG Bot of 19 March 2013. AG Bot advised the CJEU to set aside the decision of the General Court, asking for 'moderation in the performance of judicial review'[109] in view of the security-sensitive and international nature of the subject matter as well as the improvements made in the UN sanctions regime. In doing so, the AG was prepared to sacrifice the promise of the CJEU's decision in *Kadi* to secure meaningful protection to due process rights to the applicant, as for him the judicial review of assessments made by the Sanctions Committee should be confined to cases of 'flagrant error' only.[110]

In its decision, however, the CJEU disavowed the advice of the AG and confirmed the substance of its earlier ruling on the requirement of a fully fledged judicial review. The Court clarified that the right to defence and to effective judicial protection entailed that the relevant EU authority had to disclose the available evidence, on which it based its decision, to the listed individual,[111] and that it is for the EU courts to verify whether this evidence is sufficient for the listing.[112] Hence, the Court embraced the rule 'either disclose or delist',[113] clarifying that it will disregard any reason advanced by the institutions to subject an individual to restrictive measures if that institution does not or cannot furnish it with a requisite amount of substantiating material.[114] The CJEU hereby reaffirmed (albeit without quoting it) the *ratio decidendi* of the ECtHR in *A. v. United Kingdom*,[115] i.e. that secrecy and confidentiality of the material cannot serve as a general excuse for the member states or institutions to withhold it.[116] For the CJEU, this represents a 'fair balance

---

108 See Deirdre Curtin and Christina Eckes, 'The *Kadi* case: mapping the boundaries between the executive and the judiciary in Europe' (2009) 5 *International Organizations Law Review* 365.

109 *Kadi II*, Opinion of Advocate General Bot of 19 March 2013, nyr, para. 80.

110 *Ibid.*, para. 110.

111 *Kadi II*, para. 111.

112 *Ibid.*, para. 119.

113 See for a more in-depth explanation of the operation of this rule, see Fabbrini, 'Global sanctions', 299–300.

114 *Kadi II*, para. 123.

115 *A. v. United Kingdom*, Application no. 3455/05, Eur. Ct. H. R. [GC], Judgment of 19 February 2009.

116 *Kadi II*, para. 125. On the problem of the disclosure of secret evidence (or the gist thereof) see also Daphne Barak-Erez, Matthew Waxman, 'Secret evidence and the due process of terrorist detention' (2009) 48 *Columbia Journal of Transnational Law* 3 and the research paper prepared for the UK Joint Committee on Human Rights: *The Use of Secret Evidence in Judicial Proceedings: A Comparative Survey* (OUP, 2011).

between the maintenance of international peace and security and the protection of the fundamental rights and freedoms... those being shared values of the UN and the European Union'.[117]

The fact that the CJEU disregarded the influential advice of the AG[118] and reaffirmed its commitment to a strong protection of human rights in the EU legal order becomes meaningful when seen in light of *Nada* and the prospect of the accession of the EU to the ECHR. The stand of the ECtHR contributed to 'lock in' the CJEU, preventing it from lowering in *Kadi II* the standard of protection it had erected in the *Kadi* judgment of 2008. Given the looming accession of the EU to the ECHR, it became harder for the CJEU to reconsider its previous position, as *de facto* advised by AG Bot.[119] Whereas, before accession, no external scrutiny of EU standards of protection was in place, once the accession will be accomplished, EU institutions, including EU courts, will be required to comply with the guarantees of the ECtHR. A future gap of protection generated in the EU by a low-level standard of due process protection would most likely not be tolerated by the ECtHR. In our view, therefore, the existence of a prospective control by the ECtHR on the action of the EU institutions persuaded the CJEU to maintain the high due process standard it framed in *Kadi*, preventing any re-emergence of challenges of ineffectiveness in the EU constitutional system.

Conclusion: pulling together for human rights

In conclusion, the dialogue between the CJEU and the ECtHR, against the backdrop of the opening of the ECHR to the EU, proved to be of great value in securing adequate protection of human rights in the European multilevel constitutional architecture.[120] The UN Security Council raised serious challenges to an effective protection of due process rights both in Luxembourg and Strasbourg. The joint efforts by the two transnational judicial bodies were instrumental in limiting excesses by the most powerful global executive organ – the UN Security Council.

In the combined story of *Kadi* and *Nada*, it was revealed how, in the context of UN-targeted anti-terror sanctions, a rivalling yet constructive relationship between the two courts worked in a beneficial manner for fundamental rights. As we sought to demonstrate, fuelled by the continuing shortcomings of the UN sanctions regime as well as by the prospect of the EU's

---

117 *Kadi II*, para. 131.
118 See Anthony Arnull, *The European Union and its Court of Justice* (2nd edn, OUP, 2006), 15 (noticing that 'most students of the Court would probably say that it is fairly unusual – although by no means unheard-of – for the Court to depart from the Opinion of its Advocate General').
119 See also *Kadi II*, paras. 60 et seq.
120 See also Federico Fabbrini, *Fundamental Rights in Europe: Challenges and Transformations in Comparative Perspective* (OUP, 2014), ch. 2.

accession to the ECHR, the ECtHR found in *Kadi I* a powerful argument to make the case for the persisting need to exercise judicial review even in the face of the UN Security Council. Subsequently, the *Nada* judgment helped the CJEU to stand its ground in the face of voices demanding to paddle back to a more deferential approach. Hence, both Strasbourg and Luxembourg, in their competition to be a 'bulwark' of human rights pulled together for the benefit of judicial protection in Europe. From *Kadi I* to *Nada* to *Kadi II*, European courts consistently struck the balance between global security and due process rights in a way that the latter is never eclipsed by the former.

12 The autonomy of EU law

A joint celebration of *Kadi II* and *Van Gend en Loos*

Giuseppe Martinico[1]

Introduction

This chapter develops an intuition by Gattini, according to whom *Kadi* (*I*[2]) would be 'a direct, if late, offspring of the *Van Gend en Loos* and *Costa/Enel* jurisprudence'.[3] Starting from this idea and on the occasion of the 50th anniversary of *Van Gend en Loos*,[4] this chapter aims to make a comparison between *Van Gend en Loos* and *Kadi II*[5], taken as emblematic of two different stages of the EU constitutionalization process.

While in *Van Gend en Loos* the idea of autonomy was used to construct the narrative of the *sui generis* nature of the Community legal order, in *Kadi* autonomy was employed to justify the stepping in of the Court of Justice of the European Union (CJEU) to protect some fundamental goods belonging to the European Union (EU) fundamental core, even in cases of unclear jurisdiction of the Court. The connecting thread between the two cases is represented by the idea of autonomy of a legal order, constructed in two different manners by the Court of Justice,[6] and by the attention paid to the 'individual', conceived as the holder of a set of rights stemming from European sources. In order to develop a comparison between these two decisions, this chapter is based on the distinction between *definition* and *identification*. 'Definition' comes from the Latin word *finis* (border, boundary) and refers to the act of making something distinct from something else.

---

1 Many thanks to Matej Avbelj, Giuseppe Bianco, Giacomo Delledonne, Filippo Fontanelli, Leonardo Pierdominici, and Marta Simoncini for their comments.
2 Joined Cases C-402/05 P and C-415/05 P, *Yassin Abdullah Kadi and Al Barakaat International Foundation* v. *Council and Commission* [2005] ECR, II-3649.
3 Andrea Gattini, 'Joined Cases C-402/05 P & 415/05 P, Yassin Abdullah Kadi, Al Barakaat International Foundation v. Council and Commission, Judgment of the Grand Chamber of 3 September 2008' (2009) 46 *Common Market Law Review*, 213, p. 224.
4 Case 26/62, *Van Gend en Loos* [1963] ECR 3.
5 Joined Cases C-584/10 P, C-593/10 P, and C-595/10 P, *Commission, Council, United Kingdom* v. *Yassin Abdullah Kadi*, nyr (www.curia.europa.it).
6 On the principle of autonomy of EU law see René Barents, *The Autonomy of Community Law* (Kluwer Law International, 2004).

One could describe this concept through the image of the 'wall-identity' – frequently employed by scholars in identity studies – whereas the other crucial step, consisting of the positive identification of some common elements through a moment of self-reflection, has been described with the formula 'mirror-identity'.[7] Both definition (corresponding to the 'wall-identity' moment) and identification (corresponding to the 'mirror-identity' phase) are classical in any process of identity-building. In other words, in a first moment the Luxembourg Court clarified what 'Community law is not', while in a second moment it tried to show what 'Community law' is by means of some elements that are treated as an 'indicator' of its speciality, because they are supposed to belong to its unchangeable core. According to this reading, *Van Gend en Loos* was on the definition of the Community legal order as *sui generis* and autonomous, while *Kadi* was more on the identification of the untouchable core of this special legal order.[8]

Van Gend en Loos: the (external) boundaries of the autonomy doctrine

Why is everybody interested in the *Kadi* saga? Of course there are many reasons for this, but I would limit myself to three main elements – first of all, because *Kadi* deals with several substantive and procedural issues that have attracted the attention of scholars with different backgrounds (EU lawyers, constitutional lawyers, public international lawyers, legal theorists, administrative law scholars etc.). The present book is testimony to this. Secondly, the *Kadi* saga is

---

7 Furio Cerutti, 'Political identity and conflict: a comparison of definitions', in Furio Cerutti, Rodolfo Ragionieri (eds), *Identities and Conflicts* (Palgrave, 2001) 9–17. 'Furio Cerruti has, in a text dealing with group identities and political identities, suggested two metaphorical concepts that can be used as analytical tools: the mirror-identity and the wall-identity. The mirror identity is dependent on the values, normative principles, life forms and life styles, within which a group recognises itself. This process essentially consists of the group members recognising or mirroring themselves in those values, and through this mirroring they form their image as a group "Self", as something that gives sense to their behaviour as a group. The mirror identity creates a "we" but it does not create an "other". The wall-identity, on the other hand, is more ambivalent. A wall gives support; it gives consistency to a group, preventing disintegration in times of political or social crises. A wall is also enclosing; it separates the group from other groups; it efficiently shuts out the Other. Which of the two walls will dominate or prevail depends on the wall's constitutive elements (universal integrative or self centred-exclusive) as well as on the trials (e.g. existential or political threats) to which the group is subjected', K.G. Hammarlund, 'Between the mirror and the wall: boundary and identity in Peter Weiss' novel *Die Ästhetik des Widerstands*', in K.G. Hammarlund (ed.), *Borders as Experience* (Forskning i Halmstad, 2009) 117–29, p. 117.
8 For a similar point see Daniel Sarmiento, 'The EU's constitutional core', in Alejandro Saiz Arnaiz, Carina Alcoberro Llivina (eds), *National Constitutional Identity and European Integration* (Intersentia, 2013) 177–204; Nikolaos Lavranos, 'Revisiting Article 307 EC: the untouchable core of fundamental European constitutional law values', in Paolo Carrozza, Filippo Fontanelli, Giuseppe Martinico (eds), *Shaping Rule of Law through Dialogue: International and Supranational Experiences* (Europa Law Publishing, 2010) 119–46.

a *summa* of many of the traditional arguments employed in the 'Classics' of the Court of Justice[9] (*Van Gend en Loos*, *Costa/Enel*,[10] *Les Verts*,[11] *Opinion 1/91*[12] etc.). Finally, these proceedings have conveyed the image of an arena where different conceptions about the nature of EU law have fought against each other.

Indeed, almost unanimously, *Kadi I* has been seen as a perfect representation of the jurisprudential boldness of the CJEU, as it was very rich in 'constitutional intimations'[13] and 'constitutional symbolism'.[14] *Kadi I* also recalled the idea of a community based on the rule of law and, more concretely, that of a complete and coherent system of judicial protection[15] (all elements retaken from the *Les Verts* doctrine). These references marked the continuity with the jurisprudence of the foundation of Community law,[16] in particular with *Van Gend en Loos*, as Gattini and others aptly pointed out:

> On the one hand, one can not but welcome the unbending commitment of the European Court of Justice to the respect of fundamental human rights, but on the other hand the relatively high price, in terms of coherence and unity of the international legal system, that had to be paid in order to arrive at the conclusion of the invalidity of the contested Regulation, is worrying. Of course, one might argue that the ECJ was all too willing to pay that price, and that it could have even felt it as no price at all, but as a golden opportunity to bring a step further the proclaimed 'constitutionalization' and autonomy of the Community legal system. The *Kadi* judgment is a direct, if late, offspring of the *van Gend en Loos* and *Costa/Enel* jurisprudence, and, without wanting to sound too rhetorical, one might even venture to say that similarly to those decisions it will be a landmark in the history of EC law.[17]

However, a closer look at *Van Gend en Loos* reveals that the label 'constitutional' was not in the text of the decision. On the contrary, on that occasion the

9 Loïc Azoulai, Miguel Poiares Maduro (eds), *The Past and the Future of EU law. The Classics of EU law on the 50th Anniversary of the Rome Treaty* (Oxford, 2010).
10 6/64, *Costa/Enel*, [1964] ECR 1141.
11 294/83, *Parti Ecologiste 'Les Verts' v. Parliament*, [1986] ECR 1365.
12 Opinion 1/91, Draft Agreement relating to the creation of the European Economic Area [1991] ECR I-6079.
13 Neil Walker, 'Opening or closure? The constitutional intimations of the ECJ', in n. 9, Azoulai, Maduro (eds), *The Past and the Future*, 333.
14 *Ibid.*
15 See the contributions by Koen Lenaerts, 'The basic constitutional charter of a community based on the rule of law'; Jean-Paul Jacqué, '*Les Verts* v. the European Parliament'; Alemanno Alemanno, 'What has been, and what could be, thirty years after Les Verts/European Parliament', in Azoulai, Maduro (eds), *The Past and the Future*.
16 Franz Mayer, 'Van Gend en Loos: *The Foundation of a Community of Law*', in n. 9, Azoulai, Maduro (eds), *The Past and the Future*, 16–25.
17 Andrea Gattini, 'Joined Cases C-402/05 P', 224.

reference to international law came with no sign of a constitutional vocabulary. In fact, the Court of Justice used a much more ambiguous formulation to
separate the destiny of its own community from that of the other international
organizations, since it described the system of the Treaties as 'a new legal order
of international law for the benefit of which the states have limited their sovereign rights'.[18]

When commenting on these lines Franz Mayer argued that: 'The formula
used by the Court to describe the European construct, however, has evolved
over the years, replacing the reference to international law with a reference to
constitutional law.'[19] In other words, the constitutional 'vocabulary' did not
come (at least immediately) together with the ideology of autonomy.[20] This
ambiguity (neither fully international nor fully constitutional) is at the
essence of the *sui generis* narrative of supranational law and was probably unintended at that time. Yet, it has thrived over the years also for strategic
reasons, to afford the Court an escape from the straitjacket categories of
public international law and, at the same time, spare it from being subject to
the laws of the member states.[21] However, it is correct to notice that in *Van
Gend en Loos*, the Luxembourg Court proclaimed the autonomy of Community
law, but did not exhaust the revolutionary moment.

As Mayer again pointed out, this concept was not defined in an isolated
moment by the CJEU. This happened over time, through a long series of
decisions: for instance in *Costa* v. *Enel* the Court slightly changed the terminology, by describing Community law in the following terms: 'By contrast
with ordinary international treaties, the EEC treaty has created its own legal
system which, on the entry into force of the treaty, became an integral part of
the legal systems of the member states and which their courts are bound to
apply.'[22]

Going even beyond, in *Les Verts*, it finally employed the constitutional
language:

> It must first be emphasized in this regard that the European economic
> community is a community based on the rule of law, inasmuch as neither
> its member states nor its institutions can avoid a review of the question
> whether the measures adopted by them are in conformity with the basic
> constitutional charter, the treaty.[23]

---

18 *Van Gend en Loos*.
19 Franz Mayer, 'Van Gend en Loos: the foundation', 20, see n. 16.
20 Deirdre Curtin, 'The shaping of a European constitution and the 1996 IGC: flexibility as
   a key paradigm?' (1995) 50 Aussenwirtschaft 237.
21 On this process see Matej Avbelj, 'The pitfalls of (comparative) constitutionalism for
   European integration', *Eric Stein Working Paper* (2008), p. 1 (http://papers.ssrn.com/sol3/
   papers.cfm?abstract_id=1334216) (accessed 28 September 2013).
22 *Costa/Enel*.
23 *Les Verts*.

However, from the beginning many authors have described *Van Gend en Loos* as characterized by a constitutional afflatus[24] and there is no doubt that, because of this impact over the history of EU law, this decision can be defined as foundational and, therefore, constitutional in the etymological sense of the word (constitution from *constituere* = to found, to establish), despite the absence of a constitutional terminology. In order to solve this terminological impasse, it is maybe useful to recall that 'constitutonalization' has traditionally been used in two ways by EU law scholars. Normally by the formula 'constitutionalization' of the EU legal order, authors[25] mean the progressive shift of Community law from the perspective of an international organization to that of a (quasi) federal state. To this aim, the idea of direct effect (*Van Gend en Loos*) and primacy (*Costa/Enel*) have been crucial in 'federalizing' Community law, making national judges the key actors of this process of integration.[26]

However, there is also a different meaning to the constitutionalization process of the EU legal order, which refers to the progressive 'humanization' (i.e. the progressive affirmation of the human rights issue at supranational level) of the law of the common market.[27]

Of course these two meanings are related[28] and connected to a broader process of polity building (even in terms of the politicization of the Union), but it is possible to say that the foundational jurisprudence of autonomy implies a move in constitutional terms (understood *lato sensu*), while the post-*Internationale Handelsgesellschaft*[29] case law implies a move in constitutional terms understood *stricto sensu*.

In the next sections I focus on the *Kadi* saga by showing its 'added value' in the history of EU law. My point is that *Van Gend en Loos, Costa v. Enel*, and many other decisions of the foundational period marked the existence of a difference (by the means of a kind of *actio finium regundorum*), but they did not clarify the 'content' of such a special legal order. This happened later, when

24 Daniel Halberstam, 'Pluralism in Marbury and Van Gend', in Azoulai, Maduro (eds), *The Past and the Future*, 26–36, see n. 9.

25 For example, Marta Cartabia, Joseph H. H. Weiler, *L'Italia in Europa* (Mulino, 2000), 73 ff. About the ambiguity of the notion of constitutionalization in EC/EU law see Francis Snyder, 'The unfinished constitution of the European Union', in Joseph H. H. Weiler, Marlene Wind (eds), *European Constitutionalism beyond the State* (Cambridge University Press, 2003) 55–73.

26 On this idea of constitutionalization as federalisation see Eric Stein, 'Lawyers, judges and the making of a transnational constitution' (1981) 75 *American Journal of International Law* 1; Peter Hay, *Federalism and Supranational Organizations. Patterns for New Legal Structures* (University of Illinois Press, 1966); Peter Hay, 'Supremacy of Community law in national courts. A progress report on referrals under the EEC Treaty' (1968) 16 *American Journal of Comparative Law* 524.

27 On this process, see Koen Lenaerts, 'Fundamental rights in the European Union', (2000) 25 *European Law Review* 575 ff.

28 Joseph H. H. Weiler, 'The transformation of Europe', (1991) 100 *Yale Law Journal* 2403.

29 11/70, *Internationale Handelsgesellschaft*, [1970] ECR 1125.

the CJEU progressively paid attention to fundamental rights issues, conceiving the constitutionalization process no longer as a mere shift from the categories of public international law to something else (either expressly definable as constitutional or not), but also as a legal phenomenon characterized by some principles aimed at protecting fundamental goods, like human rights. This way the Court of Justice filled the empty and ideological box of autonomy.

Autonomy as 'appropriation': the *Kadi* saga

The *Kadi* saga responds to a double logic: on the one hand, it develops from a strong perception of EU law autonomy, while on the other hand it reflects the idea of the existence of a mature system in terms of fundamental rights protection. These ideas of autonomy and maturity has been used by the CJEU as a fundamental premise to justify its intervention in a rather sensitive case from a legal (and geopolitical) point of view. Indeed, at first sight, the *Kadi* saga seems to feature a progressive 'appropriation' of a question which was originally presented as an issue regulated by an external set of norms belonging to public international law (i.e. one can perceive in this saga the progressive efforts made by the Court of Justice at 'internalizing' the legal questions at stake).[30]

In *Kadi I* the former Court of First Instance admitted the possibility of reviewing the regulation that implemented the UN resolution only in case of violation of *jus cogens*, that is to say a corpus of norms originally alien to the body of EU law.[31] This was a consequence of the approach chosen by the Court of First Instance, which adopted as point of reference a set of norms that do not belong to the EU legal order understood *stricto sensu*, i.e. norms of international law. On the contrary, moving to the Opinion of Advocate General Maduro in *Kadi I*,[32] one

---

30 For a similar approach see Marise Cremona, *European Law and International Law after Kadi*, speech given at Bristol University on 3 November 2008 (available at http://denning. law.ox.ac.uk/news/events_files/European_Law_and_international_law_after_Kadi.pdf) (accessed 28 September 2013).

31 T-315/01 *Kadi* v. *Council and Commission* [2005] ECR II-3649, para. 226: 'None the less, the Court is empowered to check, indirectly, the lawfulness of the resolutions of the Security Council in question with regard to jus cogens, understood as a body of higher rules of public international law binding on all subjects of international law, including the bodies of the United Nations, and from which no derogation is possible.' See also paras. 213–15.

32 Joined Cases C-402/05 P and C-415/05 P, *Kadi and Al Barakaat*, Opinion of Advocate General Poiares Maduro [2008] ECR I-6351, especially at para. 34: 'The implication that the present case concerns a "political question", in respect of which even the most humble degree of judicial interference would be inappropriate, is, in my view, untenable. The claim that a measure is necessary for the maintenance of international peace and security cannot operate so as to silence the general principles of Community law and deprive individuals of their fundamental rights. This does not detract from the importance of the interest in maintaining international peace and security; it simply means that it remains the duty of the courts to assess the lawfulness of measures that may conflict with other interests that are equally of great importance and with the protection of which the courts are entrusted.'

can realize that his point of departure was very different, since he focused on stressing the potential violation by the United Nations (UN) resolution of some norms peculiar to EU law. By following a similar line *Kadi I* of the Court of Justice constantly referred to the autonomy of EU law[33], but the Court went even further on that occasion. Indeed, the issue of the autonomy of EU law was more emphasized, as the Court neglected what was an essential step in the Opinion of the Advocate General: the analysis of the question from the viewpoint of former art. 307 of the Treaty on the European Community (TEC).[34]

Starting from former art. 307 TEC, the Advocate General in *Kadi I* attempted to stress that no obligations envisaged therein can be interpreted 'so as to silence the general principles of Community law and deprive individuals of their fundamental rights'.[35] Coherently with this reconstruction, it was fundamental to find the right way for the European order to interact with the international legal order's obligations and judges.

It is not a coincidence that the Advocate General devoted several lines of his Opinion to recall the importance of judicial deference in the relationship between the Court of Justice and other judges. This deference, though, must find a limit in the possible risk for the fundamental values of the EU legal order: 'Consequently, in situations where the Community's fundamental values are in the balance, the Court may be required to reassess, and possibly annul, measures adopted by the Community institutions, even when those measures reflect the wishes of the Security Council.'[36]

---

33 See, for instance, para. 282 of *Kadi I* of the Court of Justice: 'It is also to be recalled that an international agreement cannot affect the allocation of powers fixed by the Treaties or, consequently, the autonomy of the Community legal system, observance of which is ensured by the Court by virtue of the exclusive jurisdiction conferred on it by Article 220 EC, jurisdiction that the Court has, moreover, already held to form part of the very foundations of the Community (see, to that effect, Opinion 1/91 [1991] ECR I-6079, paras. 35 and 71, and Case C-459/03 *Commission* v. *Ireland* [2006] ECR I-4635, paragraph 123 and case-law cited).'

34 Former art. 307 TEC (now art. 351 TFEU) reads: 'The rights and obligations arising from agreements concluded before 1 January 1958 or, for acceding States, before the date of their accession, between one or more Member States on the one hand, and one or more third countries on the other, shall not be affected by the provisions of this Treaty.

'To the extent that such agreements are not compatible with this Treaty, the Member State or States concerned shall take all appropriate steps to eliminate the incompatibilities established. Member States shall, where necessary, assist each other to this end and shall, where appropriate, adopt a common attitude.

'In applying the agreements referred to in the first paragraph, Member States shall take into account the fact that the advantages accorded under this Treaty by each Member State form an integral part of the establishment of the Community and are thereby inseparably linked with the creation of common institutions, the conferring of powers upon them and the granting of the same advantages by all the other Member States.' On this see Nikolaos Lavranos, 'Revisiting Article 307 EC'.

35 Opinion of Advocate General Poiares Maduro, para. 34.

36 *Ibid.*, para. 44.

In the Advocate General's own words, these values represent 'the constitutional framework created by the Treaty'.[37] In its reasoning, the CJEU seemed to pay more attention to the peculiar nature of the EU legal order than to its relationship with international law. This can be noticed by looking at the use of the idea of autonomy employed in the decision. Thus, one could say that the Court of Justice's initial assumptions were more unilateral, since they were not centred around the terms of the relationship between international and EU law, but rather around the constitutional and peculiar nature of EU law. This is also proved by the fact that the Court of Justice missed the opportunity to clarify the scope of art. 307, for example, specifying 'its position on the consequences if the "appropriate steps" of Member States remain unsuccessful'.[38]

In sum, in *Kadi I* the Court of Justice disregarded former art. 307 TEC following a precise argumentative strategy: the need to contextualize the question of the relationship between international and community law within the boundaries of its own legal order. It could then give the question an 'internal answer' and insist on the values of its own 'order'.

I think that *Kadi II*[39] can be read coherently with *Kadi I* of the CJEU, although the two decisions differ for some reasons – first of all for the language employed by the Luxembourg Court in *Kadi II*. Indeed, it is evident from initial analysis that *Kadi II* does not present the powerful rhetoric contained in *Kadi I*. The adjective 'constitutional' was employed 14 times in *Kadi I*, while 'constitutional' is recalled just twice in *Kadi II* and it should be stressed that in the first of these two citations[40] the CJEU was summing up the decision held in 2008. Another evident difference in the terminology employed by the CJEU is the absence of the word 'autonomy' in *Kadi II*. These remarks might lead to considering *Kadi II* as different from *Kadi I*, but when looking at the substance of the decision it is possible to find strong continuity.[41]

In *Kadi II*, the Court rejected the argument according to which the challenged Regulation enjoyed immunity from judicial review. It did so relying on its previous decision and borrowing the same reasoning, since 'there has been no change in those factors which could justify reconsideration of that position' (para. 66). As a consequence, all EU acts must be reviewed for compliance with fundamental rights (para. 67). It also confirmed that the

---

37 Moreover: 'The relationship between international law and the Community legal order is governed by the Community legal order itself, and international law can permeate that legal order only under the conditions set by the constitutional principles of the Community' (*ibid.*, para. 24).
38 Gattini, 'Joined Cases', 235.
39 Joined Cases C-584/10 P, C-593/10 P, and C-595/10 P, *Commission, Council, United Kingdom v. Yassin Abdullah Kadi*, not yet reported (www.curia.europa.it).
40 *Kadi II*, paras. 21–2.
41 *Contra* see Lavranos and Vatsov, ch. 9 this volume.

intensity of the review, in principle, must be full, thus standing by its precedent. The CJEU also showed not to suffer from the pressure coming from an international context and academic circles, as it was not afraid of the possible impact of this decision over similar delisting cases. It constructed the controversy as a 'domestic' case for at least two reasons: first, because the issue concerned an EU act; secondly, because it was about a possible violation of some fundamental rights protected by the EU legal order.

Thus, the CJEU confirmed the approach followed in *Kadi I* and the idea of autonomy stemming from that decision. In conclusion, the first way to read *Kadi II* by the CJEU is therefore the asymmetry existing between the form of this decision (which seems to abandon the bombastic approach used in *Kadi I*) and the substance of the judgment which maintains its approach towards public international law. Despite the different terminology employed, if one goes beyond form and looks at the substance one can see that the confirmation of the idea 'in principle full review' confirms the strong claims of *Kadi I*.

In order to do so, the CJEU even defended the core of the decision taken by the General Court (former Court of First Instance) in *Kadi II*.[42] On that occasion the General Court had accepted to revise its previous decision and to comply with the revolutionary decision of the Court of Justice, serving as a 'loyal soldier', despite the many doubts it had on the decision of the CJEU.[43] This is evident in those passages where the General Court wanted to recall the decisions of other courts or tribunals which had shared the original position of the former Court of First Instance[44]. In *Kadi II* the CJEU defended the core of the decision of the General Court endorsing the idea according to which the EU presents an untouchable nucleus of principles that may not be jeopardized by international law, not even by the UN Charter[45].

---

42 T-85/09 *Kadi* v. Commission [2010] ECR II-5177.

43 *Ibid.*, para. 121.

44 'It should be observed, as an ancillary point, that, although some higher national courts have adopted a rather similar approach to that taken by this Court in its judgment in Kadi (see, to that effect, the decision of the Tribunal fédéral de Lausanne (Switzerland) of 14 November 2007 in Case 1A.45/2007 Youssef Mustapha Nada v. Secrétariat d'État pour l'Économie and the judgment of the House of Lords (United Kingdom) in Al-Jedda v. Secretary of State for Defence [2007] UKHL 58, which is currently the subject of an action pending before the European Court of Human Rights (Case No 227021/08 Al-Jedda v. United Kingdom), others have tended to follow the approach taken by the Court of Justice, holding the Sanctions Committee's system of designation to be incompatible with the fundamental right to effective review before an independent and impartial court (see, to that effect, the judgment of the Federal Court of Canada of 4 June 2009 in Abdelrazik v. Canada (Minister of Foreign Affairs) 2009 FC 580, cited at paragraph 69 of the UK Supreme Court judgment in Ahmed and Others)' (*ibid.*, para. 122).

45 At the same time, the CJEU recognized that the General Court had erred in law in paras. 138–40 and 142–9 but also confirmed that these errors did not vitiate the validity of the decision under appeal.

Reading the *Kadi* saga in context: the CJEU between definition and identification

As we saw, the *sui generis* narrative created by foundational decisions like *Van Gend en Loos* and *Costa* responds to the need for a demarcation from the rest of international law without the need to further label (at least, not immediately) its nature as 'constitutional' and without the effort to determine the very peculiar content of this new legal order. In the last part of this contribution, I seek to show that *Kadi II* belongs to a new generation of decisions in which the CJEU does not merely proclaim EU law autonomy from both national and international laws, but sets out to identify a constitutional core of principles whose violation justifies its intervention even in cases of dubious jurisdiction.

As Rosas and Armati pointed out: 'in *Kadi*, the ECJ confirmed and made more explicit a tendency discernible in previous case-law according to which the EU constitutional order consists of some core principles which may prevail over provisions of the Treaties and thus of written primary law.'[46] This is evident from the wording of *Kadi I*, whereby the Court of Justice maintained that:

> Article 307 EC may in no circumstances permit any challenge to the principles that form part of the very foundations of the Community legal order, which include the principles of liberty, democracy and respect for human rights and fundamental freedoms enshrined in Article 6(1) EU as a foundation of the Union (para. 304).

When doing so, the Court of Justice acts as many Constitutional Courts do: in fact, in these cases the CJEU selects a group of principles which may not be jeopardized because their violation would imply the denial of the axiological bases on which the EU legal order is founded. At national level, constitutional law scholars call this set of principles in different ways – 'Republican form' (*'forma repubblicana'*[47]) in Italy, 'eternity clause' (*'Ewigkeitsklause'*[48]) in Germany [49] – but in the concrete task of identifying the principles that may be traced back to such an untouchable core a primary role has always been played by constitutional judges. This has happened with particular regard to human rights, whose language has been codified by national constitutions *grosso modo* since the end of World War II.

This codification of rights has made those norms aimed at protecting rights constitutional principles, and the rights protected by such constitutional principles have become fundamental rights, i.e. meta-norms of many contemporary

---

46 Allan Rosas, Lorna Armati, *EU Constitutional Law. An Introduction* (Hart, 2011) 43.
47 Art. 139 of the Italian Constitution.
48 Art. 79 para. (3) of the Basic Law (*Grundgesetz-GG*) of the Federal Republic of Germany.
49 For an overview of these claues see Francesco Palermo, *La forma di stato dell'Unione europea. Per una teoria costituzionale dell'integrazione sovranazionale* (Cedam, 2005).

legal orders. 'Fundamental rights are to be understood as encompassing those selective and substantive criteria which, together with others, enable judgments of "validity": the recognition of belonging to a legal order, legitimacy, compatibility of institutional behaviour and norms within a given legal-political system.'[50] Other evidences of this approach may be found in the case law of the CJEU. For instance, in some cases the CJEU has acknowledged the existence of a group of rights that cannot be subjected to any form of balancing, i.e. absolute rights. An example of this way to proceed is *Schmidberger*[51] where the Court of Justice distinguished between two groups of fundamental rights: the absolute rights (which admit no restrictions) and other fundamental rights. Concerning the second category of rights, the Court of Justice admitted the necessity to evaluate, through a case-by-case approach, the proportionality of their possible restrictions.[52] By doing so, the Luxembourg Court paved the way for the creation of a hierarchy of principles (and rights).

The *Kadi* saga follows a parallel line and, with *Zambrano*,[53] belongs to the moment of concrete identification of a set of values shared and which it is necessary to fight for. Scholars[54] have already compared *Kadi* and *Zambrano*, reading them as a part of an important case law concerning this process of identity

---

50 Gianluigi Palombella, 'From human rights to fundamental rights. Consequences of a conceptual distinction', *EUI Working Paper* LAW no. 2006/34, 2006 (http://cadmus.eui. eu/bitstream/handle/1814/6400/LAW-2006-34.pdf;jsessionid=57A331FDFF3245D221C 04E57E8469D36?sequence=1) (accessed 28 September 2013).

51 C-112/00 Schmidberger [2003] ECR I-5659.

52 'Thus, unlike other fundamental rights enshrined in that Convention, such as the right to life or the prohibition of torture and inhuman or degrading treatment or punishment, which admit of no restriction, neither the freedom of expression nor the freedom of assembly guaranteed by the ECHR appears to be absolute but must be viewed in relation to its social purpose. Consequently, the exercise of those rights may be restricted, provided that the restrictions in fact correspond to objectives of general interest and do not, taking account of the aim of the restrictions, constitute disproportionate and unacceptable interference, impairing the very substance of the rights guaranteed' (C- 112/00 Schmidberger [2003] ECR I-5659, para. 80).

53 C-34/09, *Gerardo Ruiz Zambrano* v. *Office national de l'emploi (ONEm)* [2011] ECR I-01177. On Zambrano see Kay Hailbronner, Daniel Thym, 'Case C-34/09, Gerardo Ruiz Zambrano v. Office national de l'emploi (ONEM), Judgment of the Court of Justice (Grand Chamber) of 8 Mar. 2011' (2011) 48 *Common Market Law Review* 1253; Anja Wiesbrock, 'The Zambrano case: relying on Union citizenship rights in "internal situations"' (9 March 2011) (http://eudo-citizenship.eu/news/citizenship-news/449-the-zambrano-case-relying-on-union-citizenship-rights-in-internal-situations) (accessed 28 September 2013); Alicia Hinarejos, 'Extending citizenship and the scope of EU law' (2011) 70 *The Cambridge Law Journal* 309. To understand Zambrano see also C-135/08 *Janko Rottmann* v. *Freistaat Bayern* [2010] ECR, I-01449; C- 434-09, *Shirley McCarthy* v. *Secretary of State for the Home Department*, [2011] ECR, I-03375; C-256/11, *Dereci and others* v. *Bundesministerium für Inneres*, nyr; C-40/11 *Iida*, nyr; Joined Cases C 356/11 and C 357/11 Judgment, *O, S* v. *Maahanmuuttovirasto* and *Maahanmuuttovirasto* v. *L.*, nyr; C 87/12, *Kreshnik Ymeraga*, nyr (available at www.curia.europa.eu).

54 For instance Sarmiento, 'The EU's constitutional core'.

building. When commenting on them, authors like von Bogdandy[55] argued the existence of an untouchable core of fundamental rights protected by EU law and opposable to the international community or to the EU member states.

These two decisions are different and similar at the same time. They have been criticized by scholars and they are both expressions of a proactive Court. Both of them are 'muscular' judgments, showing a militant conception[56] of the role of the Luxembourg Court, since they share the interventionist attitude of the Court in case of deprivation[57] of those fundamental rights belonging to this untouchable core. And they are both based on a kind of presumption in favour of the domestic (in *Zambrano*) or international (*Kadi*) level which leads the CJEU to consider its intervention as a kind of *extrema ratio*.

At the same time, they show important differences: the 'interlocutors' first of all, are the UN in the *Kadi* saga, the member states in *Zambrano*. The grounds of criticism are different: despite its diplomatic impact, in *Kadi* the intervention of the CJEU is justified by the existence of an EU legal act, while in *Zambrano* the CJEU intervened in a situation that according to many was purely internal.[58] In *Zambrano* the Court delivered a revolutionary judgment in a few pages, characterized by poor, obscure legal reasoning[59] and left many questions open; it is the product of a Court which is afraid of its own activism. *Kadi* was, instead, criticized for being too unilateral, even 'chauvinist and parochial'.[60] Many scholars were sure that another decision like that was hardly possible but the CJEU reiterated its message to the international community, confirming the boldness of the Court.[61]

This leads me to my last point. *Kadi I* (but the same applies to *Kadi II*) has been accused of being conducive to systemic conflicts, of being 'blind' from a diplomatic point of view.[62] However, when accepting the point that in *Kadi I*

---

55 Armin Von Bogdandy, Matthias Kottmann, Carlino Antpöhler, Johanna Dickschen, Simon Hentrei, Maja Smrkolj, 'Reverse Solange. Protecting the essence of fundamental rights against EU member states' (2012) 49 *Common Market Law Review* 489.

56 On the idea of militant democracy see Karl Loewenstein, 'Militant democracy and fundamental rights, I', *American* (1937) 31 *Political Science Review* 417.

57 Sarmiento, 'The EU's constitutional core', 186–7.

58 See the powerful Opinion of Advocate General Sharpston to the Zambrano case, especially para. 90 and ff.

59 For an analysis of this aspect see Urška Šadl, 'Ruiz Zambrano as an illustration of how the Court of Justice of the European Union constructs its legal arguments' (2013) 9 *European Constitutional Law Review* 205.

60 Gráinne de Búrca 'The European Court of Justice and the international legal order after Kadi' (2010) 51 *Harvard International Law Journal* 1. See also Luis. I. Gordillo Pérez, *Interlocking Constitutions: Towards an Interordinal Theory of National, European and UN Law* (Hart, 2012) 305.

61 Compare, for a different approach, the decision of the CJEU with the Opinion given by AG Bot to to *Kadi II*.

62 On this debate see Joris Larik, 'Two ships in the night or in the same boat together: how the ECJ squared the circle and foreshadowed Lisbon in its Kadi judgment' (2010) 13 *Yearbook of Polish European Studies* 149.

and *II* the CJEU assumed a constitutional approach, these considerations lose appeal and the conclusion repeated by the CJEU becomes coherent with the premises of the decision (the existence of a strong axiological core in EU law). In this sense one should look at *Kadi II* as an emblematic judgment which goes beyond the particular situation of Mr Kadi. A confirmation is given by the choice of the Court to face the question frontally in spite of the occurred delisting of Kadi[63] and of the very different approach suggested by Advocate General Bot. It is now to be seen whether *Kadi I* and *II* will influence the long list of pending cases in this field, but probably the CJEU thought it necessary to send a strong message to the UN, just to make clear the bases of a future convergence. It would not be the first time in the history of the EU, and even on a comparative level it is possible to detect similar decisions rendered by domestic courts. There they either insist on the need to preserve constitutional rights at the domestic level in order to 'justify' the breach of some international obligations (like in *Kadi*)[64] or they allow federal intervention in a state domain (like in *Rottmann* or *Zambrano*) on the basis of the necessary preservation of those homogeneity clauses through which the federal Constitution limits the fundamental charters of its member states.[65]

Indeed, those who criticize *Kadi I* and *II* may have forgotten the importance that conflicts have traditionally had in the development of the EU legal order. It is sufficient to think of the genesis of art. 6 TEU – codifying the human rights commitment of the EU – to find proof of this. Indeed, this Article was the by-product of a long confrontation between Constitutional Courts and the Court of Justice, started in the 1970s after the delivery of *Internationale Handelsgesellschaft*[66] which triggered the reaction of the national constitutional

---

63 One might argue that the Court has deliberately chosen not to exercise its discretionary power to discontinue the case for having become 'devoid of purpose' in the light of art. 149 of the Rules of Procedure, for instance. On this, see the considerations made by Fontanelli, ch. 2 this volume.

64 For instance, Madras High Court, *Novartis Novartis* v. *Union of India & Others*, Judgment of 6 August 2007 (available at http://judis.nic.in/judis_chennai/qrydispfree. aspx?filename=11121) (accessed 7 October 2013): 'We have borne in mind the object which the Amending Act wanted to achieve namely,... to provide easy access to the citizens of this country to life saving drugs and to discharge the [legislature's] Constitutional obligation of providing good health care to it's [*sic*] citizens' (para. 19). On this see Eyal Benvenisti, George W. Downs, 'National courts, domestic democracy, and the evolution of international law' (2009) 20 *European Journal of International Law* 72. More recently (on 1 April 2013) even the Supreme Court of India ruled on the case (http://supremecourtofindia.nic.in/outtoday/ patent.pdf) (accessed 7 October 2013).

65 For instance art. 28 of the Basic Law (*Grundgesetz-GG*) of the Federal Republic of Germany. On this see Francesco Palermo, *La forma di stato dell'Unione europea*.

66 11/70, *Internationale Handelsgesellschaft* [1970] ECR 1125 whereby the Court of Justice stated: 'the validity of a Community measure or its effect within a Member State cannot be affected by allegations that it runs counter to either fundamental rights as formulated by the constitution of that State or the principles of a national constitutional structure' (para. 3).

guardians with the well-known *Solange*[67] and counter-limits[68] doctrines. Without entering the debate on the similarities (and differences[69]) existing between *Kadi* and *Solange*[70], the *Solange* and the counter-limits doctrines are a perfect example of the importance of constitutional conflicts for the development of the EU legal order. They represented a potential crisis of the European process which actually served as a turning point, opening a new season in the case law of the CJEU and of the constitutional courts.

This does not mean that after that season of confrontation conflicts faded away. On the contrary, judicial clashes are still frequent in the life of the multi-level legal order. This is consistent with the explanations given by scholars interested in conflicts:[71] although the actors operating in this arena now share the necessity to respect those constitutional goods conceived as fundamental rights according to the multilevel case law, it is always possible to have interpretative disagreements. I think this is the description which best explains the current state of the relationship between constitutional courts and the CJEU: they are competitors and antagonists, but this is not pathological at all, as it also occurs in other contexts.[72]

More in general, conflicts belong to the life of constitutional polities. This has been demonstrated by scholars in sociology and political science (mainly with regard to social conflicts[73]), but conflicts also belong to the essence of

67 BVerfGE 37, 271 (*Solange I*); English translation at [1974] 2 CMLR 540; 73, 339 (*Solange II*); English translation at [1987] 3 CMLR 225. See also *BVerfGE* 89, 155, *BVerfGE* 102, 147.

68 This formula has been introduced into the Italian scholarly debate by Paolo Barile, 'Ancora su diritto comunitario e diritto interno', in *Studi per il XX anniversario dell'Assemblea costituente*, VI (Vallecchi, 1969), 33–54, 49. For this doctrine see Corte Costituzionale, Decision no. 183 of 18 December 1973; see also Decision no. 170 of 5 June 1984 and Decision no. 232 of 13 April 1989.

69 'The difference, however, is that the ECJ, in its own understanding, is not such an international supervisory body [a human rights supervisory body] but a juridical body analogous to a domestic court' (Andrea Gattini, 'Joined Cases', 234–5).

70 See Tzanakopoulos, ch. 10 this volume.

71 Chantal Mouffe, *The Return of the Political* (Verso, 1993); Chantal Mouffe, *The Democratic Paradox* (Verso, 2000); Chantal Mouffe, *On the Political* (Routledge, 2005).

72 Daniel Halberstam, 'Constitutional heterarchy: the centrality of conflict in the European Union and the United States', in Jeffrey Dunoff, Joel Trachtman (eds), *In Ruling the World? Constitutionalism, International Law and Global Governance* (Cambridge University Press, 2009) 326–55: 'In one important sense, however, the relationship between the European Union and its Member States is, of course, different from that between the United States and the several states. In the United States, the relationship between federal and state law, and, in particular, between the federal Supreme Court and the state judiciary, are fully ordered... In the European Union, by contrast, the relationship between the central and component state legal orders is fundamentally unsettled.'

73 Jack Knight, *Institutions and Social Conflict* (Cambridge University Press, 1992); Alessandro Pizzorno, *Le classi sociali* (il Mulino, 1959); Alessandro Pizzorno, *Le radici della politica assoluta* (Feltrinelli, 1993); C. Crouch, Alessandro Pizzorno, *Conflitti in Europa* (Etas libri, 1977); Ralf Dahrendorf, 'Toward a theory of social conflict' (1958) 2 *The Journal of Conflict Resolution* 170; Ralf Dahrendorf, *Essays in the Theory of Society* (Stanford University Press, 1968).

constitutionalism as such which has a 'polemical' (and not irenical) nature being funded on a never-ending friction between liberty and power, as Luciani wrote.[74] In this sense *Kadi* is the manifestation (at its best) of the 'polemical' spirit of European constitutional law:[75] it is likely that, even after the *Kadi*, conflicts – as expression of interpretative disagreement – will not magically disappear. Perhaps the *Kadi* saga will pave the way for a new season of contestation and, hopefully, for an improved protection of fundamental rights at the international level.

74 Massimo Luciani, 'Costituzionalismo irenico e costituzionalismo polemico' (http://archivio. rivistaaic.it/materiali/anticipazioni/costituzionalismo_irenico/index.html) (accessed 28 September 2013).
75 Giuseppe Martinico, *The Tangled Complexity of the EU Constitutional Process: The Frustrating Knot of Europe* (Routledge, 2012) 107–62.

13 Constitutional dimensions of administrative cooperation

Potentials for reorientation in *Kadi II*

Nele Yang

Through numerous references in academic writings, court decisions, and political discussions on institutional reform, the *Kadi* jurisprudence of the Court of Justice of the European Union (CJEU) has taken on a special aura. By now, it is not only the story of Mr. Kadi, but a foundational narrative of the European Union (EU) – a veritable saga. In this line, both its dryness and its administrative technicality may not win the European Court of Justice's (ECJ) *Kadi II* first place for a sparkling performance. Yet, it is precisely the focus on administration, which lets the judgment gleam with issues of constitutional relevance for the EU. Both in the area of EU-United Nations (UN) relations and fundamental rights protection, *Kadi II* holds potential to reorient the EU constitutional order.

From ships in the night to administrative cooperation

The tone of the ECJ's *Kadi II* stands in marked contrast to the constitutional flourish of the preceding *Kadi* decisions – administrative technicality dominates the shortest decision of the *Kadi* jurisprudence. However, the Court's pressure on the EU administration to request more information from the UN level could make the judgment a critical juncture for the Union's self-understanding.

Building suspense

One of the most memorable features of the *Kadi* line is Advocate General Maduro's evocation of ships in the night which sail past each other without taking notice[1] – a metaphor for legal orders operating in self-sufficient ignorance, without any regard to each other. Evocatively, the Advocate General characterized questions of the relationship with the UN as constitutional issues for the EU. Following in the rhetorical footsteps of Maduro, the Court drew on the full arsenal of constitutional rhetoric in its 2008 *Kadi* decision.

---

1 Joined Cases C-402/05 P and C-415/05 P, *Kadi and Al-Barakaat*, Opinion of Advocate General Poiares Maduro [2008] ECR I-06351, para. 22.

It brandished 'the basic constitutional charter, the EC Treaty',[2] and 'the very foundations of the Community'.[3] The decision smacked of grand design and the Court's will to be the designer. In 2010 the General Court (GC) added its share[4] – the constitutional glamour of *Kadi* seemed as incessant as the sparkle in the eyes of the legal scholars referring to it.

In the October 2012 oral hearing of the ensuing appeal, the Commission, Council, and the impressive number of intervening member states had not grown tired of emphasizing one central point: the improvements in UN delisting, with the Ombudsperson procedure as their latest exponent, must be considered. This would require the Court to interpret its 2008 dictum of 'in principle full review' deferentially. Picking up on this line, Advocate General Bot's opinion was all about the standard of review as an overarching mechanism to structure the relationship between the EU legal order and the UN Security Council.[5] Thus, Bot connected patterns from French administrative law doctrine with the grand constitutional issue of the EU's autonomy. All eyes were now certainly on the ECJ in suspense. One author echoed common expectations when he forecast 'another legal blockbuster',[6] and another hinted that a second ECJ decision in favor of Mr. Kadi would be 'redolent of high constitutional principle'.[7]

The anticlimax: abandoning constitutional rhetoric

But the ECJ defies expectations and brushes aside the openings which would have allowed it to continue in the vein of its 2008 rhetoric. Whereas the 2008 decision was about the EU v. UN legal order, the 2013 decision is phrased in terms of courts v. administrations. Curtness dominates both the section on the issue of scope v. intensity and the Court's dismissal of the UN delisting procedure. Instead of offering constitutional sparkle, the Court condenses the grounds of appeal to a question about flows of information between administrations.[8]

Asymmetries of information characterize the sanctions regime. Because of UN members' reluctance to disclose potentially sensitive information, the EU administration and, in turn, listed individuals have very scarce information

2 Joined Cases C-402/05 P and C-415/05 P, *Kadi and Al-Barakaat* [2008] ECR I-06351, paras. 81, 281.
3 *Ibid.*, paras. 282, 290, 304.
4 Case T-85/09 *Kadi v. Commission* [2010] ECR II-05177, paras. 98, 119, 125.
5 *Kadi II*, Opinion of Advocate General Bot of 19 March, nyr.
6 Armin Cuyvers, 'The *Kadi II* Judgment of the General Court' (2011) 7 *European Constitutional Law Review* 481.
7 Conor Gearty, 'Kadi II' (25 March 2013) (available at http://eutopialaw.com) (accessed 20 September 2013).
8 *Kadi II*, para. 103.

on the grounds for listing. The Court faces the same scarcity – unless the EU administration takes the initiative to request more information from the UN.

The Court stops short of explicitly obligating the Commission to adopt such action. Yet, it hints at the possible detrimental consequences non-action might have for the Commission's implementing regulation. The Court's reasoning in this respect vacillates between strictness and leniency. However, what emerges clearly is the pressure on the EU authorities to understand their relationship with the UN Sanctions Committee as one which requires them to make direct contact more intensively.

The Court asserts that 'it is for [the competent EU] authority to assess ... whether it is necessary to seek the assistance of the Sanctions Committee ... in order to obtain ... the disclosure of information or evidence ... to enable it to discharge its duty or careful and impartial examination'.[9] In other words, when exercising its administrative obligation to examine carefully and impartially an individual's contestation of their listing, the Commission has discretion to decide whether it will need to contact the UN level for more information. According to the Court, an obligation to request more information follows neither from the UN Security Council's sanctions resolution nor from the implementing EU regulation,[10] nor from the right to effective judicial protection.[11]

In between, however, the ECJ makes some less generous additions. For one, when deriving from the rights to the defense and the right to effective judicial protection an obligation of EU authorities to disclose the information on which the listing decision is based, the Court clarifies that by this information it means 'at the very least' the summary of reasons.[12] Thus, there are cases in which the Commission will be obliged to exercise its discretion in such a way as to request further information from the UN Sanctions Committee or UN member states. The contours of these cases remain blurry. The line would certainly have to be drawn where the information contained in the summary of reasons is so scarce that it holds no probative value for the Court, let alone appropriately substantiates the reasons for listing. But the Commission is left adrift with regard to when and whether its discretion would be reduced at this line. Instead, the ECJ has put a sword of Damocles into place: the Court itself will have the final word when it comes to the probative value of the evidence and to whether this evidence substantiates the reasons for listing sufficiently. So Commission and Council are not obliged to go beyond the statement of reasons, but they had better provide more information to dispel the risk of having their decisions annulled by the Court.

---

9 *Ibid.*, para. 115.

10 *Ibid.*, paras. 107–8.

11 *Ibid.*, para. 139. Tzanakopoulos appears to ignore these statements when claiming that the Court establishes a legal obligation on EU authorities to request more information from the UN level – Antonios Tzanakopoulos, 'Kadi showdown' (19 July 2013) (available at www.ejiltalk.org) (accessed 20 September 2013).

12 *Kadi II*, para. 111.

A glint of glamour

That the Court addresses the administration is significant for the EU's relationship with the UN and for EU fundamental rights protection. The reason why, of all cases, it is the ECJ's *Kadi II* judgment which could become a critical juncture here, is that it essentially is about the interpretation of the Court's 2008 *Kadi* judgment. The latter is both the epicenter and vanishing point of a wealth of academic production, which uses the decision to praise, criticize, or construct various concepts of the relationship between the EU and the UN in particular, and of legal orders in general. The 2008 *Kadi* judgment has also been referred to frequently by EU and UN bureaucracies and by non-governmental organizations (NGOs) in the ongoing discussion on sanctions regime reform, and it has been used recurrently by the CJEU in assessing sanctions implementation. It has, moreover, become a standard reference for arguments concerning fundamental rights protection. In interpreting its *Kadi* 2008 decision, the ECJ is doing no less than working out the meaning of the central point of orientation for the EU's self-understanding.

The external constitutional dimension: EU-UN relations

The issue of the relationship between the EU legal order and the UN is by now almost an old hat in the *Kadi* discourse but certainly one that has not come out of fashion yet. But it also carries much import for the EU as a constitutional order. One of the core elements of such an order is the capacity to define by itself its relations with other legal orders.[13] For lack of a clear statement in EU law, it has been for the ECJ to pronounce itself on this issue. This has engendered jurisprudence as rich and labyrinthine as the academic literature trying to make sense of it.[14] *Kadi II* may appear like just another puzzling point to this maze. However, the judgment has the potential to reorient the discourse on EU-UN relations in the realm of sanctions toward an understanding that requires direct, sustained engagement of all actors.

External relations as an internal affair

There is a concept that has dominated discussions on the proper arrangement of UN-EU relations: the duty to take into account. The CJEU and its Advocates General, EU institutions at large, and legal academics have all referred to this duty when discussing how EU and UN actors should behave

13 On external relations as a dimension of EU constitutional law, see Daniel Thym, 'Foreign affairs' in Armin von Bogdandy, Jürgen Bast (eds), *Principles of European Constitutional Law* (2nd edn. Hart, 2010), 309–43.
14 Of the more recent efforts, see Enzo Cannizzaro, Paolo Palchetti, Ramses A. Wessels (eds), *International Law as Law of the European Union* (Martinus Nijhoff, 2012); Mario Mendez, 'The legal effect of Community agreements' (2010) 21 *European Journal of International Law* 83.

toward one another. The use of this concept, however, covers a broad spectrum of meanings.

On one end of the spectrum, some actors interpret taking into account as mainly meaning that the EU should refrain from any action which could jeopardize the attainment of UN objectives. For the EU administration, taking into account UN objectives means not questioning the assessment made by the UN Sanctions Committee. Accordingly, in the *Kadi II* oral hearing, the Commission underlined that sanctions implementation did not require it to be a 'sort of second chamber of the UN Security Council'. Hence, the Commission saw no necessity to enter into contact with the UN Sanctions Committee beyond the limited exchange explicitly foreseen in the EU implementing Regulation.[15]

A different interpretation disconnects the recognition of the UN objective of countering terrorism from the necessity to accord this objective the same weight as the UN order does. In his 2008 Opinion, Advocate General Maduro underlines that the ECJ and the Court of First Instance 'take judicial notice' of international obligations.[16] But for Maduro, this does not mean that the Community should blindly follow the UN Security Council in sanctions implementation. The Court's practice of interpreting UN sanctions implementing acts echoes this understanding. In 2008, the ECJ asserted that the Community would have to 'take due account of the terms and objectives' of the UN sanctions resolution.[17] Through use in subsequent cases, this dictum has ossified into a formula for the interpretation of sanctions-implementing measures. However, the fight against terrorism has not always prevailed as an objective that trumps all others.[18]

Even a grammatically opposed conduct has been labeled a form of taking into account: challenges of the UN sanctions regime by the ECJ. Judgments like the 2008 *Kadi* decision have been seen as contesting the UN Security Council's primacy in matters of international peace and security because the ECJ *de facto* exercised a review of the original sanctions resolution.[19] But in doing this, the Court actually gives an impulse for change toward the protection of the fundamental rights that are enshrined in international law, and it therefore respects

---

15 Council Regulation (EC) No 881/2002 of 27 May 2002, as amended by Regulation 1286/2009 of 22 December 2009, arts. 7, 7 (a) and 7 (c). Whether such contact could be comprised by 'all necessary contacts with the Sanctions Committee for the purpose of the effective implementation of [the] Regulation' remains open to exploration.

16 Joined Cases C-402/05 P and C-415/05 P *Kadi and Al-Barakaat*, Opinion of Advocate-General Poiares Maduro [2008] ECR I-06351, para. 22.

17 Joined Cases C-402/05 P and C-415/05 P *Kadi and Al-Barakaat* [2008] ECR I-06351, para. 296.

18 Case C-340/08, *M & Others* [2010] I-03913; *Kadi II*, Judgment of 18 July 2013, nyr.

19 Most salient, Larissa van den Herik, Nico Schrijver, 'Eroding the primacy of the UN system of collective security' (2008) 5 *International Organizations Law Review* 330, 335; Riccardo Pavoni, 'Freedom to choose the legal means for implementing UN Security Council Resolutions and the ECJ *Kadi* Judgment' (2009) 28 *Yearbook of European Law* 627.

rather than challenges the objectives of that order, the argument goes.[20] Thus, the contrast between challenging the international legal order and promoting international rights protection seems to be unmasked as an artificial one. This is a rash conclusion, however, if one considers what is challenged and what is protected. The challenge is directed against an overemphasis on the UN objective of countering terrorism, while support is voiced for safeguarding fundamental rights, another UN objective. Moreover, those who take this to mean that the ECJ takes into account international human rights guarantees focus on the impact instead of the reasoning of the ECJ's decisions. This is illustrated nicely by the counter-example of commentators who laud the outcome of the 2008 *Kadi* decision but at the same time complain that the Court did not take into account the international legal order because it did not cite international human rights treaties.[21]

Taking into account can also mean actively pursuing the other order's objectives, even in the absence of a practice of implementation. To this effect, Feinäugle interprets the UN's duty to respect the interests of its member states in a UN sanctions regime in accordance with the rule of law: according to him, respecting these interests means pursuing them – entailing action as wide-ranging as the creation of an independent judicial body at UN level for the examination of delisting requests.[22]

The analysis of interpretations of what it means to take into account another order's objectives reveals a range of different understandings. Nevertheless, an underlying commonality remains: cooperation appears as something that is exercised internally, by looking at the other legal order, its courts' decisions, its legal acts, its objectives. But not necessarily by making contact with actors from the other legal order beyond citing or criticizing what they produce, that is to say beyond engaging with the acts instead of with the actors themselves.

The potential: sustained and direct engagement

With a reference to art. 220 (1) of the Treaty on the Functioning of the European Union (TFEU) and the 'spirit of effective cooperation',[23] the Court takes

---

20 See Stephan Schill, 'The interface between national and international energy law' in Kim Talus (ed.), *Research Handbook of International Energy Law* (Elgar Publishing, forthcoming), who argues this with reference to *Kadi* in order to speak about a division of labors between national and international law in the area of energy law; Isabelle Ley, 'Verfassung ohne Grenzen?' in Ingolf Pernice *et al.* (eds.), *Europa jenseits seiner Grenzen* (Nomos, 2009), 91–126, 118.

21 Daniel Halberstam, Eric Stein, 'The United Nations, the European Union and the King of Sweden' (2009) 46 *Common Market Law Review* 64, 68; Gráinne de Búrca, 'The European Court of Justice and the international order after Kadi' (2010) 51 *Harvard International Law Journal* 41–2; Andrea Gattini, 'Joined Cases C-402/05 P & 415/05 P' (2009) 46 *Common Market Law Review* 231–2.

22 Clemens A. Feinäugle, *Hoheitsgewalt im Völkerrecht* [*The Exercise of Public Authority in International Law*] (Springer, 2011), 101–24, 250–1. For an English language summary of the argument, see pp. 357–60.

23 *Kadi II*, para. 115.

Advocate General Bot up on the idea of closer cooperation between EU authorities and the UN. For the first time, the Court uses the term 'cooperation' with reference to the relationship between the EU and UN administrative authorities.

Only thinly veiled by the dry language, this passage of the judgment resonates with annoyance in the face of EU administrative practices regarding requests for information on listings. In the oral hearing, the judges were aghast at the fact that the Commission's only source of information with respect to reasons for Mr. Kadi's listing had been the French permanent representative to the UN. Unfazed by this, the Commission had insisted that it would only ask the Sanctions Committee for further information if the Court requested it on a case-by-case basis. The Court's annoyance with this nonchalance translates into the bottom line: the Council's and Commission's task is broader than simply to synchronize the EU implementing Regulations with the UN consolidated lists. It pertains to them to also engage directly with the UN level, and thus to stimulate, not just to simulate.

One could be tempted to conclude that, in putting pressure on Commission and Council to request further information from the UN level in *Kadi II*, the Court is simply enlisting the EU administration in its drive for the contestation of deficient UN procedures. This may be true. But it makes all the difference.[24]

Unlike courts, the administration has the inherent capacity to negotiate continuously and strategically.[25] Unlike courts, it does not have to limit itself to planting an impulse and then watching the repercussions in the hope of being able to curb or intensify them in later decisions – it is able to answer back immediately, since it does not depend as much as courts do on individual claims being brought before it. Thus, communication by the EU administration can induce proactive cooperation of other actors like the UN sanctions bodies. A single pronouncement on legality, on the other hand, is a tough medium to use to effect more than just incremental change. Also, the administration may choose to behave proactively, something a court could, if at all, only do in *obiter dicta*. Excessive *obitering* can damage a court's reputation, just as attempts of judges to take proactive steps might do, for example through declarations in the media or press releases.[26] Moreover, courts are mostly dependent on other actors to supply information. In cases where courts are not inherently dependent on the parties to the case but can adopt measures of inquiry, these

---

24 On the importance of institutional choice, see Neil Komesar, *Imperfect Alternatives* (University of Chicago Press, 1994).

25 Along the same lines, see Kevin Banks, 'Trade, labor and international governance' (2011) 32 *Berkeley Journal of Employment and Labor Law* 113 et seq.

26 See, for example, criticism on the German Federal Constitutional Court's *obiter dicta* by Hans-Peter Schneider, 'SOS aus Karlsruhe – das Bundesverfassungsgericht vor dem Untergang?' (1996) *Neue Juristische Wochenschrift* 2631. This court's current president, Andreas Voßkuhle, has incurred harsh criticism for his declarations in the media on public policy and on pending cases.

are limited to the case at hand. The idea of courts as negotiators vis-à-vis another legal order[27] may be helpful to clarify that courts, in decision-making, have to juggle a number of objectives. But calling courts 'negotiators' masks the fact that the frequency and scope of interactions is mostly not up to the court to determine.

Because of the inherent capacities of administrative institutions, the focus on the cooperation of the Commission and Council with the UN level points to a mode of engagement in which making direct and sustained contact with UN actors is paramount beyond 'taking into account' UN objectives. This does not mean that one should completely shut out the CJEU or try to construe it as some kind of administrative entity. After all, the features which make the CJEU unfit for sustained direct negotiation – dependence on claims brought, the specific procedure, yardstick and format for arriving at a decision most often concerned with past events – are those which justify its existence as a court.[28]

Implications: an open constitutional order

Embracing administrative cooperation as a powerful way to enter into contact with the UN sanctions bodies would have implications for the EU constitutional order as a whole. The cases on UN sanctions have long come to stand for the relationship of EU law with international law in general even though the CJEU has not approached all of international law in the same way.[29] Thus, cases like *Kadi II* play an important role in perception-building as to what kind of constitutional order the EU understands itself to be. Conceptualizing it as an autonomous legal order necessarily entails delimitation from international law. Some 45 years after *Van Gend en Loos*, the Court's 2008 *Kadi* decision perpetuated this foundational truism, this time rendering it in the form of a statement about yardsticks. Activating the institutional capacities of the EU administration to really converse with the UN administration and seeing this as an inherent part of the administrative role points the way to a constitutional order which acknowledges and internalizes that sanctions operation and legitimacy is not a purely internal affair. The focus on administrative cooperation works against the paradigm of separation without completely leveling differences between legal orders – rather, it addresses mutual dependencies and the necessity to act on them.

---

27 Often contributions that use game theory to analyze courts implicitly convey this idea, for example Arthur Dyevre, 'Judicial non-compliance in a non-hierarchical legal order' (2012) (available at www.ssrn.com).

28 See Christoph Möllers, *Gewaltengliederung* (Mohr Siebeck, 2005) 95–97, 260–264.

29 Compare only Case C-366/10 *ATAA*, Judgment of 21 December 2011, nyr (customary international law); Case 308/06 *Intertanko* [2008] ECR I-4057 (UN Convention on the Law of the Sea); Case C-149/96 *Portugal* v. *Council* [1999] ECR I-8395 (WTO/GATT); Joined Cases C-120/06 and 121/06 P *FIAMM and Fedon* [2008] ECR I-6513 (from the meandering case law on WTO Dispute Settlement Body decisions).

For the EU, this idea has been captured in the concept of *Verbund*, first used in German constitutional law scholarship as a battleground for competing visions of Europe, but then tamed and brought to fame by administrative law scholarship.[30] Describing the EU as a composite structure encompassing Union and member state authorities, the *Verbund* concept shows mutual dependencies in law implementation, functionality, and legitimacy. It subsequently demands cooperation as the normal state of affairs, understood also in terms of sharing resources like information within the composite structure.

In the realm of UN targeted sanctions resolutions, the involved EU and UN authorities exist at a level of dependence that necessitates seeing them as actors in a *Verbund*, too.[31] The Sanctions Committee depends on UN members and the EU to implement targeted sanctions, no matter how well-defined the targets. This operative dependence also reflects in the worries of many authors that UN counterterrorism will break down if domestic courts annul implementing measures.[32] This worry further signals legitimatory dependence. International organizations and their bodies to a large extent draw their *raison d'être* from an effective fulfillment of their mandate.[33] The UN Security Council as a body whose mandate is to protect international peace and security is no exception to this. Thus, fading compliance with its resolutions and the ensuing ineffectiveness of the sanctions regime – even if only perceived as such – weaken the Security Council's legitimacy.[34] The EU implementing acts to targeted sanctions, in turn, also depend on the UN level for their legitimacy: the Commission and Council need to justify their implementing decisions in accordance with the rule of law, one of the principles on which the legitimacy of the exercise of public authority is built.[35] For justificatory material, they depend on the UN sanctions bodies.

30 Eberhadt Schmidt-Aßmann, 'EU administrative law' in Rüdiger Wolfrum (ed.), *The Max Planck Encyclopedia of Public International Law* (OUP, 2012), vol. 3, pp. 723–33, para. 8; Oswald Jansen, Bettina Schöndorf-Haubold, *The European Composite Administration* (Intersentia, 2011).

31 About the *Verbund* as a useful analytical and normative concept for international law: Armin von Bogdandy, Philipp Dann, 'International composite administration' in Armin von Bogdandy *et al.* (eds), *The Exercise of Public Authority by International Institutions* (Springer, 2010), 883–912; Schill, 'The interface'.

32 See footnote 19 above.

33 Kirsten Schmalenbach, 'International organizations or institutions, general aspects', in Rüdiger Wolfrum (ed.), *The Max Planck Encyclopedia of Public International Law* (OUP, 2012), vol. 5, pp. 1126–53, para. 39.

34 On the importance of perceptions of legitimacy, see Iain Hurd, 'Legitimacy, power, and the symbolic life of the UN Security Council' (2002) 8 *Global Governance* 35, who, however, sees compliance only as a consequence of perceived legitimacy, not as a factor contributing to that perception.

35 See Armin von Bogdandy, 'General principles of international public authority' in Armin von Bogdandy *et al.* (eds), *The Exercise of Public Authority by International Institutions* (Springer, 2010), 727–60.

In sum, dependencies between the EU and the UN in the realm of targeted sanctions are such that information should be seen as a common resource of this *Verbund*. This can be a yardstick for how the EU administration behaves toward the UN sanctions bodies. Conceptualizing their behavior as taking place in a composite structure helps balance the autonomy of the EU as a constitutional order with dependencies vis-à-vis the UN.[36] Granted, UN members and sanctions bodies are reluctant to disclose information and are quick to justify this reluctance by expressing security concerns. But this does not discredit the idea of information as a common *Verbund* resource. If anything, it implies that those possessing the information should bear the burden to give reasons, beyond general concerns, why they do not want to disclose certain information.

The internal constitutional dimension: procedural rights

However, the Court's focus on flows of information, and its accompanying drive to make itself the hub of these flows, have a more problematic potential: to lose the focus on the individuals whose rights the Court is supposed to protect.

Foundational focus: individual rights

The EU has evolved into an order that sees its foundation not so much only in the common market but rather also – and increasingly – in the protection of fundamental rights. Procedural rights play an important role in this development, as they provide a connection between the traditional idea of a legal community and the idea of an EU constitutional order at whose very foundation lie fundamental rights.

The potential: losing the focus?

The ECJ's efforts to make itself the only and final EU institution for the evaluation and control of information on listings potentially could lead to losing this foundational focus. Harbingers of this potential loss are a skewed conception of the relation between individual rights in administrative procedure and in judicial procedure as well as the Court's obiter on *in camera* proceedings.

The duty of an administrative authority to state the reasons for its acts is linked to the important individual right to have these reasons stated and to have access to them. This has several purposes: it provides an opportunity for the administration to check itself the justification of its act; the affected individual

---

36 On the need to balance EU autonomy and dependencies on international organizations, see Ramses A. Wessel, Steven Blockmans (eds), *Between Autonomy and Dependence* (T.M.C. Asser, 2013).

is supposed to be given the best possible basis on which to make an informed decision on further action, for example contestation of the administrative act in court; and if the matter gets to court, the justification of the act enables the court to review the act effectively.[37] In *Kadi II*, the first two purposes lose importance. There is no mention of administrative self-control. The Court originally deduces the duty to state reasons only from the right to effective judicial protection. It also displays the role which administrative procedure plays for individual rights protection as an emanation of the right to effective judicial protection. Administrative procedure thus appears largely as a prelude serving the judicial procedure. In the course of its reasoning, the Court eventually deduces the duty to state reasons from both the individual's rights of the defense and the right to effective judicial protection. However, it remains unclear whether the evaluation of the reasons as 'sufficiently detailed and specific'[38] also refers to their sufficiency for a meaningful hearing at the administrative stage. The Court is blatantly keen to examine all reasons, no matter how scarce. Altogether, this creates the impression that the duty to state reasons serves only to enable the CJEU to scrutinize the act; the right to defense in administrative procedure simply becomes a derivative of the right to effective judicial protection.

This skews the basic idea that administrative and judicial procedures are mutually exclusive and at the same time fulfill their tasks in interaction with each other.[39] The rights of the defense in administrative procedure and the right to effective judicial protection are interdependent rights and certainly one is not secondary to the other. Such complementarity further permits the idea that deficits in one type of procedure may be compensated by the other. In the reasoning of the ECJ, this relationship is skewed as well. According to the general understanding, compensation can either mean giving individuals an enhanced opportunity to be heard in court if their right to be heard in the administrative procedure has not been honored, or subjecting to closer judicial scrutiny an act which has come into existence through a deficient administrative procedure.[40] The limit of compensation is reached where the deficits in the administrative procedure are such as to result in too little information to actually exercise closer judicial scrutiny. In cases like this, courts have held that the right to effective

---

37 Martin Gellermann, 'Art. 296' in Rudolf Streinz (ed.), *EUV/AEUV* (C.H. Beck, 2012), para. 5. If one approaches administrative procedural rules from an efficiency v. protection dichotomy (Hanns Peter Nehl, Principles of Administrative Procedure in EC Law [Hart, 1999], 20-26), the first purpose would be part of the efficiency rationale, whereas the second and third purpose would belong to the protective rationale.

38 *Kadi II*, para. 130.

39 Fritz Scharpf, *Die politischen Kosten des Rechtsstaats* (Mohr Siebeck, 1970), 26–38; Martin Shapiro, Alec Stone Sweet, *On Law, Politics, and Judicialization* (OUP, 2002), 38.

40 On the idea of compensation, see Heike Jochum, *Verwaltungsverfahrensrecht und Verwaltungsprozessrecht* (Mohr Siebeck, 2004), 66–71. See also Joined Cases C-478/11 P to C-482/11 P *Gbagbo and Others*, Opinion of Advocate General Cruz Villalón of 19 December 2012, nyr, paras. 46–52; Case T-85/09 *Kadi v. Commission* [2010] ECR II-05177, para. 144.

judicial protection had been infringed precisely because the deficits in the administrative procedure were so grave that they prevented the judges from exercising effective protection.[41] Contrastingly, however, the ECJ in *Kadi II* asserts that it will exercise substantive review in any case, no matter how scarce the informative material. It is to be doubted whether the individual gains anything from this in terms of rights protection. Skeletal reasons may be easier to rebut for the applicant than a fuller account. But it is even easier to base a rights violation on the very scarcity of information, without putting the individual in additional limbo. As it stands, however, the emphasis on the Court as the central EU organ for in-depth scrutiny of any listing information has the potential to block out the individual.

Most telling in this regard is the Court's suggestion to employ *in camera* proceedings where confidentiality prohibits the disclosure of information. The fact that the suggestion is an *obiter dictum*, since confidentiality was not invoked in *Kadi II*, signals that this is a general line. Recent developments outside the courtroom confirm the impression: the obiter echoes the General Court's proposal to amend its rules of procedure so as to allow the use of confidential information in proceedings for annulment. Bar associations and NGOs from the UK have already voiced concerns about this and have written to ECJ president Skouris to demand a consultation. This shows strong public awareness for the fact that this would be a major step. The Court, on the other hand, does not appear willing to recognize it as such.[42]

Implications: a constitutional order serving the Court

The issue of fundamental rights protection touches deeply on the question of the Union's finality, that is, the purpose at the heart of European integration.[43] The *Kadi* jurisprudence has played an important role in converging lines of case law on rights protection, thus reaffirming and entrenching it as the foundational core of the Union.[44] Together with the Court's decisions on EU citizenship, this has provided a solidified anchor point for thinking of the EU as a constitutional order built on fundamental rights, and therefore, serving the individual. The Court – like other courts around the world – has been criticized for using fundamental rights as an instrument for self-empowerment. This

---

41 Recent examples from the CJEU include Case C-399/06 P *Hassan and Ayadi* [2009] ECR I-11393 and Case T-86/11 *Bamba* [2011] ECR II-02749.

42 See Maya Lester, 'Organizations call on European Court to consult on classified evidence rule change' (27 July 2013) (available at http://europeansanctions.com) (accessed 20 September 2013).

43 Ulrich Haltern, 'On finality' in Armin von Bogdandy, Jürgen Bast (eds), *Principles of European Constitutional Law* (2nd edn Hart, 2010).

44 On this 'special primary law', see Nikolaos Lavranos, 'Revisiting Article 307 EC', in Filippo Fontanelli, Giuseppe Martinico, Paolo Carrozza (eds), *Shaping Rule of Law through Dialogue* (Europa Law, 2010), 119–46.

instrumental use may occur, but it does not have to be negative if fundamental rights are better protected as a result. The use in *Kadi II*, however, is of a different quality: the Court could have declared the implementing act incompatible with Union law simply for lack of information. Instead, it maneuvers the listed individual into a situation where annulment, but also protection of the right to an adversarial procedure, becomes uncertain. The prospect of a constitutional order serving the Court is a depressing one for the EU.

Tapping the positive and curbing the negative potential: missing steps

To curb the loss of attention to the individual and to tap more fully the potential of administrative cooperation, some steps are still missing – notably, a legal obligation of the EU administration to request more information, and the integration of the UN Ombudsperson. That the Court did not take these two most important steps has one root: the Court's distrust toward the institutions of its own legal order and toward the UN bureaucracy. This is certainly not unfounded, seeing the Commission's reluctance and UN members' unwillingness to provide more information. But the Court's behavior is bound to entrench these positions.

Establishing a legal obligation

The problem is not so much finding a legal basis for an obligation of the EU administration to engage with the UN. As seen above, the problem rather is that the Commission and Council in the realm of sanctions implementation as yet follow a conception of EU-UN relations that does not comprise high-frequency direct contact with the UN level to negotiate for information. To effectively activate administrative capacities in the direction of an open constitutional order, the Court would have to exert more influence on the Commission's and Council's understanding of their institutional role. The Court could have done this by defining the meaning of cooperation, in other words: by establishing a legal obligation of the EU administration to proactively acquire more information from the UN.

Interpretation in light of the *Verbund* concept could open up 'forms of appropriate cooperation' in art. 220 (1) TFEU as the basis for such a legal obligation. However, there might be a problem with the competence of the Court to stipulate this, as the competence to concretize cooperation with international organizations lies with the High Representative (art. 220 (2) TFEU). Alternatively, one could think of expanding the administration's obligation of diligent and impartial examination, which also entails the duty to obtain information.[45] Here, conceptualizing EU-UN relations in the area

---

45 See Paul Craig, *EU Administrative Law* (2nd edn OUP, 2012), 335–7.

of targeted sanctions as a *Verbund* indicates that obtaining information is not limited to sources within the EU.

Now, after *Kadi II*, it is unclear when the Court will consider the probative value of information insufficient because the information is confidential or can, if at all, only be provided in abridged form. This uncertainty can backfire and cause a feeling of resignation with the Commission and Council. The difference between not supplying additional information and supplying too little or too confidential information appears indiscernible and indeed irrelevant if the Court would opt for full substantive review anyhow. Thus, motivation to engage in negotiations for more information at all is likely to stay at the present low. A legal obligation would work against this. Additionally, granting the administration discretion in assessing the probative value of the information would offer motivation to follow that obligation; it would attenuate the strained emphasis on the Court and would be in tune with the idea of complementarity of administrative and judicial procedures.

What seems to have stood in the way is the text of the implementing Regulation, but also distrust toward the Commission and Council. Distrust appears to be the stronger one of these factors, as the Court's conception of cooperation already exceeds the scarce secondary law text.

Integrating the Ombudsperson

Secondly, integrating the Ombudsperson could have been a step toward alleviating asymmetries of information and fully acknowledging administrative capacities. It is one of the tasks of the Ombudsperson to gather information from listed individuals, from UN members, and from the Sanctions Monitoring Team, which is the UN Sanctions Committee's go-between when it comes to assessing information. In contrast, the Sanctions Committee only has a mandate to receive information, not to gather it on its own initiative.[46] The Ombudsperson has managed to establish herself as the main source of listings information at the UN; she has notably concluded agreements on the provision of confidential information with some UN members. Thus, she may not be a comprehensive source but certainly is an important actor when it comes to access to information in a request for delisting or a contestation of a (re)listing.

Recognizing this, some authors have proposed different ways of integrating results from the Ombudsperson delisting procedure into CJEU decisions. Making the procedure an admissibility criterion for GC annulment proceedings probably goes too far[47] and making assumptions as to when deficits in

---

46 UNSC Resolution 1267(1999), para. 6.
47 On the proposal, see Juliane Kokott, Christoph Sobotta, 'The Kadi case: constitutional core values and international law. Finding the balance?' (2012) 23 *European Journal of International Law* 1015; Nele Yang, 'Comment on Kokott/Sobotta' (14 January 2013) (available at www.ejiltalk.org) (accessed 20 September 2013).

the Ombudsperson procedure would play out in the final decision of the Sanctions Committee[48] amounts to much guesswork. But the Court could have made the Ombudsperson a mandatory interlocutor of the EU administration while still signaling that it did not consider the UN delisting procedure sufficiently in tune with procedural rights standards. With the non-inclusion of the Ombudsperson, the Court misses the opportunity to use her as an established negotiator with UN members.

Treating the Ombudsperson almost as non-existent as part of the UN sanctions administration might just encourage the Security Council's efforts to give this rather progressive UN institution the narrowest possible scope. On the other hand, it might help to expand the idea of direct, sustained communication between EU and UN administrations more easily to UN targeted sanctions regimes like the Taliban list and sanctions against Iranian nuclear proliferation, which lie outside the Ombudsperson's mandate.

Conclusion: loose ends and new beginnings

Although the focus on administrative technicality seems like a step back from the previous *Kadi* decisions, what makes the ECJ's *Kadi II* a dry read potentially has reorienting power for the EU as a constitutional order. A new path has been opened: the active role the EU bureaucracy can assume in engaging directly with the UN level and recognizing dependencies while at the same time preserving Union autonomy and fundamental rights protection. However, the Court should be cautious not to create asymmetries between itself and the EU administration and between itself and the individual. So, although some loose ends remain, *Kadi II* holds potential for new beginnings. The saga is far from over. It just needs a new hero.

---

48 Andreas von Arnauld, 'Der Weg zu einem "Solange ½"' (2013) 2 *Europarecht* 236–46, works with this idea to integrate results of the Ombudsperson procedure into CJEU decision-making.

14 Multilevel judicial protection of 'access to justice' and the EU's duty to contribute 'to the strict observance and development of international law'

Ernst-Ulrich Petersmann

Introduction: 'access to justice' requires multilevel 'judicial governance' of international public goods

The statues of the ancient Greek and Roman goddesses of justice (*justitia*) in courthouses all over the world – with a blindfold (symbolizing impartiality), holding a balance (symbolizing fair procedures like 'hear the other side', proportionality) as well as a sword (symbolizing authority, independence, peace, rule of law) – illustrate that principles of procedural and substantive justice remain the primary paradigms for peaceful settlement of disputes and reasonable justification of law and governance in 'courts of justice' in response to the perennial, individual, and political quests for protecting and clarifying 'principles of justice'.[1] Individual access to justice and to justification of law and governance can be viewed as the most basic human right so as to transform 'rule by law' into 'rule of law' by empowering individuals to realize their individual and democratic self-development and invoke and enforce their rights in order to hold all government agents accountable for the rule of law and obtain redress for violations of rights.[2] The United Nations (UN) Charter and the Universal Declaration of Human Rights (UDHR, 1948) emphasize these interrelationships between justice, human rights, and rule of law, for instance by reaffirming: '[w]hereas it is essential, if man is not to be compelled to have recourse, as a last resort, to rebellion against tyranny and oppression, that human

---

1 Judith Resnik, Dennis Edward Curtis, *Representing Justice. Invention, Controversy, and Rights in City-States and Democratic Courtrooms* (Yale University Press, 2011). On the diversity of theories of justice justifying international economic law see Ernst-Ulrich Petersmann, *International Economic Law in the 21st Century. Constitutional Pluralism and Multilevel Governance of Interdependent Public Goods* (Hart Publishing, 2012), ch. VI.
2 Examples for guarantees of 'access to justice' in human rights law include art. 8 UDHR, art. 13 ECHR, art. 47 EU Charter of Fundamental Rights, arts. 3 and 7 African Charter of Human and People's Rights, arts. 8 and 25 Inter-American Charter of Human Rights; see Francesco Francioni (ed.), *Access to Justice as a Human Right* (OUP, 2007); Antônio Augusto Cançado Trindade, *The Access of Individuals to International Justice* (OUP, 2011). On the human right to justification, Rainer Forst, *The Right to Justification. Elements of a Constructivist Theory of Justice* (Columbia University Press, 2012).

rights should be protected by the rule of law' (Preamble UDHR); and 'faith in fundamental human rights' is necessary for establishing 'conditions under which justice and respect for the obligations arising from treaties and other sources of international law can be maintained' (Preamble UN Charter).

As coherent legal systems of 'primary rules of conduct' and 'secondary rules of recognition, change and adjudication'[3] require clarification of the applicable law through impartial dispute settlement and adjudication, the UN Charter art. 93 provides for the International Court of Justice (ICJ) as 'the principal judicial organ of the United Nations'. In view of the frequent indeterminacy of rules (e.g. of customary law) and 'general principles' of international law, art. 38 ICJ Statute recognizes 'judicial decisions' as 'subsidiary means for the determination of rules of law' (para. 1 (d)), just as other international dispute settlement procedures (like art. 3 of the World Trade Organization (WTO) Dispute Settlement Understanding) explicitly acknowledge the judicial function to 'clarify the existing provisions of [WTO] agreements in accordance with customary rules of interpretation of public international law' (para. 2). The more globalization continues to transform national 'public goods' (PGs) into international 'aggregate PGs' (like the international monetary, financial, trading, environmental, development, and rule of law systems) demanded by citizens, the more important become international law and multilevel governance institutions for the collective supply of international PGs, including the ever larger number of international courts of justice protecting multilevel rule of law systems through impartial and independent, judicial identification, interpretation, and application of the rules of law and legally binding adjudication in conformity with procedural and substantive 'principles of justice' and 'due process of law'. The proliferation of international courts and their judicial 'clarification' and the related development of international law remain uneven, however; the 'judicial function' is more developed in mutually beneficial international economic law (IEL), human rights law (HRL), and international criminal and administrative law (e.g. as applied by the increasing number of international criminal and administrative courts) than in most other areas of international relations.[4]

Similar to global economic, environmental, and technological integration, the effectiveness of multilevel political, legal, and judicial governance requires connecting local, national, regional, and worldwide legal and judicial institutions so that rule of law systems function in mutually coherent ways as required by the 'consistent interpretation' and 'judicial comity' requirements

---

3 On the characteristics of 'legal systems' as a union of 'primary rules of conduct' and 'secondary rules of recognition, change and adjudication' see H.L.A. Hart, *The Concept of Law* (OUP, 1994), ch. V.
4 For a classification of ten different types of international courts and tribunals see Benedict Kingsbury, 'International courts: uneven judicialization in global order' in James Crawford, Martti Koskenniemi (eds.), *The Cambridge Companion to International Law* (CUP, 2012), 203.

of national and international legal systems. 'Judicial dialogues' and cooperation among 'overlapping jurisdictions' are all the more important because, in
contrast to national judicial systems, most international courts coexist without institutional and legal hierarchies and enforcement powers similar to
national courts; their 'judicial authority' depends on communication and
justification of rules vis-à-vis governments and citizens required to comply
with international judicial decisions settling disputes over the application of
rules of international law through legally binding procedures of interpretation and adjudication. How should national, regional, and worldwide 'courts
of justice' cooperate in protecting transnational rule of law for the benefit of
citizens without unduly limiting their own authority and often 'exclusive
jurisdiction' (e.g. pursuant to art. 344 of the Treaty on the Functioning of the
European Union (TFEU), art. 23 WTO Dispute Settlement Understanding)
for interpreting and enforcing their respective legal systems? How should
such 'exclusive jurisdiction clauses' be interpreted and coordinated in multilevel governance of interdependent PGs, for instance in view of the fact that
international agreements binding on the European Union (EU), such as the
WTO Agreement, become an integral part of the EU legal system governing
relations among EU institutions, EU member states, EU citizens, and other
non-governmental actors also inside the EU (e.g. as regulated in the customs
union exceptions in the General Agreement on Tariffs and Trade (GATT) art.
XXIV and the General Agreement on Trade in Services (GATS) art. V)?[5]

Legitimate diversity of multilevel judicial governance systems

The term 'governance' (*gubernare*, meaning 'to steer' and 'to regulate') refers to
the image of steering a ship (e.g. the 'state ship'). Governance differs from
government by its different performance of government functions without a
unifying authority, as illustrated by the decentralized performance of information, allocation, coordination, and sanctioning functions through common
market law, competition rules, and intergovernmental network cooperation in
the EU. Even inside states with a *centralized government authority* controlling the
state, there are many diverse forms of decentralized governance (e.g. through
market mechanisms), centralized governance (e.g. through regulatory agencies), multilevel governments (e.g. in federal states), and 'network governance'
(e.g. among central banks). National government systems for the supply of
national PGs legitimately differ even among constitutional democracies.
Similarly, international regulatory systems for multilevel governance of *international PGs* differ depending on their diverse, regulatory challenges, as illustrated by the diverse memberships, jurisdictions, applicable law clauses, and
procedures of the ICJ, the International Tribunal for the Law of the Sea

5 Cf. Enzo Cannizzaro, Paolo Palchetti, Ramses Wessel (eds), *International Law as Law of the European Union* (Martinus Nijhoff Publishers, 2012).

(ITLOS), the WTO dispute settlement system, the International Criminal Court, international administrative tribunals, regional economic and human rights courts, and arbitral tribunals; as multilevel legal systems often define the 'judicial functions' and their relationships to democratic and international law-making differently, the interpretative and judicial methodologies applied by judges for the settlement of disputes over the identification, interpretation, and application of rules and principles of law may likewise differ in response to their diverse legal contexts.

Multilevel governance through legislative, administrative, and judicial institutions entails an increasing fragmentation of central government authority in nation states – notably in the field of economic policy – and more diverse, public and non-governmental governance institutions, regulatory systems, and 'private–public partnerships' at local, national, regional, and worldwide levels for the collective supply of 'aggregate PGs'. Due to the comparatively more limited law-creating processes in *international* compared with *national legal systems*, judicial identification and application of often indeterminate international rules and principles may also be more important in international law compared with domestic legal systems. The functional reallocation of regulatory and judicial powers – both upwards to *international* and downwards to *subnational institutions* – results in new overlapping jurisdictions (like commercial arbitration, regional and worldwide dispute settlement systems) challenging traditional government functions, related legal hierarchies, concepts (e.g. of state sovereignty), democratic accountability, and 'participatory democracy'. Due to the divergent roles (e.g. as ad hoc dispute settlers or permanent courts guarding rule of law) and functions of international courts (e.g. for rule-clarification and adjudication vis-à-vis states, individuals, and other non-governmental actors), their cooperation with domestic courts differs from one area to the other (e.g. in the context of legally binding 'preliminary rulings', non-binding 'preliminary opinion' procedures, 'prior exhaustion of local remedies' requirements, supervision of transnational arbitration, recognition and enforcement of arbitral awards by national courts).

Need for connecting multilevel judicial governance systems

This section begins with a brief reminder of the tensions between the rule of law principles in EU law and the reluctance of the Court of Justice (CJEU) to accept and comply with the jurisprudence of other multilevel dispute settlement systems – e.g. of the WTO, the ITLOS, the International Center for the Settlement of Investment Disputes (ICSID), the European Court of Human Rights (ECtHR), and the European Economic Area (EEA) – as legally binding or 'relevant context' for CJEU jurisprudence. The next section emphasizes the customary law requirement of clarifying 'principles of justice' and the diverse 'contexts of justice' in the interactions between national and international 'courts of justice', including five different approaches to justifying IEL in terms of 'principles of justice'. The *Kadi* and *Solange* jurisprudence of European courts remain unique European models of multilevel judicial protection of 'constitutional justice' for the benefit of citizens (see the following section). The next section discusses alternative models of 'Westphalian justice' and of 'cosmopolitan justice' in the external relations law of the EU and criticizes the lack of effective judicial remedies against arbitrary EU violations of the EU's WTO obligations to the detriment of EU citizens and other non-governmental 'violation victims' as well as 'retaliation victims'; it is suggested that the successful multilevel judicial protection of cosmopolitan commercial rights, investments, and human rights offers more convincing models of 'constitutional justice' protecting transnational rule of law for the benefit of citizens in their mutually beneficial economic cooperation across frontiers than arbitrary disregard by EU institutions for their multilevel legal and judicial obligations under the interdependent WTO and EU legal and dispute settlement systems.

The chapter concludes that multilevel judicial protection of transnational rule of law in the external relations of the EU requires linking the EU's multilevel judicial protection of individual rights to other multilevel judicial governance systems, for instance, in international conventions (like the 1958 New York Convention) on the recognition and enforcement of foreign arbitral awards, the 1965 World Bank Convention establishing the ICSID, and the multilevel legal and dispute settlement systems of other worldwide agreements such as the WTO and the UN Convention on the Law of the Sea (UNCLOS). Rather than *promoting* 'strict observance and the development of international law' in conformity with art. 3 (5) of the Treaty on European Union (TEU) as illustrated by the *Kadi* jurisprudence, the EU Court's judicial self-restraint (e.g. vis-à-vis WTO dispute settlement rulings) *reduces* the legal, democratic, and judicial accountability of EU governance institutions for their harmful violations of the rule of law – without convincing justifications vis-à-vis adversely affected citizens and their legitimate reliance on the rule of law principles underlying both the EU and WTO legal and dispute settlement systems.

Access to justice and its limits in the international relations law of the EU

EU law protects 'justice' – as one of the 'values common to the Member States' of the EU (art. 2 TEU) – in diverse ways. For instance:

- as an *objective* of EU law (e.g. in art. 67 (2) TFEU: 'The Union shall facilitate access to justice');
- as corresponding *fundamental rights* (e.g. in art. 47 of the EU Charter of Fundamental Rights of the EU protecting the 'right to an effective remedy and to a fair trial' so as 'to ensure effective access to justice');
- and as *constitutional principles* for EU institutions like the 'Court of Justice' of the EU (cf. art. 19 TEU) and the EU 'area of freedom, security and justice' (arts. 67–76 TFEU).

Constitutional requirements of 'judicial comity' among 'courts of justice'?

European law provides for a more comprehensive system of multilevel legal and judicial protection of constitutional and other individual rights than any other international treaty system.[6] The commitment of EU law to 'the rule of law' (art. 2 TEU), including 'the strict observance and the development of international law, including respect for the principles of the United Nations Charter' (art. 3 TEU), suggests that the common goal of the multilevel legal and judicial remedies is – as stated in art. 19 TEU – to 'ensure that in the interpretation and application of the Treaties the law is observed' for the benefit of the 500 million EU citizens as 'agents of justice' and 'democratic principals' of European and national governance institutions.[7] In Opinion 1/91 on the 1991 Agreement establishing an EEA, the CJEU acknowledged:

> An international agreement providing for... a system of courts is in principle compatible with Community law. The Community's competence in the field of international relations and its capacity to conclude international agreements necessarily entails the power to submit to the decisions of a court which is created or designated by such an agreement as regards the interpretation and application of its provisions.[8]

The same judgment also recognized that – just as international agreements binding on the EU are an 'integrating part of the Community legal system'[9] with a legal rank below EU 'primary law' but above EU secondary law – judgments of international courts set up under such agreements may be legally binding on all EU institutions including the CJEU.[10] In practice, however, the CJEU only rarely recognizes the legally binding character of such court decisions and refers to such dispute settlement jurisprudence (e.g. of WTO dispute settlement bodies, the ECtHR) only selectively as relevant precedents for EU law.[11]

---

6 For a comprehensive analysis see EU Agency for Fundamental Rights, *Access to Justice in Europe: An Overview of Challenges and Opportunities* (2011).

7 Cf. Advisory Opinion 1/09 of the CJEU of 8 March 2011, para. 69: 'the national court, in collaboration with the Court of Justice, fulfils a duty entrusted to them both of ensuring that in the interpretation and application of the Treaties the law is observed.'

8 Advisory Opinion 1/91, ECR 1999 I-6079, para. 40.

9 According to the ECJ, international agreements concluded by the EC become an 'integral part of the Community legal system' (Case 181/73, *Haegeman* ECR 1974 449). In *International Fruit Company* (Joined Cases 21-24/72, ECR 1972 1219), the ECJ recognized that – due to the legal succession of the EC to the GATT rights and obligations of EC member states – GATT law had also become an integral part of the Community legal system.

10 Advisory Opinion 1/91, para. 39.

11 Bruno de Witte, 'The use of the ECHR and convention case law by the European Court of Justice' in Patricia Popelier, Catherine Van de Heyning, Piet Van Nuffel (eds), *The Human Rights Protection in the European Legal Order: The Interaction between the European and the National Courts* (Intersentia, 2011), 17 ff.

Is this focus on protecting the autonomy of EU institutions compatible with the constitutional requirements of 'upholding', 'promoting', and 'contributing to' the EU's constitutional values such as 'protection of its citizens' and 'the strict observance and the development of international law' (art. 3 (5) TEU)? As customary law requires interpreting treaties and settling related disputes 'in conformity with the principles of justice and international law', including 'human rights and fundamental freedoms for all' (as codified in the Preamble and art. 31 of the 1969 Vienna Convention on the Law of Treaties): why does the CJEU fail to indicate any 'principles of justice' justifying its lack of cooperation with other international dispute settlement systems (e.g. of the WTO)?

Why does the CJEU refrain from 'judicial balancing' of public and private interests in certain areas of the foreign relations law of the EU?

This contribution praises the CJEU's *Kadi* jurisprudence as a model for multi-level judicial protection of fundamental rights in multilevel governance of PGs. Yet, even though the CJEU emphasizes that the 'judicial system of the European Union is a complete system of legal remedies and procedures designed to ensure review of the legality of acts of the institutions',[12] the lack of cooperation by the CJEU with other international dispute settlement systems entails that individual access to justice is not effectively protected – also inside the EU – in many other areas of transnational cooperation among citizens and related multilevel governance of international PGs demanded by citizens. The jurisprudence of the CJEU reveals a distinct reluctance on the part of the Court to limit its legal and institutional autonomy by cooperating with other international dispute settlement systems outside the EU, as illustrated by judgments and advisory opinions by the CJEU denying the consistency with EU law of EU participation in international dispute settlement systems, e.g. as provided for in the 1976 Draft Agreement establishing a European laying-up fund for inland waterway vessels,[13] in the 1991 EEA Agreement,[14] in earlier proposals for EU membership in the European Convention on Human Rights (ECHR) and its ECtHR,[15] or in a 2010 draft agreement providing for a new European and Community Patents Court.[16]

---

12 Advisory Opinion 1/09, para. 70.
13 Advisory Opinion 1/76, ECR 1977 741.
14 Advisory Opinions 1/91.
15 Advisory Opinion 2/94, ECR 1996 I-1759.
16 Cf. note 7 and for an analysis of the CJEU's 'selfish attitude' protecting its own authority and prerogatives against rival international dispute settlement mechanisms Bruno de Witte, 'A selfish court? The Court of Justice and the design of international dispute settlement beyond the European Union' in Marise Cremona, Anne Thies (eds), *The Role of the Court of Justice of the EU and EU External Relations Law: Constitutional Challenges* (Hart Publishing, 2013).

In its judgment on the *Mox Plant* dispute, the CJEU agreed with the claim of the EU Commission that Ireland – by submitting the dispute to bilateral arbitration and to the ITLOS – had breached the prohibition laid down in art. 344 TFEU of submitting disputes relating to EU law to outside dispute settlement mechanisms.[17] The *FIAMM* and *Intertanko* judgments[18] of the European Court of Justice (ECJ) suggest that – contrary to the constitutional mandate of art. 21 TEU that the 'Union's action on the international scene shall be guided by the principles which have inspired its own creation, development and enlargement, and which it seeks to advance in the wider world', as convincingly defended in the *Kadi* judgments discussed below – the ECJ has decided to grant legal and judicial immunity to violations by the EU of its obligations under WTO law and the UNCLOS, without offering adversely affected EU citizens and EU member states judicial remedies. As neither EU law nor WTO law provides for any lawful discretion of EU institutions to violate the EU's international legal obligations, the ECJ justifies its refusal to review the legality of alleged EU violations of GATT/WTO obligations as 'integral parts of the Community legal system' by relying on power-oriented claims by the political EU institutions that they need 'freedom of manoeuvre' to continue violating international law even if the 'reasonable period' for implementing legally binding dispute settlement rulings (e.g. by WTO dispute settlement bodies) has expired.[19]

In contrast to the *Kadi* judgment's defence of the 'autonomy of the EU legal order' in order to enhance legal protection for individuals and respect for human rights, the ECJ's refusal to cooperate with WTO and UNCLOS dispute settlement bodies in protecting 'strict observance of international law' *undermines* the EU's rule of law system, including the EU's 'strict observance of international law' (art. 3 TEU), without any regard to the rights of EU citizens (e.g. their democratic rights to rely on 'strict observance' of international agreements ratified by parliaments for the benefit of EU citizens). The more the CJEU prioritizes claims by EU politicians for 'freedom of manoeuvre' to violate UN law, WTO law, and other treaty obligations of the EU ratified by parliaments – without even requiring the political EU institutions to justify how EU non-compliance with WTO legal obligations and related WTO dispute settlement rulings can serve legitimate 'Community interests' in 'the rule of law' (art. 2 TEU) – the more it becomes necessary to review and challenge such power politics by the EU's political and judicial institutions and their often arbitrary claims that the 'nature and structure' of worldwide agreements and

---

17 Case C-459/03, *Commission* v. *Ireland*, ECR 2006 I-4635.

18 Joined Cases C-120 and C-121/06 P, *FIAMM*, ECR 2008 I-6513; C-308/06, *Intertanko*, ECR 2008 I-4057.

19 This term continues to be used by both the political EU institutions and the CJEU (e.g. in Joined cases C-120 and C-121/06 P, *FIAMM*, para. 119) as the only justification for their disregard of legally binding WTO rules and WTO dispute settlement rulings.

dispute settlement systems exclude effective judicial remedies inside the EU holding EU institutions accountable for their violations of international agreement ratified by parliaments for the benefit of EU citizens.

The need for clarifying 'principles of justice' justifying the multilevel judicial protection of the 'rule of law'

All UN member states have human rights obligations under the UN Charter and under UN, regional, and national HRL as universally recognized in hundreds of human rights instruments like the UN Convention on the Rights of the Child ratified by more than 190 states. Many human rights instruments confirm that '[a]ll human rights are universal, indivisible and interdependent and interrelated'; and 'it is the duty of States, regardless of their political, economic and cultural systems, to promote and protect all human rights and fundamental freedoms'.[20]

According to art. 21 TEU,

> [t]he Union's action on the international scene shall be guided by the principles which have inspired its own creation, development and enlargement, and which it seeks to advance in the wider world: democracy, the rule of law, the universality and indivisibility of human rights and fundamental freedoms, respect for human dignity, the principles of equality and solidarity, and respect for the principles of the United Nations Charter and international law.

In her speech of 16 June 2010, the EU High Representative for Foreign Affairs, Catherine Ashton, confirmed to the European Parliament that 'human rights, democracy and rule of law... will run like a silver thread' through the EU's foreign policies.[21] Hence, the EU has included into its international trade agreements with more than 100 third countries 'human rights clauses' and additional provisions on 'human rights dialogues' and 'human rights assistance', thereby also recognizing fundamental rights as a matter of justice in trade relations. Even though human rights and 'principles of justice' often remain contested and offer no precise guidelines for designing IEL, the customary rules of international treaty interpretation – as codified in the Vienna

---

20 Vienna Declaration and Programme of Action adopted at the UN World Conference on Human Rights by more than 170 states on 25 June 1993 (A/CONF.157/24, para. 5). This 'universal, indivisible, interrelated, interdependent and mutually reinforcing' nature of human rights was reaffirmed by all UN member states in numerous human rights instruments such as UN Resolution 63/116 of 10 December 2008 on the '60th anniversary of the Universal Declaration of Human Rights' (UN Doc A/RES/63/116 of 26 February 2009).
21 For a recent analysis see Michal Golabek, *'Weaving a Silver Thread.' Human Rights Coherence in EU Foreign Affairs and Counter-Terrorism* (EUI doctoral thesis, 2013).

Convention on the Law of Treaties (VCLT) – require interpreting treaties and settling related disputes 'in conformity with the principles of justice and international law', including 'universal respect for, and observance of, human rights and fundamental freedoms for all' (Preamble and art. 31 VCLT). As HRL also protects individual and democratic diversity, it recognizes 'margins of appreciation' for implementing human rights in domestic legal systems with due respect for the legitimate reality of 'constitutional pluralism' and 'reasonable disagreement' among individuals, peoples, and governments on how legal obligations to respect, protect, and fulfil human rights should be construed, prioritized, and legally protected. Governments also often disagree on how 'equal freedoms' as 'first principle of justice' (J. Rawls) should be protected in IEL, for instance in common law countries (protecting 'common law freedoms') compared with constitutional democracies (e.g. in the EU) protecting 'common market freedoms', general consumer welfare, and non-discriminatory conditions of competition through fundamental rights and judicial remedies. The human rights to justification and 'access to justice' are recognized in ever more national, regional, and worldwide legal instruments (e.g. in HRL and IEL), for instance in terms of rights to justification, effective legal and judicial remedies, fair and public proceedings, timely resolution of disputes, legal aid if necessary, and adequate redress.[22]

Need for distinguishing the diverse 'contexts of justice'

The UN Charter principles of 'sovereign equality of states' (art. 2) and 'self-determination of peoples' (arts. 1, 55) aim at protecting international peace by legally recognizing the territorial status quo (e.g. in terms of governmental and popular control over a territory) even though the related distribution of natural resources is as arbitrary from a moral point of view as the distribution of natural human capacities among individuals. The UN legal obligations to respect, protect, and fulfil 'human rights and fundamental freedoms for all' (cf. arts. 1, 55, 56) limit the injustices deriving from power-oriented allocation of rights (e.g. to the rulers controlling a national territory) and from natural inequalities among individuals (e.g. in terms of genetics, health and human capacities) by protecting equal individual and popular rights to liberty and self-development so as 'to establish conditions under which justice and respect for the obligations arising from treaties and other sources of international law can be maintained' (Preamble UN Charter). In contrast to the comprehensive definition of 'principles of justice' in EU law in terms of fundamental rights and principles of democratic constitutionalism, the UN Charter specifies neither its 'principles of justice' nor the human rights obligations of all UN member states; in view of the fact of 'reasonable disagreement'

---

22 See notes 2 and 6.

among individuals and people with diverse constitutional traditions, resources, democratic preferences, and conceptions for a 'good life' and 'political justice', the progressive clarification and legal realization of human rights depend on their constitutional, legislative, administrative, and judicial protection and prioritization in conformity with other 'principles of justice' in national and international legal systems.

Yet, both UN law and EU law proceed from 'constitutional recognition' of equal individual and popular rights to liberty ('constitutional' and 'allocative justice') limiting state sovereignty, and protect the freedom of individuals, people, and states to conclude ever more private and public 'social contracts' specifying principles of 'distributive', 'corrective' and 'commutative justice', and 'equity' through more specific principles and rules on mutually beneficial cooperation (e.g. 'human rights and fundamental freedoms for all', 'difference principles' protecting poor people against harmful distributive consequences of formally equal treatment, principles of reciprocity, *pacta sunt servanda*, good faith protection of 'legitimate expectations', principles for benefit sharing, fair play, tort law, correction of 'unjust enrichment'). Such principles are important for resolving disputes in 'courts of justice' whenever conflicting claims are made upon the design of social and legal practices, and persons insist and disagree on what they consider their rights. In order to settle disputes over such complaints and social practices peacefully and clarify indeterminate principles and rules through fair procedures, national and international legal systems protect 'access to justice' and 'administration of justice' by independent and impartial tribunals.[23] The diversity of e.g. civil, commercial, labour, criminal, administrative, and constitutional courts illustrates that the 'judicial administration of justice' must take into account the diverse 'contexts of justice' (e.g. the different dimensions of human autonomy rights) in economic regulation, such as:

- *private freedoms* of citizens (e.g. in families and associations) to define and develop one's individual identity in private communities with due respect for the legitimate diversity of individual and social conceptions of a 'good life';
- *moral freedoms* of all members of global humanity (e.g. to respect for, and protection of, 'inalienable' and 'indivisible' human rights) in their relationships with other human beings inside and beyond states;
- *legal freedoms* of citizens to equal treatment and participation in legal communities, including 'negative freedoms' from unjustified government

---

23 This contribution focuses on *judicial* administration of justice rather than on constitutional, legislative, and administrative protection of principles of justice at national, transnational, and international levels of governance and regulation (on the latter see Ernst-Ulrich Petersmann, (note 1).

restrictions and 'positive freedoms' of participation and development of one's human capacities;

- *political freedoms* of citizens to participate as co-authors of democratic legislation in the democratic exercise of national governance powers;
- *cosmopolitan freedoms* of citizens (e.g. in their roles as producers, investors, traders, and consumers cooperating in the global division of labour) to be recognized and legally protected as 'world citizens' in national and international law in order to be able to exercise their collective responsibility for jointly supplying transnational public goods, including entitlement 'to a social and international order in which the rights and freedoms set forth in this Declaration can be fully realized' (art. 28 UDHR).[24]

Five competing approaches to justifying IEL in terms of 'principles of justice'

Investments and trade are of existential importance for producing and consuming scarce goods and services demanded by citizens for their survival and self-development. Trade and investments are closely interrelated, for instance due to the fact that investments into the production of goods and services necessarily precede cross-border trade of the goods and services produced. Hence, transnational trade and investment regulation belong to the oldest fields of national and international legal systems, as illustrated by ancient trade agreements concluded between Mediterranean city republics, the Roman *jus gentium*, and the Medieval law merchant (*lex mercatoria*). Yet, in contrast to the systems of bilateral trade agreements linked by most-favoured-nation clauses (e.g. in Europe following the 1860 Cobden–Chevalier trade agreement between England and France, in the Americas following the US Reciprocal Trade Agreements Act of 1934), the about 3000 bilateral and plurilateral investment agreements in force today have never led to a worldwide investment agreement similar to GATT (1947) and WTO (1994) with substantive 'primary rules of conduct', 'secondary rules' of recognition, change, and adjudication, and worldwide institutions with legislative, administrative, and judicial functions.

The 1965 World Bank Convention on the Settlement of Investment Disputes between States and Nationals of other States provides for institutionalized dispute settlement and enforcement procedures without – as in the case of GATT/WTO law – specifying the applicable *substantive rules* of conduct. Whereas the ICJ, regional courts, and GATT and WTO dispute

---

24 The different private, legal, and political 'contexts of justice' in particular communities, and of moral and cosmopolitan principles in the world community of human beings, have been recognized in human rights declarations since the *Déclaration des droits de l'homme et du citoyen* of 1789; cf. Rainer Forst, *Contexts of Justice: Political Philosophy beyond Liberalism and Communitarianism* (University of California Press, 2002).

settlement bodies are 'community-originated dispute settlement institutions', investor–state arbitral tribunals tend to be 'party-originated dispute resolution mechanisms'[25] which are likely to settle disputes (e.g. about legal claims involving or affecting multiple responsible actors) in different ways (e.g. without multilateral adoption and surveillance of dispute settlement findings by a worldwide institution like the WTO Dispute Settlement Body). Why have commercial, trade, and investment adjudication evolved into such diverse dispute settlement rules, procedures, and institutions even though some regional and worldwide economic agreements (like the still-born 1948 Havana Charter for an International Trade Organization) and international courts with universal jurisdiction (like the ICJ) aimed at their 'integrated regulation'?

From the perspective of 'normative individualism' underlying both HRL and consumer-driven markets regulated by IEL, trade and investment law and adjudication must also be evaluated in terms of respecting, protecting, and fulfilling human rights and 'human welfare'.[26] The UN Charter and HRL explicitly recognize 'principles of justice' as integral parts of modern international and national legal systems. The Bretton Woods Agreements, GATT, and the WTO agreements do not explicitly refer to 'principles of justice' in view of the 'reasonable disagreement' among governments on human rights and justice dimensions of IEL. Yet, the customary law requirement of interpreting IEL, and settling related disputes, 'in conformity with principles of justice' and 'human rights and fundamental freedoms for all' also requires clarifying how IEL can be justified in terms of fundamental rights and other 'principles of justice'. Five competing approaches to promoting 'principles of justice' in IEL can be distinguished.

(1) Justice as international order protected by power (e.g. GATT 1947)

National *political realism* focuses on states as the main international actors in a 'billiard ball model' of 'international law among egoist states' driven by power-politics so as to maximize national security. Realists claim that, as state-centred international law reflects the status quo distribution of power rather than 'principles of justice', 'international adjudication is [also] unable to impose effective restraints upon the struggle for power on the international scene'.[27] International courts can only be effective 'in those spheres which do not affect

---

25 On these two different categories of courts see David D. Caron, 'Towards a political theory of international courts and tribunals' (2007) 24 *Berkeley Journal of International Law* 401–23.

26 On the necessary limitation of economic 'gross domestic product' approaches by human rights approaches and complementary 'capabilities' and 'human development approaches' to international economic regulation see Martha C. Nussbaum, *Creating Capabilities. The Human Development Approach* (Harvard University Press, 2011).

27 Hans J Morgenthau, *Politics among Nations. The Struggle for Power and Peace* (McGraw-Hill Education, 1951), 224.

the security and existence of the state'.[28] 'Political disputes' over the use of force and the distribution of power underlying the applicable rules of international law risk eluding judicial control and being 'non-justiciable', as illustrated by the fact that the Permanent Court of International Justice (PCIJ) considered only once such an international dispute.[29] Similarly, *national courts* also tended to be ineffective in constraining democratic revolutions challenging power-oriented, authoritarian legal systems (e.g. in England in the 17th century, America and France in the 18th century). Colonialism and the intergovernmental power politics in the context of 'GATT 1947', which was not ratified by the US Congress, prior to the establishment of its Legal Office in 1982/83 illustrate the IEL dimensions of 'political realism' relying on political rather than judicial dispute settlement methods.

(2) Justice as national democratic decision-making (e.g. the Bretton Woods agreements)

The foreign policies of liberal states tend to be guided in diverse ways by their domestic 'principles of justice'.[30] *Wilsonian liberalism* believed that, following World War I, the USA could protect international peace through promoting liberal democratic values and institutions for the peaceful resolution of international disputes. But the rejection by the US Congress of US membership in the League of Nations and of US acceptance of the compulsory jurisdiction of the PCIJ illustrated that democratic people might also refuse projecting national democratic and judicial institutions on to international levels of governance in a world including non-liberal and 'outlaw states'. Neither under the League of Nations nor under the UN has it been possible to institute effective 'world parliaments' and 'world courts' with universal compulsory jurisdictions. *Democratic New Haven approaches* to US foreign policies following World War II succeeded in persuading other states to ratify the UN Charter, the Bretton Woods Agreements, and UN Specialized Agencies on the basis of drafts prepared by the US government. Yet, the policy-oriented 'democratic participant perspective' of the New Haven School also justified US legal privileges (e.g. veto rights in UN and Bretton Woods institutions), unilateral military interventions, US refusals to participate in international PGs regimes (like compulsory jurisdiction of the ICJ, the International Criminal Court, the Kyoto Convention on climate change prevention), and discriminatory economic sanctions (e.g. by means of s. 301 of the US trade law); such 'power politics in disguise' has prompted

---

28 Edward Hallet Carr, *The Twenty-Years Crisis 1919–1939* (Macmillan and Company Limited, 1940), 249.
29 Cf. Morgenthau, *Politics among Nations*, 224 (discussing the PCIJ advisory opinion on the dispute over the German–Austrian Customs Union, PCIJ Ser. A/B, no. 41).
30 Frank J. Garcia, *Global Justice and International Economic Law: Three Takes* (CUP, 2013), 67 ff.

criticism of 'the miracle of New Haven' endorsing whatever policy justifications are advanced by the US State Department and US interest groups.[31] Also John Rawls' proposals for a *Law of Peoples* justify the existing principles of UN law for the national pursuit of international justice in an international society of liberal states, non-liberal but 'decent states', outlaw states, and states burdened by unfavourable conditions,[32] without proposing a theory of global justice based on cosmopolitan or communitarian principles limiting the perceived 'justice deficits' of international law. Arguably, the legitimacy of the Bretton Woods Agreements derives more from their parliamentary ratification by democratic states than from their 'hegemonic elaboration' (notably by the USA and the UK) and multilevel monetary and financial governance dominated by industrialized donor countries.[33]

(3) 'Constitutional justice' as multilevel constitutional protection of constitutional rights (e.g. UN HRL, EU law)

All UN member states have adopted national (big C) Constitutions (written or unwritten) that recognize the importance of international law and institutions for the collective supply of international 'aggregate public goods' (PGs) demanded by citizens, including functionally limited (small c) 'treaty constitutions' (*sic*) establishing UN Specialized Agencies like the International Labor Organization (ILO), the World Health Organization (WHO), the Food and Agriculture Organization (FAO), and the UN Educational, Scientific, and Cultural Organization (UNESCO). The functionally limited treaty constitutions constitute multilevel governance powers (the *enabling function* of constitutions); subject governments to legal and institutional restraints (the *limiting function* of constitutions); commit government policies to protecting PGs (like protection of human rights, 'sustainable development') through agreed regulatory instruments (the *regulatory function* of constitutions); and legitimize law and governance by 'principles of justice' (the *justificatory function* of constitutions), such as labour rights justifying ILO law, human rights to education and

31 Academics claim that the interdisciplinary 'New Haven methodology' of analysing national and international law as decision-making processes that are both 'authoritative and controlling' in the pursuit of a 'public order of human dignity' should be based on a 'five-step interdisciplinary analysis' of '(1) the parameters of the social ill or problem the law has to address; (2) to review the conflicting interests or claims; (3) to analyse the past legal responses in light of the factors that produced them; (4) to predict future such decisions; and (5) to assess the past legal responses, invent alternatives and recommend solutions better in line with a... public order of human dignity' (cf. S. Wiessner, 'The New Haven school of jurisprudence: a universal toolkit for understanding and shaping the law' (2010) *Asia Pacific Law Review* 18, 45–61, p. 48.

32 John Rawls, *Law of Peoples* (Harvard University Press, 1999), 59 ff.

33 Frank J. Garcia, 'Global justice, the Bretton Woods institutions and the problem of inequality' (2007) 10 *Journal of International Economic Law*, 461–82.

democratic governance justifying **UNESCO** law, rights to health protection justifying **WHO** law, and freedom from hunger justifying **FAO** law. Yet, the inadequate legal, democratic, and judicial accountability of governments dominating UN decision-making processes entails that most UN institutions fail to protect international PGs effectively for the benefit of all citizens (like UN HRL, transnational rule of law). EU common market law and the regional implementation of UN HRL through the ECHR protect fundamental rights more effectively.

(4) 'Commutative justice' in functionally limited PGs regimes (e.g. WTO law)

The WTO Agreement establishes a multilevel legal, governance, and dispute settlement system outside the UN legal system aimed at promoting reciprocal liberalization and regulation of a multilateral trading system based on mutually agreed 'commutative *justice principles*',[34] like reciprocal market access commitments (e.g. GATT arts. II, XXVIII) subject to sovereign rights to protect non-economic PGs (e.g. arts. XIX–XXI GATT). Yet, similar to UN law, WTO law also remains dominated by 'inter-governmental decision-making' and fails to protect its treaty objectives (like 'sustainable development') effectively due to inadequate regulation of 'market failures', 'governance failures', and of 'accountability mechanisms'.

(5) 'Cosmopolitan justice regimes' (e.g. commercial and investment law)

Cosmopolitan conceptions of law[35] aim at multilevel legal and judicial protection of commercial, property, and other cosmopolitan rights of citizens through institutionalized networks of national and transnational courts and arbitral tribunals. Transnational commercial and investment law and arbitration, rights-based free trade agreements like the EEA, or international criminal law and related adjudication have proven to protect international PGs (like transnational rule of law, fundamental rights) more effectively than

---

34 The Latin term 'commutare' means 'to exchange'; 'commutative justice' refers to mutual agreements on functionally limited 'treaty principles of justice' like the economic efficiency principles underlying the legal ranking of economically 'optimal trade policy instruments' in GATT/WTO law (e.g. non-discriminatory domestic regulation and subsidies rather than border discrimination, tariffs rather than non-tariff trade barriers, sanitary regulations on the basis of science-based 'risk-assessments' rather than on the basis of discriminatory protectionism).

35 The Greek term 'cosmopolite' refers to a 'citizen of the world' recognizing all human beings as morally equal and constituting a single world community that should avoid national prejudices. Alec Stone Sweet, 'A cosmopolitan legal order: constitutional pluralism and rights adjudication in Europe' (2012) 1 *Global Constitutionalism* p. 53 defines a 'cosmopolitan legal order' as 'a transnational legal system in which all public officials bear the obligation to fulfil the fundamental rights of every person within their jurisdiction, without respect to nationality or citizenship'.

'Westphalian legal regimes' that prioritize rights of governments over rights of citizens without effective legal, democratic, and judicial accountability of governments vis-à-vis adversely affected citizens.[36] Cosmopolitan regimes are characterized by the proliferation of international courts – like the European Free Trade Area (EFTA) Court in the EEA, the arbitration and annulment procedures of the ICSID, and the more than half a dozen of international criminal courts complementing national criminal jurisdictions – which cooperate with domestic courts in their joint enforcement of transnational legal orders governing mutually beneficial, transnational cooperation among citizens, governmental, and non-governmental actors for the collective supply of PGs (like common markets, human rights, transnational rule of law).

The multilevel 'judicial governance' is complemented by intergovernmental cooperation and by ever more transnational governance networks of regulatory agencies (like central banks, competition authorities, food safety, environmental and other regulatory agencies) subject to legal, democratic, and judicial account-ability mechanisms that promote legitimacy and domestic political support.[37] Arguably, the justification of multilevel governance in terms of protecting cosmopolitan rights and the reality of transnational cooperation among sub-state actors (e.g. in the context of transnational 'supply chains' for energy and food security) strengthens the 'constitutional functions' of multilevel rules and institutions for protecting international PGs demanded by citizens.[38]

'Constitutional justice' protecting human rights: the European *Kadi* – and Solange jurisprudence

Article 47 of the Charter of Fundamental Rights of the EU protects the right to an effective remedy and to a fair trial as a cosmopolitan right of 'everyone', including alleged foreign terrorists. The four *Kadi* judgments of the General Court and CJEU since 2005 relate to EU regulations implementing UN Security Council sanctions adopted under art. 41 UN Charter vis-à-vis Mr Kadi and other alleged terrorists in response to the terrorist attacks of 11 September 2001. The Security Council had identified Mr Kadi (a wealthy citizen of Saudi-Arabia) as a possible supporter of Al-Qaida and had ordered the freezing of his assets. In the first judgment of 2005 on Mr Kadi's legal challenge of the EU regulation implementing the Security Council sanctions, the General Court refused to fully review the EU regulation in view of the judicial immunity of the Security Council sanctions; the Court only reviewed whether the Security Council had violated fundamental rights of Mr Kadi

---

36 Petersmann, (note 1), 145 ff.
37 On this emergence of a 'new disaggregated world order' and 'judges constructing a global legal system' see Anne Marie Slaughter, *A New World Order* (Princeton University Press, 2004), 65 ff.
38 Petersmann, (note 1), chs. I–IV.

protected by *jus cogens* and did not find such infringements. On appeal, the CJEU fully reviewed the lawfulness of the EU implementing regulation on the ground that all EU legal acts must remain consistent with the fundamental rights protected by EU law, even in case of implementation of UN Security Council sanctions; the Court also found – without pronouncing on the legality of the UN Security Council measures – that the EU implementing regulation had violated the claimant's fundamental right to be informed of the grounds for his subjection to sanctions, his right to be heard, his access to effective judicial review, and the right to protection of property.[39]

As the EU Commission and Council decided to maintain the sanctions, Mr Kadi appealed to the General Court once again. In its judgment of 2010, the General Court annulled the contested EU sanctions vis-à-vis Mr Kadi on the ground of infringements by the EU institutions of the rights of the defence, the right to respect for property, and the principle of proportionality, and also of the right of Mr Kadi to effective judicial review. In its judgment of 18 July 2013, the CJEU rejected the appeal and concluded that effective 'judicial review is indispensable to ensure a fair balance between the maintenance of international peace and security and the protection of the fundamental rights and freedoms of the person concerned, those being shared values of the UN and the European Union'.[40]

The judgment mentions a number of improvements in the UN Security Council procedures for delisting and *ex officio* re-examination of sanctions at UN level (such as the creation, in 2009, of the office of an independent Ombudsperson processing requests to be delisted from the UN sanctions list). Yet, the CJEU concurred with a previous finding of the ECtHR that these procedural improvements do not guarantee the listed persons effective judicial protection.[41] The *Kadi* judgment may be construed in conformity with the *Solange* jurisprudence of the German Constitutional Court as well as of the ECtHR to the effect that 'as long as' (which means *Solange* in German language) the higher level of law (i.e. UN law in the *Kadi* cases, EU law in the *Solange* jurisprudence of the German Constitutional Court) does not guarantee equivalent protection of fundamental rights, the courts at lower levels of multilevel legal and judicial systems must guarantee such fundamental rights. Just as the German Constitutional Court and the ECtHR refrained from exercising their jurisdiction 'as long as' the CJEU protects fundamental rights in ways equivalent to the constitutional protection under German constitutional law and the ECHR respectively, the CJEU might limit its judicial review of EU measures implementing UN Security Council sanctions once UN law offers equivalent procedural and substantive legal protection of

---

39 Case C-402/05P and C-415/05, *P. Kadi and Al Barakaat Foundation* v. *Council and Commission*,
    ECR 2008 I-6351.
40 Joined Cases C-584/10P, C-593/10P, and C-595/10P, para. 131 (not yet reported).
41 *Ibid.*, para. 133.

individual rights of the defence, property rights, and effective judicial protection.[42] As UN and regional human rights conventions leave states 'margins of appreciation' for implementing and protecting higher standards of human rights in their national legal systems, this contribution argues more generally that multilevel legal regulation and judicial protection of civil, political, economic, social, and cultural rights should be based on legal principles of mutually consistent interpretations and 'judicial comity' (e.g. regarding the local remedies rule in HRL), 'subsidiarity', and 'loyal cooperation' among the different levels of governance, and respect for the sovereign rights of states to guarantee higher levels of constitutional protection at national levels than at international levels of governance.[43] Yet, international trade and investment law differ from HRL by the fact that WTO law and bilateral investment treaties (BITs) often protect higher standards of economic freedoms, property rights, non-discrimination, and transnational rule of law than those in national trade and investment legislation permitting discriminatory border discrimination against foreign goods, services, and investments.

From 'Westphalian justice' in the ICJ and the WTO to multilevel cosmopolitan adjudication in HRL and IEL

The ICJ takes it for granted that 'Whatever the legal reasoning of a court of justice, its decisions must by definition be just, and therefore in that sense equitable';[44] and 'Equity as a legal concept is a direct emanation of the idea of justice. The Court whose task is by definition to administer justice is bound to apply it'.[45] Yet, similar to the deferential jurisprudence of the PCIJ towards state sovereignty (e.g. in terms of presumptions against limitations of national sovereignty, narrow interpretations of such treaty limitations), the contribution of the ICJ to the development of HRL has remained so limited during the first 50 years of ICJ jurisprudence making it 'necessary to question whether the International Court is a court of law, let alone a court of justice'.[46] For, as only states (i.e. legal constructs empowering the rulers over a population in a given territory, often without guarantees of democratic representation) may

---

42 Cf. Juliane Kokott, Christoph Sobotta, 'The Kadi case – constitutional core values and international law – finding the balance?' (2012) 23 *European Journal of International Law* 1015–24.

43 On the different judicial methodologies applied by the CJEU, the EFTA Court, and the ECtHR (e.g. regarding national 'margins of appreciation') see Ernst-Ulrich Petersmann, 'Multilevel judicial governance in European and international economic law' in Samantha Besson, Andreas R Ziegler (eds), *The Judge in European and International Law* (Schulthess, 2013), 45, 58 ff.

44 North Sea Continental Shelf Judgment ICJ Reports 1969, pp. 48–9, para. 88.

45 Continental Shelf (*Tunisia* v. *Libyan Arab Jamahiriya*), Judgment ICJ Reports 1982, p. 60, para. 71.

46 Philipp Allott, 'The international court and the voice of justice' in Vaughan Lowe, Malgosia Fitzmaurice (eds), *Fifty Years of the International Court of Justice* (CUP, 1996), 17, 27.

be parties in cases before the ICJ and the Court's jurisdiction is limited to cases submitted with the consent of the defendant state, large parts of the global social reality (e.g. citizens, the more than 2 billion poor people living without effective protection of their human rights, the global economy, international organizations) have no effective access to the ICJ and are not effectively represented in disputes before the ICJ.

'Principles of justice' in intergovernmental economic adjudication

As long as the diplomatic presentation of states in intergovernmental UN institutions and in the ICJ is left to rulers and their diplomats pursuing political self-interests (e.g. in limiting their legal, democratic, and judicial accountability vis-à-vis citizens adversely affected by, for instance, the 'resource privilege' and 'lending privilege' of governments to appropriate scarce resources for the benefit of the rulers), UN institutions can neither effectively protect justice vis-à-vis citizens nor rule-of-law for the benefit of citizens. Principles of justice and of equity continue to be important in the ICJ jurisprudence on procedural 'due process of law' and the settlement of border disputes (e.g. the delimitation of adjacent 'territorial seas' and 'continental shelves'). Yet, notwithstanding references to human rights in some ICJ judgments and advisory opinions since the *Corfu Channel* case (1949), it is only since the 1990s that the ICJ uses HRL as *ratio decidendi* for limiting certain abuses of government powers and 'feudal deference' towards governmental rulers.[47] In spite of the 'optional protocols' to some UN human rights conventions enabling individual complaints to political UN bodies, UN law continues to fail protecting human rights and other 'principles of justice' effectively vis-à-vis individuals and peoples exploited by non-democratic rulers or not protected through the traditional means of 'diplomatic protection'. The few investment disputes decided by the ICJ have been criticized as proving the inadequacy of ICJ proceedings for protecting investor rights and human rights by means of 'diplomatic protection', the prior 'exhaustion of local remedies', and ICJ judgments more than 20 years after the contested governmental interferences into the investor rights (e.g. in the ELSI case).[48] The deliberate avoidance by the ICJ, up to its *Genocide* case in 2007, of references to

---

47 For detailed analyses of the ICJ jurisprudence on human rights see the two contributions by Judge Bruno Simma, 'The ICJ and human rights' and by Judge Abdulqawi Ahmed Yusuf, 'The ICJ and the development of human rights law' in Società Italiana di Diritto Internazionale (ed.), *La Tutela Dei Diritti Umani e il Diritto Internazionale* (Editoriale Scientifica, 2012), 3–30, 573–81.

48 Judge Stephen M. Schwebel, 'The treatment of human rights and of aliens in the ICJ' in Vaughan Lowe, Malgosia Fitzmaurice (eds), *Fifty Years of the International Court of Justice* (CUP, 1996), 327, 350. The ICJ Judgment of November 2010 in the *Diallo Case* (*Guinea* v. *Congo*) seems to be the first economic dispute in which the ICJ assessed breaches of human rights treaty obligations referring to the jurisprudence of UN and regional human rights bodies.

judgments of other international courts, and the limited ICJ jurisdiction for human rights treaties,[49] further illustrate the narrow conceptions of procedural and substantive 'principles of justice' in UN law and in ICJ jurisprudence focusing on 'sovereign equality of states' and the ICJ as 'the principal judicial organ of the UN' (art. 92 UN Charter) without effective judicial protection of 'access to justice' as a human right and 'judicial dialogues' with other jurisdictions in order to clarify 'principles of justice'.

Also GATT/WTO dispute settlement procedures are limited to GATT/WTO members and have so far never applied the human rights obligations of all UN member states as applicable law or 'relevant context' for interpreting GATT/WTO obligations. Governments appear unwilling – in the UN (e.g. in the ICJ and UN treaty bodies established by human rights conventions) as well as in GATT/WTO – to submit genuine human rights disputes to international adjudication. International judges have to respect 'party autonomy' (as illustrated by the prohibition of going *ultra petita partium*). The intergovernmental structures of ICJ and GATT/WTO dispute settlement proceedings entail that legal responsibility in ICJ and GATT/WTO dispute settlement proceedings remains essentially 'Westphalian responsibility' by states/governments vis-à-vis other states/governments, often without effective remedies and enforcement mechanisms (e.g. no reparation of injury and no collective enforcement in GATT/WTO jurisprudence). The GATT/WTO dispute settlement system goes beyond the inter-state structures of ICJ dispute settlement proceedings, for instance by

- protecting 'access to justice' not only for states, but also for economically independent 'customs territories' (like Hong Kong, Macao, Taiwan), customs unions (like the EU) as well as access by individual and corporate actors to domestic courts;[50]
- protecting 'violation complaints' on the basis of legal presumptions that every violation of a GATT/WTO 'primary rule of conduct' justifies the presumption of 'nullification or impairment' of treaty benefits due to distortions of competition;
- extending legal responsibility through the admissibility of 'non-violation complaints' protecting 'commutative justice' (e.g. in the sense of the mutually agreed balance of reciprocal trade commitments) against lawful trade distortions provided the complainant can prove the unexpected upsetting ('nullification or impairment') of the agreed balance of reciprocal, competitive benefits;

49 Only five of the major human rights conventions include a compromissory clause providing for ICJ jurisdiction, and none of these clauses seems to have been used so far by states for challenging human rights violations by other states in the ICJ; cf. Simma, 'The ICJ and human rights'.
50 Ernst-Ulrich Petersmann, *The GATT/WTO Dispute Settlement System* (Kluwer, 1997), 194 ff., 233 ff.

- permitting 'situation complaints' that may protect sovereign rights and legitimate expectations even beyond 'violation' and 'non-violation complaints' (e.g. in case of an unforeseen economic depression or environmental crisis threatening human, food, and health security and the corresponding human rights to an adequate standard of living for oneself and one's family, cf. art. 11 of the UN Covenant on Economic, Social and Cultural Rights = ICESCR);[51]
- providing for compulsory and exclusive jurisdiction of WTO dispute settlement bodies in the WTO Dispute Settlement Understanding (DSU) (cf. arts. 6, 23 DSU); and
- regulating compliance with WTO dispute settlement rulings and 'retaliation powers' in ways which set incentives for termination of illegal WTO measures 'consistent with the findings contained in the panel or Appellate Body report adopted by the DSB or an arbitration award rendered under this Understanding' (cf. arts. 22, 23 DSU).

Yet, the WTO's focus on the justice dimension of reciprocal market access commitments among governments and on sovereign rights to protect non-economic public interests (e.g. pursuant to GATT arts. XIX–XXI) fails to protect justice vis-à-vis individuals. As stated by the WTO dispute settlement panel in US ss. 301–10 of the Trade Act of 1974:

> under the doctrine of direct effect, which has been found to exist most notably in the legal order of the EC but also in certain free trade agreements, obligations addressed to States are construed as creating legally enforceable rights and obligations for individuals. Neither the GATT nor the WTO has so far been interpreted by GATT/WTO institutions as a legal order producing direct effect. Following this approach, the GATT/WTO did not create a new legal order the subjects of which comprise both contracting parties or Members and their nationals.[52]

Due to the domination of GATT/WTO decision-making procedures by governments and their self-interests in limiting their legal and judicial accountability vis-à-vis citizens adversely affected by governmental violations of GATT/WTO obligations, the domestic legislation implementing GATT/WTO law inside some GATT/WTO members (like the EU and the USA) purports to exclude individual rights to invoke and enforce the GATT/WTO

---

51 On the six different kinds of legal complaints under GATT art. XXIII and similar provisions in other WTO rules, and on the controversial relationship between 'non-violation complaints', 'good faith principles', and explicit WTO rules (e.g. on 'actionable subsidies'), see Petersmann, *The GATT/WTO*, ch. 3. The human right 'to a social and international order in which the rights and freedoms set forth in this Declaration can be fully realized' (art. 28 UDHR), and the extraterritorial human rights obligations of promoting 'universal respect for human rights' (cf. the Preamble of the ICESCR), could offer relevant context for interpreting the contested scope of 'situation complaints' in GATT/WTO law.

52 WT/DS152/R, para. 7 (72).

obligations of governments in domestic courts.[53] At the request of self-interested governments, many domestic courts (e.g. inside the EU) also neglect the 'consistent interpretation' – and 'judicial comity' – requirements underlying WTO law (e.g. art. XVI (4) WTO Agreement and the DSU) and interpret and apply domestic trade laws without regard to WTO legal obligations and WTO dispute settlement rulings.

Judicial protection of 'cosmopolitan justice' in IEL

In transnational commercial and investment law, regional economic integration law (e.g. in the EU, the EEA, the North American Free Trade Agreement (NAFTA), and the Andean Common Market), and HRL, by contrast, international treaty provisions are increasingly construed by national and international courts and arbitral tribunals as protecting not only rights of governments, but also rights of citizens. Following the recognition of human rights and other 'principles of justice' as integral parts of national and international legal systems, ever more national and international courts throughout Europe have interpreted international guarantees of economic freedom, non-discrimination, and rule of law for the benefit of citizens even if the international rules were addressed to states without explicitly providing for cosmopolitan rights:

> the fact that certain provisions of the Treaty are formally addressed to the Member States does not prevent rights from being conferred at the same time on any individual who has an interest in compliance with the obligations thus laid down (see Case 43/75 *Defrenne v Sabena* [1976] ECR 455, par. 31). Such consideration must, *a fortiori*, be applicable to art. 48 of the Treaty, which... is designed to ensure that there is no discrimination on the labour market.[54]

Almost a century ago, the German jurist Rudolf Jhering noted that the 'life of the law' often depends on citizens struggling for their rights; such 'struggle for his rights' may be a 'duty of the person whose rights have been violated' as well as a 'duty to society'.[55] In US antitrust law as well as in European economic law, individual plaintiffs invoking and enforcing competition and common market rules have been likened to 'attorney generals' promoting 'community interests' (e.g. in rule of law) rather than pursuing only individual self-interests.[56] As illustrated by the *Kadi* cases, the increasing legal and judicial guarantees of 'access to justice' and of cosmopolitan rights offer individuals incentives to enforce HRL and IEL in decentralized and de-politicized ways against illegal

---

53 Petersmann, *The GATT/WTO*, 18 ff.
54 Case C-281/98, *Angonese* [2000] ECR I-4139.
55 Rudolf Jhering, *The Struggle for Law* (Callaghan and Company, 1915), chs. II–IV.
56 This conception was emphasized by the CJEU in its *Van Gend en Loos* judgment (Case 26/62, ECR 1963, 1), where the CJEU stated that 'the vigilance of the individuals concerned to protect their rights amounts to an effective supervision in addition to the supervision entrusted by (ex) arts. 169 and 170 to the diligence of the Commission and the Member States'.

government restrictions and irresponsible interest group politics. The need for legal and judicial 'balancing' of civil, political, economic, social, and cultural human rights makes 'constitutional justice' (e.g. multilevel judicial protection of equal freedoms, human rights, and transnational rule of law) and 'legal balancing' the 'ultimate rule of law'.[57] This is also true for IEL reconciling economic freedoms with non-economic rights and public interests subject to the requirements of transparency, non-discrimination, 'suitability', necessity, 'proportionality *stricto sensu*', and legal accountability. Legal and judicial protection of cosmopolitan rights promotes not only more inclusive 'public reason' and more democratic conceptions of the relevant 'rules of recognition' as 'tests' for legitimate interpretations of IEL and justifications of its principled coherence with HRL and other 'principles of justice'. It also justifies reviewing the 'Westphalian methodologies' of WTO dispute settlement bodies and 'investor biases' in investment arbitration in order to protect reasonable citizen interests more effectively. As national parliaments have not transferred any powers to the EU for arbitrary violations of international law, European courts should also protect EU citizens against welfare-reducing violations of the EU's WTO obligations rather than disregard legally binding WTO dispute settlement rulings on the ground that EU politicians claim 'freedom of maneuver'[58] to violate international law without any evidence that illegal trade restrictions can serve legitimate 'Community interests' in 'strict observance of international law' (art. 3 TEU).

EU law requires mutually consistent interpretations and 'judicial comity' in multilevel judicial governance systems protecting cosmopolitan rights of citizens

The more globalization transforms *national PGs* demanded by citizens into international '*aggregate PGs*' that national constitutions can protect only together with international law and multilevel governance institutions, the more important become multilevel guarantees of 'access to justice' extending legal and judicial remedies beyond civil and political rights of citizens. For instance:

- Some national Constitutions have responded to systemic governance failures by providing for broad legal and judicial remedies whenever 'rights are violated by public authority' (art. 19 (4) German Basic Law).
- Some free trade agreements concluded by the EU (such as the EEA Agreement with EFTA states) are explicitly committed to facilitating 'access to justice', 'rule of law', and 'rights to an effective remedy and to a fair trial' by providing for the establishment of independent courts (like the EFTA Court) protecting judicial remedies of states and non-governmental actors.

---

57 Cf. David M. Beatty, *The Ultimate Rule of Law* (OUP, 2004).
58 Cf. note 19 and E.U. Petersmann, 'Can the EU's disregard for "strict observance of international law" (art. 3 TEU) be constitutionally justified?' in M. Bronckers, V. Hauspiel, R. Quick (eds.), *Liber Amicorum for J. Bourgeois* (2011), 214–25.

- The GATT and the WTO Agreements include a large number of requirements to make available judicial, arbitral, or administrative tribunals
and independent review procedures not only at international governance levels among WTO members, but also in domestic legal systems
in the field of GATT (cf. art. X), the WTO Antidumping Agreement
(cf. art. 13), the WTO Agreement on Customs Valuation (cf. art. 11),
the Agreement on Pre-shipment Inspection (cf. art. 4), the Agreement
on Subsidies and Countervailing Measures (cf. art. 23), the General
Agreement on Trade in Services (cf. art. VI GATS), the Agreement on
Trade-Related Intellectual Property Rights (TRIPS) (cf. arts. 41–50, 59
TRIPS), and the Agreement on Government Procurement (cf. art. XX).
- In international investment law, the legal guarantees of access to justice
at national and international levels (e.g. in the ICJ) have become supple-
mented by about 3000 bi- and pluri-lateral treaty guarantees of indi-
vidual access to transnational arbitration.
- Some environmental conventions – like the 1998 Aarhus Convention on
Access to Information, Public Participation in Decision-Making, and Access
to Justice in Environmental Matters – protect individual 'access to a review
procedure before a court of law or another independent and impartial body
established by law' (art. 9) in transnational environmental regulation.
- UN and regional human rights covenants (e.g. art. 34 ECHR, the
Optional Protocol to the UN Covenant on Economic, Social and Cultural
Rights) increasingly extend protection of individual access to legal and
(quasi)judicial remedies in case of violation of economic and social rights
beyond national courts subject to prior exhaustion of local remedies.

Arguably, the constitutional and human rights obligations of the EU and EU
member states and their reciprocal duties of cooperation in areas of shared
competences (like international 'mixed agreements' concluded by both the
EU and its member states) constitutionally limit the role of the CJEU as

- 'gatekeeper' regarding the entry and effect of international law into the
EU legal system; as well as
- 'judicial protector' of the autonomy of the EU legal order and of its 'rule
of law system' protecting access to justice and other fundamental rights
of citizens.

The Court's acceptance of other multilateral dispute settlement systems if
they enlarge the powers of the CJEU[59] contrasts with the Court's reluctance

---

59 Cf. Opinion 1/00 on the establishment of a European Common Aviation Area and the 'Discussion
Document' adopted by the CJEU on 5 May 2010 suggesting to provide – in the negotiations on
EU accession to the ECHR – for an explicit rule prohibiting the ECtHR to decide on applications against the EU without first allowing the CJEU to examine those complaints in the light
of the EU's HRL (cf. T. Lock, 'Walking on a tightrope: the Draft ECHR Accession Agreement
and the Autonomy of the EU Legal Order' (2011) 48 *Common Market Law Review* 1025 ff.).

to interpret EU law in conformity with the jurisprudence of international courts other than the EFTA Court and the ECtHR; the rare references by the CJEU to judgments of other international courts make clear that the CJEU acknowledges only in theory, but not in practice that judgments of other international courts (like the WTO Appellate Body) may also have legally binding effects for the CJEU.[60] Since the 1972 *International Fruit Company* cases,[61] the GATT/WTO jurisprudence of the CJEU continues to be characterized by biased misinterpretations of GATT/WTO legal and dispute settlement obligations aimed at limiting the legal and judicial accountability of EU institutions for their frequent violations of GATT/WTO obligations ratified by parliaments for the benefit of EU citizens by denying both citizens and EU member states rights to invoke and enforce the EU's GATT/WTO obligations in national and EU courts, for instance on the ground that

- GATT/WTO rules are not sufficiently 'precise and unconditional' notwithstanding the fact that many GATT/WTO prohibitions of tariffs and non-tariff trade barriers and trade discrimination are more precise and unconditional than the often vague EU customs union rules based on GATT/WTO law;
- lack of 'reciprocity' by other GATT/WTO members prevents direct applicability of GATT/WTO rules inside the EU notwithstanding the Court's more convincing jurisprudence that lack of reciprocity in domestic judicial enforcement of free trade area rules is no impediment to their direct applicability in EU courts;
- the existence of 'safeguard clauses' require denying 'direct applicability' of GATT/WTO obligations in European courts even if such safeguard clauses have not been invoked by EU institutions;
- the 'structure and objectives' of GATT/WTO law exclude the application of GATT/WTO rules in European courts notwithstanding the explicit GATT/WTO guarantees of individual access to justice in domestic courts and arbitration procedures and the WTO requirement of ensuring the conformity of domestic 'laws, regulations and administrative procedures with [the] obligations as provided in the annexed Agreements' (art. XVI (4) WTO Agreement); or
- the WTO/DSU provision (art. 22 DSU) mentioning the possibility of avoiding lawful trade retaliation in response to EU non-compliance with WTO obligations through mutually agreed compensation prevents the CJEU of applying legally binding WTO dispute settlement rulings on the illegality of EU trade measures and their obligatory termination after

---

60 Cf. Marco Bronckers, 'The relationship of the EC courts with other international tribunals: non-commital, respectful or submissive' (2007) 44 *Common Market Law Review* 601–27.
61 Joined Cases 21-24/72, ECR 1972 1219.

the 'reasonable period of time' determined through WTO dispute settlement rulings.[62]

The deliberate misinformation by the EU Commission of the CJEU regarding GATT jurisprudence (e.g. in the *Dürbeck* case where the GATT panel finding against the EC was not yet publicly available) and the longstanding disregard by the CJEU for the EU's WTO obligations (e.g. of 'prompt compliance with recommendations or rulings of the DSB' requiring termination of illegal measures, cf. arts. 21–3 DSU) illustrate that the GATT/WTO jurisprudence of the CJEU pursues institutional self-interests of EU institutions (e.g. avoidance of judicial accountability of the political EU institutions vis-à-vis the 'violation victims' and 'retaliation victims' of WTO-inconsistent EU measures, judicial autonomy of the CJEU vis-à-vis other international courts) without any judicial regard to the reasonable interests of EU citizens in 'strict observance of international law' (art. 3 TEU). If the CJEU exceptionally refers to WTO dispute settlement rulings, it is to bolster its own interpretations of trade and intellectual property rules (e.g. of TRIPS provisions) rather than to review the legality of EU measures.[63]

Following some 15 GATT/WTO dispute settlement panel, appellate body, and arbitration awards since 1991 against the illegal EU import restrictions on bananas, the agreement of 8 November 2012 between the EU and 10 Latin American countries on the final settlement of this longest-running series of trade disputes in the history of the multilateral trading system[64] reminds EU citizens of how rent-seeking economic lobbies also inside the EU – including the EU's few banana trading companies – may be powerful enough to lobby the political EU institutions to persistently violate the 'rule of law' principles of EU and GATT/WTO law to the detriment of EU consumers, whose annual 'protection costs' from these illegal import restrictions were estimated to be the equivalent of an illegal tax amounting to several billion Euros per year for the benefit of a handful of EU trading companies importing bananas from (former) colonies of a few EU member states. The persistent refusal of EU politicians to grant EU citizens legal and judicial remedies against EU violations of international trade rules, even if the 'reasonable period' for implementing legally binding WTO dispute settlement rulings has expired, confirms that 'rule of law' also inside the EU risks not being stronger than in a 'banana republic'. The systemic risks of undermining the democratic legitimacy of EU law by persistent violations of treaties ratified by parliaments was illustrated more dramatically

---

62 For a detailed discussion of the legally unconvincing GATT/WTO jurisprudence of the CJEU see Petersmann, (note 58) and Anne Thies, *International Trade Disputes and EU Liability* (CUP, 2013).

63 Cf. Case C-245/02 *Anheuser-Busch*, ECR 2004 I-11018, para. 49.

64 Cf. WTO Press Release of 8 November 2012 on 'Historic signing ends 20 years of EU–Latin American banana dispute'.

when – following the financial crisis in 2008 – more than 20 out of the 27 EU member states continued to violate the agreed EU legal disciplines for fiscal, debt, and economic convergence policies (cf. art. 126 TFEU), ushering in private and public debt defaults (i.e. violations of contract law) necessitating bailouts in ever more over-indebted EU member states (like Greece, Portugal, Ireland, Spain, Cyprus) and of bankrupt banks at the expense of European taxpayers, undermining rule of law, protection of human rights (e.g. in Greece), and the democratic legitimacy of European governance.

Conclusion: EU law, HRL, and WTO law require multilevel judicial protection of transnational rule of law for the benefit of citizens

This contribution has argued that the 'constitutional justice approach' of the *Kadi* and *Solange* jurisprudence of European courts should also serve as a model beyond HRL so as to protect mutually beneficial cooperation among citizens and among interconnected judicial and 'rule of law' systems across frontiers. Rather than referring to the comparatively most developed worldwide WTO dispute settlement system as a justification for undermining rule of law and judicial remedies for the 'violation victims' and the 'retaliation victims' inside the EU, the CJEU should admit that the multilevel legal WTO guarantees of 'access to justice' at national and international levels justify European leadership in promoting 'strict observance and development of international law', as required by EU law (e.g. arts. 3, 21 TEU). Contrary to the 'Westphalian claims' by the political and judicial EU institutions, neither EU law nor WTO law provides for EU discretion to violate the WTO agreements ratified by parliaments for the benefit of EU citizens without any 'balancing' of the public and private interests affected by the judicial toleration of – in case of WTO dispute settlement rulings against the EU and the expiry of the 'reasonable period' for terminating illegal restrictions – obviously illegal trade discrimination and resultant competitive distortions.[65]

The fundamental rights of adversely affected EU 'violation victims' and 'retaliation victims' – such as their rights to protection of private property, 'freedom to conduct a business in accordance with Union law' (art. 16 EU Charter of Fundamental Rights), protection of legitimate expectations in rule of law, and other fundamental rights (e.g. to non-discrimination)[66] – suggest that, as stated by the CJEU in the *Kadi* cases – the EU courts must 'ensure the review, in principle the full review of the lawfulness of all [EU] acts in the light of the fundamental rights forming an integral part of the general principles of [EU] law'.[67] Such review and judicial protection of fundamental

---

65 Cf. Thies, *International Trade Disputes*, 100–1.
66 *Ibid.*, 140–7 on potential infringements of these rights.
67 Case C-402/05P and C-415/05, *P. Kadi and Al Barakaat Foundation* v. *Council and Commission*, ECR 2008 I-6351, paras. 281 ff., 326.

rights 'must be considered to be the expression, in a community based on the rule of law, of a constitutional guarantee stemming from the [EU treaties] as an autonomous legal system which is not to be prejudiced by an international agreement'.[68] Neither EU law nor WTO law bars the European courts from 'maintaining EU law standards vis-à-vis individuals with regard to EU conduct'.[69]

As the most developed regional organization in the world for multilevel governance of international PGs demanded by citizens, it is in the EU's reasonable self-interest to 'lead by example' in protecting the 'consistent interpretation' and 'judicial comity' requirements underlying national and international legal systems,[70] subject to exceptional situations if the political EU institutions should ever be capable of convincingly justifying violations of international law as being necessary for protecting human rights and other legitimate 'Community interests'. Hence, as stated in many judgments by the CJEU regarding free trade agreements concluded by the EU, precise and unconditional prohibitions of trade discrimination should be presumed to be directly applicable and judicially enforceable for the benefit of adversely affected EU citizens and EU member states unless the political EU institutions can convincingly justify the necessity of 'political exceptions' (e.g. in the sense of Anglo-Saxon 'political question doctrines'). The fact that EU and WTO trade diplomats did not intend to assume such legal, democratic, and judicial accountability vis-à-vis citizens does not justify violating the EU constitutional requirements of 'rule of law' and 'strict observance of international law'. Diverging interpretations of WTO legal obligations by national courts could contribute to the citizen-driven development of WTO rules and could be limited and corrected through 'preliminary rulings' by the CJEU and WTO dispute settlement findings clarifying 'public reason' through multilevel 'judicial dialogues' with domestic courts and multilevel judicial protection of transnational rule of law.

In citizen-driven areas like the rules-based world trading system, legitimate and effective governance of interdependent national, regional, and global 'aggregate PGs' depends on multilevel judicial protection of transnational rule of law for the benefit of citizens linking governmental duties to respect, protect, and fulfil human rights and other PGs to multilevel democratic, judicial, and other accountability mechanisms limiting abuses of public and private power. The EU Court's selfish focus on state-centred 'Westphalian conceptions of justice' – without any judicial balancing of governmental self-interests in 'freedom of manoeuvre' with the reasonable interests and rights of EU citizens (e.g. in 'strict observance' of international treaty obligations ratified by parliaments for the benefit of citizens) – amounts to a regrettable 'denial of justice'

---

68 *Ibid.*, para. 316.

69 Cf. also Thies, *International Trade Disputes*, 198.

70 *Ibid.*, 105 ff., on the *Fediol* – and *Nakajima* – exceptions in the CJEU jurisprudence based on the so-called 'implementation principle', which seem to have hardly ever been used in EU practice; and *ibid.*, 110 ff., on the incoherent EU application of the 'consistent interpretation principle'.

for EU citizens participating in, and benefitting from, the global division of labour based on WTO rules.

Just as international rule of law in commercial and investment transactions is ever more often protected through multilevel cooperation among international and national courts (e.g. by national courts in the 'venue jurisdiction' as well as in the 'enforcement jurisdiction' of transnational arbitration), European courts should also take the lead in promoting multilevel judicial governance in related areas such as international trade law, regional economic integration law, HRL, and international criminal law.[71] Modern theories of justice explain why the progressive 'institutionalization' of 'principles of justice' through constitutional, legislative, administrative, and judicial rule-making at national and international level of governance often depends on impartial and independent judicial reasoning as 'exemplar of public reason' (J. Rawls) justifying law and governance vis-à-vis citizens not only in terms of 'conservative justice' (e.g. rule-following) but also in terms of 'reformative justice' protecting 'equity' and human rights in individual disputes.[72] The EU's legal advocates defending 'freedom of manoeuvre' of the political EU institutions perceive 'the Community as a somewhat State-like actor' justifying Westphalian power politics.[73]

This contribution has defended the opposite view that EU citizens and their national parliaments have established the EU as an international organization with limited powers that derive their legitimacy from multilevel protection of human rights and transnational rule of law in close cooperation with other multilevel governance regimes ratified by European and national parliaments for the benefit of citizens. As in the field of multilevel judicial protection of transnational rule of commercial law, investment law, human rights, and criminal law, national, transnational, and international dispute settlement systems in international trade law should also be construed and enforced in mutually coherent ways for the benefit of citizens, as required by the 'consistent interpretation' – and 'judicial comity' – requirements and multilevel 'access to justice' guarantees of WTO law (e.g. art. XVI (4) WTO Agreement, art. 3 DSU). The 'nature and structure' of multilevel governance regimes in citizen-driven areas of international relations – including the art. 3 DSU requirement of 'providing security and predictability to the multilateral trading system' – should be construed in conformity with principles of 'constitutional' and 'cosmopolitan justice' (e.g. the multilevel human rights and rule-of-law guarantees of EU law) – rather than of Westphalian

---

71 Cf. W.W. Burke-White, 'Proactive complementarity: the International Criminal Court and national courts in the Rome system of international justice' (2008) 49 *Harvard International Law Journal* 53 ff.

72 Cf. Ernst-Ulrich Petersmann, 'The judicial task of administering justice in trade and investment law and adjudication' (2013) IV *Journal of International Dispute Settlement* 5–28.

73 Pieter Jan Kuijper, '"It shall contribute to… the strict observance and development of international law…" The role of the Court of Justice' in Court of Justice of the European Union (ed.), *The Court of Justice and the Construction of Europe. Analyses and Perspectives on Sixty Years of Case-Law* (CJEU, 2013) 589, p. 590.

justice – so as 'to establish conditions under which justice and respect for the obligations arising from treaties and other sources of international law can be maintained' (Preamble UN Charter). 'Freedom of manoeuvre' of EU institutions to violate international agreements ratified by parliaments – without offering adversely affected citizens and member states effective judicial remedies, and without justifying how welfare-reducing WTO violations can serve reasonable interests of EU citizens – is inconsistent with the 'access to justice', rule-of-law, and constitutionally limited democratic governance principles of EU law as well as with the constitutional duties of national and EU courts to 'ensure… that in the interpretation and application of the Treaties the law is observed' and 'effective legal protection' is provided for everyone (art. 19 TEU).

Index

For Product Safety Concerns and Information please contact our EU
representative GPSR@taylorandfrancis.com
Taylor & Francis Verlag GmbH, Kaufingerstraße 24, 80331 München, Germany